THE
100 BEST
TECHNOLOGY
STOCKS
YOU CAN BUY
2012

THE
100 BEST
TECHNOLOGY STOCKS
YOU CAN BUY
2012

- Tips to identify growth technologies
- Strategies to blend tech stocks into portfolios
- Advice on balancing short- and long-term gains

PETER SANDER AND SCOTT BOBO

AVON, MASSACHUSETTS

Published by
Adams Media, a division of F+W Media, Inc.
57 Littlefield Street, Avon, MA 02322. U.S.A.
www.adamsmedia.com

ISBN 10: 1-4405-3273-7
ISBN 13: 978-1-4405-3273-3
eISBN 10: 1-4405-3286-9
eISBN 13: 978-1-4405-3286-3

Printed in the United States of America.

10   9   8   7   6   5   4   3   2   1

Library of Congress Cataloging-in-Publication Data
is available from the publisher.

This publication is designed to provide accurate and authoritative information
with regard to the subject matter covered. It is sold with the understanding that
the publisher is not engaged in rendering legal, accounting, or other professional
advice. If legal advice or other expert assistance is required, the services of a
competent professional person should be sought.

—From a *Declaration of Principles* jointly adopted by a Committee of the
American Bar Association and a Committee of Publishers and Associations

Many of the designations used by manufacturers and sellers to distinguish their
product are claimed as trademarks. Where those designations appear in this
book and Adams Media was aware of a trademark claim, the designations have
been printed with initial capital letters.

This book is available at quantity discounts for bulk purchases.
For information, please call 1-800-289-0963.

Contents

Part I

THE ART AND SCIENCE OF TECHNOLOGY STOCK INVESTING

The Art and Science of Investing in Technology

Welcome, tech investors, to the first edition of *The 100 Best Technology Stocks You Can Buy*. This book will serve as your guide to adventure in one of today's most dynamic investing spaces, known informally as the "tech sector," or just plain "tech." Here we will introduce you to the technology companies that we feel are best positioned as candidates for your personal investment portfolio. Along the way we will give you information and background that will help you understand and interpret the volumes of sometimes bewildering data that issue daily from Wall Street, not to mention Silicon Valley, the Pacific Rim, and elsewhere.

The tech landscape can be pretty intimidating to even the most astute investor. There are a great many unfamiliar concepts and a great many unfamiliar business models. The terrain can change dramatically over time, and companies that had been high-flyers can be grounded by market shifts, upstart competition, or a disruptive technology that renders their business obsolete practically overnight. Our goal here at *100 Best* is to guide you through the turbulence and, ultimately, to inspire you to chart your own course—one that suits your needs, your budget, your time, and your vision.

You are holding a copy of the first edition of what we hope will be many to come for this new title. It's good to focus some attention on one of the fastest-moving areas of the investment markets but, as the cliché goes, it isn't just about the destination, it's about the journey. Many people come to the technology sector looking for the sexy stock and quick returns. What brings you here? What's the appeal of technology for you?

If it's a gambling opportunity you're looking for, you might be disappointed. We expect you're here because you want to own something, rather than bet on something. What we'd like to offer is closer to a Sure Thing, although we can't promise that either. Anyway, if you've been in the world of individual, do-it-yourself investing, you've seen enough Sure Things already.

In fact, this is why we've created this book, the latest in the *100 Best* series. Our goal is not only to offer a fresh perspective on individual investing, but also to shed some light on one of the more mysterious corners of the market. In addition, we offer our 2012 picks for the best technology stocks to invest in. As in the other books in our *100 Best* series, we offer fish *and* some helpful advice on fishing.

Okay, another tired cliché, perhaps. And perhaps not even accurate, for the "fish" we offer aren't really cooked and ready to eat. The 100 fish we offer take the form of selected companies, their stories and their upside and downside potential. They're meant to be bait, not fish. They're ideas for you to pursue further, research further, and to consider against your own interests, intuitions, and investing strategies. They are food for thought.

Okay, since we're running out of clichés, perhaps it's time to get down to business and talk about the phrase *Best Technology*. What does *Best* mean in this context? What's a "technology" stock? And why do we need a book on the world of technology stocks?

The Mother Ship

Our story starts with the mother ship: *The 100 Best Stocks You Can Buy*. Many—perhaps most—of you have seen that book. You may have the 2012 edition already; you may have even purchased it along with this book. You may be one of the loyal readers who have followed *100 Best Stocks* and all of its lessons and recommendations from its inception fifteen years ago.

This book is built on the approach established in *100 Best Stocks You Can Buy* but extends it further into the specific area of technology stocks. The value-based investing methods described in that book are employed here but are applied to the technology sector alone. The same rules apply—there's no secret sauce for investing in technology as opposed to the broader market. Both books have their place, and both belong on your investing bookshelf.

The 100 Best Stocks You Can Buy 2012 and all previous editions provide you with what we feel are, overall, the *100 Best Stocks* you can own. They balance safety and current income with long-term success and growth. They represent the best of all worlds, companies you'll do well with primarily over the long term. These are companies that would constitute an appealing, diversified portfolio for 2012 that balances risk and return.

The stocks that we recommend in *The 100 Best Technology Stocks You Can Buy* represent the best stocks in what is inherently a more volatile and riskier segment of the overall market. Because of the two well-known tech bubbles of the past decade, some people may feel the sector is too volatile and is not where they want to be. Fair enough. We don't think anyone should lose sleep worrying about his or her investments. Others, though, understand that good companies, companies with stable markets and sound management, do well in up cycles and down cycles and the specter of the bubble is nothing to fear. These are the companies we look for. But these aren't investments you can make one day and ignore for twenty years; all investments these days must be watched and managed as you would manage a business. The world just changes too fast to do anything else.

In *The 100 Best Technology Stocks You Can Buy 2012*, we provide you with what we feel are the best choice of stocks in the technology sector. Certainly, we don't recommend that an individual investor buy all 100 issues; a manageable portfolio should provide diversification, and technology stocks should represent only part of that mix. What we've done here is to provide you with insight on a selection of issues that are safe, well positioned for growth, and appropriate for most investors.

Why Stock Investing Is Important

In our (naturally) biased opinion, we all should own some of the *100 Best Stocks* somewhere in our portfolio. In fact, perhaps, in a large portion or even a majority of our portfolio.

And in our world view, one of the major premises of owning stocks is to keep up with economic progress. As an alternative, you could buy a bond. What are you doing? You're lending money to a company to do something with it; you'll be paid back with interest eventually. But do you participate in the growth of that company's business, its productivity, or market share? Do you get a share of its better ideas or new products? No, you get a fixed, predetermined return, the value of which may well be diminished by inflation, the interest rate climate, or God forbid, an all-out default if the company goes belly up.

Put your money in a CD or some other fixed investment and you avoid the last risk, but you still face the other two. Buy a commodity or a commodity future and your success is left to the whims of supply and demand, with no management team or any other guidance working to make sure that things turn your way. And real estate? Well, we all know what happened with that one in 2008.

Not that these alternative investments are necessarily bad; they have their place. Companies have risks, too. Bad management, technology shifts, a poor response to competition—the list is long. Any shareholder in Enron or Eastman Kodak or Etrade can tell you from experience.

But if you want to participate in growth—growth that can come in the form of an increase in the share value and in the cash dividends returned (which can grow too, as so many forget), you should buy companies. That is, if you don't have the whim and wherewithal to start your own. (Or even if you do, for you shouldn't put all your business eggs in one basket.)

So, we feel that you should own at least some stocks. They offer not only the best chance to get ahead, but also the best chance to keep up.

A Little Further, a Little Faster

Now, assuming you're on board with the idea of hitching your wagon to companies, American companies primarily, to keep up with or even get a little ahead of the pack, should you participate in the real growth opportunities in today's economy? Technology? Productivity? Efficiency? New, cool technologies such as digital music, digital photography, alternative energy, or less sexy but still new ideas like plastic composite backyard decking? LED lighting? The latest and greatest in semiconductors or semiconductor manufacturing equipment? Do you participate in recently realized economic necessities like replacing older generation computer hardware, networking, and software solutions? Do you participate in new business models such as streaming video or mobile wallets or cloud computing?

Life is expensive. And as many have found out the hard way, it gets more expensive the older you get. Health care costs rise through the roof. Ditto the costs of college for those kids and grandkids, and until recently, housing costs. While that is all going on, personal incomes have hardly kept up, to say nothing of the near elimination of interest on personal savings or other fixed returns. We had a professor of physics way back when who offered a pithy summary of the Second Law of Thermodynamics: You can't win, you can't break even, and you can't quit the game. Personal finance feels that way from time to time, particularly if you only invest for modest returns, even using our *100 Best Stocks* as a guide. Life *demands* more wealth and hence greater returns, and at the same time, all things equal, it *produces* weaker ones.

Another notable physicist, Wayne Gretzky (more of an experimentalist, but you get the point), was asked why he was so far ahead of his contemporaries in the game of hockey. He replied that instead of chasing the puck, he "tried to be where the puck was going." Wonderfully simple in concept, blindingly difficult in practice, but there it is.

That's where *100 Best Technology Stocks You Can Buy 2012* comes in. We have developed this book to help you see where the puck is going by focusing on technology, where growth and innovation are rewarded handsomely and failure is often punished severely (or, strangely, ignored altogether). Again, we don't recommend technology across your entire portfolio, not by a long shot. But to be where the puck is going, your portfolio demands that some portion of your investing capital belongs in this, one of the most dynamic and lucrative investment sectors of the past thirty years. If our suggestions make sense, if our discussions inspire you, you may come around to our way of looking at the technology sector, which is a place of great promise and potential. We hope to give you some ideas on how to hitch your wagon to the future, to see where the puck is going in today's economy and lifestyle— and make some money in the process.

AMERICAN AS APPLE PIE?

If you read closely just a few paragraphs ago, you may have caught our phrase "American companies, primarily." Now, with all the headlines you read today about growth in China and so forth, why would we stick to American companies?

While we acknowledge that many foreign economies are growing faster, and that many foreign counterparts to American companies and American technological leadership are becoming more formidable, we still for the most part choose to "buy American" when it comes to investing. Why? Two reasons: First, American companies are easier to understand. Financial and accounting standards are better known and more consistent. Second, American companies with good products sell prolifically into foreign economies, often for over half of their overall revenue. So you get exposure to the "good" of foreign growth without many of the inherent risks.

And a Couple of Sister Ships

So we come back to the earlier question: mother ship, or sister ship? Did *100 Best Stocks You Can Buy* give birth to the *100 Best Technology Stocks You Can Buy*? Indeed it did. There is plenty of *100 Best* DNA in *100 Best Technology*. If there hadn't been a *100 Best*, there probably wouldn't be a *100 Best Technology*. And in fact, the best technology stocks in *100 Best* also make an appearance here (we hope that's not too surprising).

If you're really paying attention to our evolving *100 Best* series, you probably also know about (or own) our recently released *The 100 Best Aggressive Stocks You Can Buy 2012*. Aggressive stocks? Technology stocks? Sisters, yes, and a healthy family resemblance. In fact, about forty of the *100 Best Technology* stocks are also on the *100 Best Aggressive* list. But the *100 Best Aggressive* list also holds many companies nowhere near the tech space, like cardboard box maker Temple Inland or used auto retailer CarMax.

Aggressive stocks include some tech stocks, but also include healthy growth and turnaround prospects in other industries.

But for you as an investor, it makes more sense to treat the books as sisters: *100 Best Stocks* to help you with the foundations of your investing portfolio and *100 Best Aggressive* and *100 Best Technology* to get more on board with growth-focused companies, and to provide some lift as well as thrust to your investing returns in the process.

Who Are We to Write This Book?

Well, okay, first of all, we're the authors and creators of *100 Best Stocks You Can Buy*, and have been since the 2010 edition. That qualifies us, right?

Yes, it does help. We understand the idea of crafting useful tools for individual investors. We understand the idea of culling down thousands of stocks into a useful *100 Best* list serving a composite of investors with a composite of best company attributes aligned to the idea of investing for value.

We are value finders, regardless of how that value is delivered. The value may be anchored to safety and current cash returns, or it may come in the form of growth and growth potential. With the *100 Best Technology* list, we think we have found stocks of good businesses in good technology-centered industries that can provide very attractive returns and that also happen to be good values at today's prices.

We function as a team. But a team is made up of individuals, so here is a brief summary of who we are, where we came from, and how our experiences relate to bringing you the *100 Best Technology* stocks. If you've read the sister *100 Best Stocks You Can Buy*, these bio sketches will look familiar.

Peter

Peter is an independent professional researcher, writer, and journalist specializing in personal finance, investing, and location reference, as well as other general business topics. He has written twenty-five books on these topics, done numerous financial columns and independent privately contracted research and studies. He came from the corporate world, a veteran of a twenty-one-year career with a major West Coast technology firm.

He is most definitely an individual investor. And has been since the age of twelve, when his curiosity at the family breakfast table got the better of him. He started reading the stock pages with his parents. He had an opportunity during a one-week "project week" in the seventh grade to read about, and learn about, the stock market. He read Louis Engel's *How to Buy Stocks*, then the pre-eminent—and one of the only—books about investing available at the time (it first appeared in 1953 . . . he thinks he read a 1962 paperback edition). He read Engel, picked stocks, and made graphs of their performance by hand with colored pens on real graph paper. He put his hard-earned savings into buying five shares of each of three different companies. He watched those stocks like a hawk and salted away the meager dividends to reinvest. He's been investing ever since, and in combination with twenty-eight years of home ownership and a rigorous, almost sacrificial savings regimen, he has done quite well in the net worth department, pretty much on his own.

Yes, he has an MBA from a top-rated university (Indiana University, Bloomington), but it isn't an MBA in finance. He also took the coursework and certification exam to become a certified financial planner (CFP). But by design and choice, he has never worked in the financial profession. His goal has always been to share his knowledge and experience in an educational way, a way helpful for the individual as an investor and a personal financier to make his or her own decisions.

He has never made money giving investment advice or managing money for others, nor does he intend to.

When starting out with a *Fortune* 50 tech firm in the early 1980s, Peter was stationed for three years right in the heart of Silicon Valley during some of its most exciting years (for instance, when Apple Computer went public). He witnessed firsthand the incidence and development of some of the world's premier tech companies and many of the tech industries still in play today. He's been a tech stock aficionado ever since.

Outside of an occasional warm Friday evening at the harness track or a nickel-dime-quarter poker game with former work buddies, Peter just doesn't gamble. Not that he thinks it's unethical; he just doesn't like to lose hard-earned money on games of chance. But when it comes to investing, Peter can be fairly aggressive. Not with all of his investments, but with a portion. He is a classic Buffetonian value investor in most ways, investing for value in businesses he understands. He occasionally will make a big bet on something that appears to be an obvious winner. A couple of his biggest bets can be found in another of our companion books, *The 100 Best Aggressive Stocks You Can Buy 2012.*

Scott

Scott is relatively new to the professional writing game but has been an investor since age fourteen, when he made the switch from analyzing baseball box scores to looking at the numbers and charts in the business section. Cautious from the start, his first stock purchase was an electric utility with a spicy dash of dividend reinvestment. Unfortunately, his investing career was cut short by the typical high schooler's lack of investment capital, and eight years later his brokerage firm was nice enough to send him a letter asking him if he was still alive and would he mind terribly taking his business elsewhere. As it turned out, that was the real start of his investing career, since he then had an income and lived five minutes from a brokerage with half a dozen open terminals.

As a Silicon Valley resident with twenty-plus years in engineering and technology management, he's learned that a unique product value proposition is important to the success of any company, but has also learned (the hard way) that proper financial fundamentals are just as critical. From a development manager's perspective, comprehending a new product's risk/reward proposition is one of the keys to a company's success. From an investor's perspective, it's also one of the keys to successful value investing in a dynamic, innovation-driven market.

Like Peter, Scott has always been a value investor. Picking a company to buy based on momentum or popularity won't always result in a bad pick, just usually. And while there are plenty of companies out there that can point to a history of increasing stock prices, there are far fewer that can point to a future of the same. Looking hard at the numbers, picking through the pretenders, and finding the contenders is where Scott adds his own value.

Scott plays poker too, and finds the atmosphere around a poker table to be a bit like the stock market. Everyone knows there's money to be made, but not everyone is willing to do the math. Rather than figure out if they've got a reasonable chance of achieving financial gain with the cards (or stocks) they see in front of them, some simply bet on a combination of hope and the theory that "if you don't bet, you can't win." And while that's true, it's also true that if you don't bet, you can't lose. You only have so much money to play with—make the most of it by understanding what you're betting on and what you're up against. This is where this book can help.

So What Does *Best Technology* Really Mean?

To understand what a term or expression really means it's sometimes helpful to take it apart. We'll give that a try here—what do we mean by *Best Technology*? We'll do one word at a time, starting with *technology*.

Thank You, Justice Stewart

An agreed-upon definition of the word *technology* is surprisingly elusive. Dictionaries provide no consensus. We did find that the word's earliest common usage in English is in reference to "the useful arts," which probably says more about the other arts than it does about technology. Much later popular definitions, such as "the way we do things around here" are not much help either, although we did like "organized inorganic matter." But are these useful for picking technology *stocks*? Not so much.

The best definitions we see all involve the concept of tools and the *application and manipulation of raw science in order to solve a problem or serve some other purpose*. This turns out to be a very useful description and one that could be applied to every stock in this book. Unfortunately, it's a definition that also works for a manufacturer of axes, shovels, and sledgehammers. And as it turns out, there are no sledgehammer manufacturers in the Standard & Poor's Technology Sector listing. So even though they fit the definition, we couldn't really see our way clear to include *all* tools in our definition.

Clearly, if we're going to be a technology investor, we want the technology that we invest in to more or less mirror the technology investments made by the market at large. As someone once said, follow the money. Companies that stand to gain by spending as much as 10 percent of their revenue on R & D are companies that will lead, or even define, their particular market. Companies that receive little benefit from advancing the state of their tools or products don't spend that money.

There's not a lot of money being spent on R & D in the axe business, although they do have a lot of cutting-edge products. Sorry. But the point is made—if your products or business will benefit from a high level of R & D, you generally make that investment. If they will not benefit, or your company is not making that investment for other reasons (lack of funds, short-sighted management), then as a technology investor we're probably not all that interested in your stock.

There are a lot of companies that rely on technology in order to get their products out the door. Procter and Gamble, for instance, not only uses a lot of technology but also generates a great deal of its own patentable technology in the making of its products. Is P&G a technology company? A case could be made that it is, but for our purposes the answer is no. What it sells is not technology but rather soap, toothpaste, and diapers (among other things). Though the diapers it produces may be the highest-tech diapers in the business, they're still diapers. P&G's success in its businesses has far less to do with its technology and far more to do with its enormous marketing clout.

So if using or producing technology is not sufficient, does selling technology qualify a company as a technology stock? We're probably getting closer to the matter with that definition, but it's starting to look like Supreme Court Justice Potter Stewart had the right idea when he was asked to rule on, and thus define, pornography. To quote the wise Justice: "I shall not today attempt further to define the kinds of material but I know it when I see it."

Here at *100 Best* we've applied some of this logic to our stock selection process. In part, we know it when we see it. For our purposes, a technology stock is the stock of a company *that generally relies on technology as either a key component of the products it produces or as a primary differentiator of its business model.* These are the two areas where technology provides its greatest leverage. Your offices and building may be technological marvels, and your staff may be outfitted with the latest productivity tools, but this does not qualify you as a technology company.

The companies that we've included in this book are generally recognized throughout the investment community as *technology* stocks, with a few exceptions. Companies such as Avnet and Arrow are technically distributors (although they also provide technology services and value-add), and we've also included a few companies whose business falls outside the boundaries of the mainstream *technology* sector. We recognize and defend those exceptions based on their customer lists, their business cycles, or other factors that match that of the sector at large.

The reason we've taken the time to try to define *technology* is that the definition is a big part of why the technology sector is attractive as an investment area. Technology's very nature makes it a weathervane for value. We can see this as we go back to that definition of *technology* as the application of raw science in order to solve a problem. Technology is innovation, and the innovator, the first one to do something new and useful, always has a great deal of pricing power. We remember Intel's early stranglehold on the CPU market for consumer PCs—when AMD showed up with one of the first compatible processors, it made a good business charging less than 25 percent of Intel's then-current price. Intel, being first to market, enjoyed (and still enjoys, in some cases) the benefits that come with having a 100 percent market share.

Recognizing the economic power of innovation, investors naturally gravitate to technology stocks, like moths to an LED. It's been that way since the Industrial Revolution, when manufacturers learned that innovative machinery was able to not just add to the productivity of a workforce, but to actually multiply it. In more recent times, the success of IBM in the early 1960s marked the dawn of the information technology industry, and IBM became the first tech stock (practically the only one, at the time) to really capture the imagination of investors. IBM took a huge risk in the development of SABRE, the reservations system they developed for American Airlines, spending nearly $500 million in 2011 dollars. But soon after

SABRE was up and running, IBM was contracted to build similar systems for Delta and PanAm. This sort of technological leverage, this approach of "solve the problem once, sell the solution everywhere," was what sold corporate America on the power of information technology. The financial leverage it generated was what drew investors to IBM's stock, in droves. IBM was the darling growth stock through much of the 1960s, a decade that saw nearly zero growth in the market at large.

Goals, Strategies, and Tactics

But let's focus on what growth investing really *does* mean. The goal is simple: to achieve higher returns than market averages or "average" investments. It is to make more money faster.

Where the rubber really meets the road is the "how"—the strategies, tactics, and investment mentality deployed to meet the goal. For us, investing in technology is about getting ahead of the investing public. It means getting on board with newer technologies. It also means seeing where the puck is going not only with technology but also with business and business models in general.

For example, did IBM remain tied to its PC business in 2005 when the marketplace was clearly engaged in a race to the bottom? Nope. They saw margins declining, they saw market share eroding, and they saw the cost of the operation's cash generation climbing higher and higher. And what were they getting out of it? A leg up on the competition in terms of technology? Not even close—the PC uses commodity hardware and software innovation that had long ago been stifled by Microsoft's very restrictive licensing agreements. So what was IBM getting out of this business? Not much at all. Looking back, the signs were clear, but most of us were still surprised when IBM, the inventor (more or less) of the personal computer, left the business. It saw where the market was going, and it knew it's better to sell a business one year too early than one year too late. We would encourage everyone to think like IBM—investing for growth means doing the homework, being diligent about your chosen businesses, and moving on when being the leader means losing out on other opportunities.

Investing for growth can also mean finding the *next* leader, the company soon to emerge from the pack. Or, the next revolution or serious evolution in technology, like Apple with digital music or Starbucks with excellent, intellectually stimulating "third places" to replace the corner tavern. It can, of course, mean hooking up with leaders and strong niche players in exciting, futuristic industries such as alternative energy today or computer networking twenty years ago. A rising tide will float all boats, but in the business world, some boats will rise faster than others.

But Isn't Technology Inherently Risky?

Yes, there is a component of risk in investing in new technologies or new business models or reinvented old ones—they might not work, or your company might turn out not to have the best technology or solution. Investing in technology can mean taking on more risk, both in the success of the technology and the success of the company involved.

Additionally, leading companies in evolving industries tend to attract a lot of investor attention, and may be expensive to buy. So yes, there often is more risk, and a technology investor needs to recognize it and be willing to take more risk to achieve a higher return. But, just as in value investing, if you understand the company and the market, and you can determine that the company is a dominant player in a good business or good niche, the risk can be reduced considerably. Technology investing is not *necessarily* risky investing.

We'll discuss risk management a bit more later on.

Volatility Versus Cyclicality

No, we're not introducing the competitors in an investment boxing match (cyclicality would win). But since over a quarter of our recommended stocks are in the semiconductor and semiconductor equipment sector, we want to highlight the differences between these two concepts, particularly as it pertains to the semiconductor industry.

Everyone talks about the cyclical nature of the semiconductor industry, but its root causes are rarely explained to the satisfaction of the individual investor. Understanding the nature of an industry is a big part of making wise investments and managing risk, so let's get into semiconductors for a bit. We'll start by talking about cars.

Automobiles are another cyclical industry, but we've grown so accustomed to the "model year" concept that it just seems natural, like the changing of the tides. In fact, there's nothing really driving the model year "model" other than appealing to consumer's changing tastes. In the semiconductor industry, this "model year" concept doesn't exist, but there's still a cyclical nature to the business, and it's driven not by consumer tastes but by two major events—changing process nodes and changing wafer size.

A "process node" is a feature-size definition for the integrated circuit fabrication process. Way back in the stone age, around 2002, Neanderthals were pounding out integrated circuits with a feature size (a measure of the size of a single transistor) of around 90 nanometers (or "nm"—.090 microns, or 90 billionths of a meter). All of the capital equipment and tools in the fabrication process were built or customized to support this feature size, and so a fab designed to produce integrated circuits on the 90nm process node represented a very large investment in that 90nm technology.

In the time since 2002, there have been three process node changes, to 65nm, 45nm, and 32nm feature sizes. Every time a process node changes, the equipment used to produce the integrated circuits has to be recalibrated, refitted, or replaced. Replacement is very expensive and is only required every other node change, at most, but replacement is also the major driver of revenues in the semiconductor equipment industry. This replacement cycle is one of the two major drivers of cyclicality. Fortunately for semiconductor manufacturers (and for us), not every integrated circuit or semiconductor requires ever-shrinking feature size support. The ones that do are those that have the most transistors per die, and those are processors and memory.

The other major driver of cyclicality is wafer size changes. Wafers are the silicon discs on which the integrated circuits are built, and the larger the size of the wafer the more parts you can build in a given amount of time. Three wafer sizes currently account for the bulk of semiconductor volumes (150mm, 200mm, and 300mm), with specialty parts typically built on smaller processes. Wafer size changes are far less common than node changes and we don't expect to see another one for at least three years.

With that discussion out of the way, the difference between volatility and cyclicality should be clear. Cyclicality is driven by the supply side of the business, while volatility is driven by the demand side. The semiconductor industry's volatility may be unpredictable, but its cyclicality is less so. Keep an eye on the news from the big manufacturers like Global Foundries, TSMC, Samsung, and Intel to see when you can expect increased capital investment activity in the sector.

Reasonable Expectations

With regard to any type of investing, it's right to ask: What is a reasonable objective? Surely, we all want to double, triple, quadruple our money. We're thrilled at the idea of the "ten baggers" we've heard about at cocktail parties. But is that realistic? How many IBMs, Microsofts, or Apples are there? How many companies are so successful that their stocks just seem to keep on going, going, going to many multiples of their original offering price? As you know, not very many, and they're hard to find.

There are stocks that gain 40 or 50 percent in a year, but even these are hard to find and often come with risks many might not find acceptable. So as a result, we choose not to shoot the moon with our picks. We're not trying to find the can't-miss winners, the glamour stocks of the age that everyone is piling into, although some of our picks are inevitably popular.

Instead, we seek something more modest but still very lucrative to your portfolio: stocks that we feel are well positioned to achieve a 20 percent return per year and can perform in that range over a sustained period. These are not stocks that will double this year and lose 50 percent (back to zero return) the next. While these are not stocks you can buy and ignore for years or even months, we feel that if you own them, you'll be able to sleep at night.

If our picks as a whole achieve a 20 percent sustainable annual return, with at least some strength in a down market, we will feel that we've more than done our job.

20 PERCENT RETURNS—JUST HOW MUCH BETTER *IS* THAT?

Some may wonder why it's really so important to do better than "market" returns. After all, if you make money at all, that's a good thing, right? And your friends talk about doubling their money, hitting four baggers (quadrupling it), ten baggers, and the like. So why did you just spend sixteen bucks on this book to try to get some portion of your portfolio up to a 20 percent annual return?

The answer lies in the sometimes subtle, sometimes not-so-subtle power of compounding; that is, the return on your money and the returns on the returns that materialize, at first slowly, then begin to snowball ahead. Einstein once called it "the most powerful force in the universe."

If you earn more on your investment, and leave those earnings on the table to compound, the results can be staggering. Even a little more return will eventually produce some pretty amazing returns. Imagine investing $1,000. Check out Table 1 below to see what happens to your money.

▼ **Table 1: 100 Best Technology Stocks**

THE BENEFITS OF EXCEEDING MARKET RETURNS

$1,000	years:	1	2	5	10	15	20	30	40
Market return	5.0%	$1,050	$1,103	$1,276	$1,629	$2,079	$2,653	$4,322	$7,040
Beat by 5%	10.0%	$1,100	$1,210	$1,611	$2,594	$4,177	$6,727	$17,449	$45,259
Beat by 10%	15.0%	$1,150	$1,323	$2,011	$4,046	$8,137	$16,367	$66,212	$267,864
Beat by 15%	20.0%	$1,200	$1,440	$2,488	$6,192	$15,407	$38,338	$237,376	$1,469,772

If you invest $1,000 at a market return of, say, 5 percent, you'll earn $50 after one year—simple enough. If you leave that money on the table, invested at 5 percent, the return on the original investment plus the earnings will grow nicely, more than doubling it in fifteen years and almost quintupling it to $4,322 in thirty years. If you invest, say, $100,000 now, that's $432,200 when you retire, perhaps, and that's if you don't add another dime to the kitty.

Now kick that rate of return up to 10, 15, or even 20 percent. What happens? At 20 percent annually for fifteen years, you would end up with fifteen times your original investment; at thirty years, you'd have 237 times your original investment! Now if you invested $100,000, that's what, $23 million? You can see why 20 percent is a big deal. And you can also see why Warren Buffett, with his 30 percent returns over the course of forty years, is one of the world's top three net worth individuals.

Heck, we'd even take 5 percent better than market returns. Though less than our desired objective of 20 percent, a 10 percent return over thirty years still generates more than four times the cash nest egg as compared to a 5 percent "market" return.

Doesn't that $16 spent on this book start to look better now?

Best Means Best

Okay, so we've got a handle on what we're looking for in a technology stock, what it really is, and why we're interested. What about *best*? We should be able to find something pretty good in a standard dictionary, and sure enough the *Random House Dictionary* comes through with two definitions, both relevant:

1. Of the highest quality, excellence, or standing—*the best work, the best students*; 2. Most advantageous, suitable, or desirable; *the best way.*

These definitions capture what we're trying to do with *100 Best Technology Stocks*. We culled through long lists of stocks and companies, both established and emerging, to come up with the best possible assortment. That assortment takes into account many characteristics, which boil down eventually into reward and risk. The characteristics, which will be illuminated a bit more later on, combine hard facts and intangibles into a *story*.

It's a bit more complicated than this, but, bottom line, we've chosen the 100 technology companies with the most compelling stories—the greatest potential to turn your invested dollars into sizable returns without incurring too much risk.

Growth Versus Value?

Our approach to stock analysis and selection is still a "value" approach, even though many investing professionals don't associate "value" principles with growth stock investing. We think these professionals (and many financial journalists) are wrong, for a company's value can clearly be based on its growth, both in principle and in tangible calculations. As we just saw in the last sidebar, a stream of growing cash returns can have considerable value.

And in case you think this flies in the face of the Buffettonian view of value, it doesn't. Unlike his predecessor and teacher Benjamin Graham, who tended to count only a company's assets, liabilities, and current income in the value equation, Warren Buffett clearly includes growth in his intrinsic value equation.

In the sister book *100 Best Stocks You Can Buy*, we identify what we feel to be the 100 best values overall. In this book, The *100 Best Technology Stocks You Can Buy*, we are finding the 100 best values among stocks within the dynamic technology sector.

Best Growth Investing Strategies

Growth stock investing in general—and technology growth stock investing in particular—can be challenging. Why? Because most companies in their initial growth phases don't have a long, solid track record of financial, or for that matter, marketplace performance. It becomes more important to have a good crystal ball. The past doesn't predict the future, because there isn't very much past to go on.

As we explain in more detail in our sister book *The 100 Best Stocks You Can Buy*, analyzing a company for the purposes of investing is similar, if not the same, as analyzing the purchase of the entire business. You want to look at the numbers stuff—the financials—revenues, margins, profits, assets, cash flow. You also want to look at the intangibles—brand, marketplace acceptance, market share, management quality, channel excellence, and supply chain excellence—that lead to *future* financial excellence.

This model may oversimplify a bit, but essentially calls for examining the *results*—the financials—and the *story*—the business model and intangibles that sell the goods and bring in the cash.

We carry this same thought process into *The 100 Best Technology Stocks You Can Buy*. But since many of the companies we analyze are young, and are still waiting to some degree to be defined by their future, we place more emphasis on the intangibles, that is, the story. Not that we ignore the financials completely; we can't. We simply choose to look more into the future prospects for the company and less into the past results. You'll see that in the write-ups that follow.

Putting Yourself at the Helm

If you're reading this, you're probably a do-it-yourself investor. You may be an investor relying on others to make your investments, but you want to know what they're talking about. Either way, you're reading this because you want to get beyond throwing darts at stocks hoping to hit winners. You also want to get beyond relying on blind faith and throwing your investments over the wall to others.

So to do better than throwing darts, and to invest with a rational thought process and methodical approach, you need to have an investing *strategy*.

What Do We Mean by *Investing Strategy*?

Now, the notion of an investing strategy may sound kind of scary—weeks, months on end with highly paid consultants going over tools and techniques and four-quadrant grids and all sorts of things—expensive and at the end of the day so complex nobody can really use it, right?

We feel that adherence to a few guiding investing principles is easier and more effective for an individual running his or her own investing show. Not absolute adherence, mind you—if that worked, you could simply write a software program to do your investing for you and head to the white sands of the Cayman Islands. No, of course it isn't that simple.

So here we offer what might be considered, rather than a full-blown strategy, a series of standalone stratagems or principles or *rules* that a technology might follow. These principles help guide a technology investor to better stock picks, but—*disclaimer*—won't necessarily guarantee success. Followed as guidelines, they should produce better results with less pain and less risk.

Here, in no particular order or combination, are seven such guiding principles:

Play Tailwinds

Anyone who has thrown a Frisbee or hit a golf ball knows that it's easier and faster to go downwind than upwind. Not that upwind is impossible, but downwind just works better. And it's easier.

The same concept applies to investing. Why invest in a stock in a dying or out-of-favor industry? Why invest in a good homebuilder when home-building as a whole is going to heck in a handbasket? Sure, that one home-builder may make a great product and may be poised to capture a lot of market share when the market rebounds, and you can make a case to buy that homebuilder. But for the most part, picking growth stocks is easier if you pick a timely or "in favor" industry.

If an industry is in favor, a company within it is more likely to be in favor. More to the point, the industry itself is growing, and so the players within it will have an easier time meeting or exceeding growth expectations.

So part of the process in picking growth stocks involves identifying "tailwind" industries. Such tailwind industries can normally be categorized into one of three types:

1. *New or emerging industries.* These are industries where the technologies—and the key players—are still being sorted out. Today, cloud computing is an excellent example. By way of illustration, personal computers were big in the 1980s and early 1990s, and Internet stocks in the 1995–2001 era, and for that matter, railroad stocks in the 1870s through 1900.
2. *Strong growth cycle industries.* These industries have risen beyond inception to be well understood and accepted by the market. Major players have already been sorted out, and are now enjoying the rising tide of the entire industry. Computer networking, design automation, and Internet retail are current examples, as were personal computing in the late 1990s and automakers perhaps in the 1950s. Care must be taken here to choose an industry with plenty of growth left, still operating well in advance of a maturing or consolidation phase (like PCs are today) bound to hamper growth prospects for all.
3. *Re-emergent industries.* The electrical infrastructure in the United States is starting to sag under the weight of higher peak and average demands. In addition, the usage patterns have changed as the population has shifted from the industrialized Midwest to Sun Belt and coastal states. This system, which wasn't designed with a great deal of redundancy in the first place, has been patched and propped up well beyond its

original planned capacity. Enron learned how to manipulate the system's shortcomings and basically turned California on and off at will. The solution to this problem is more capacity, certainly, but also an improved transmission network, smarter control, and considerably better analytics. Re-engineering the transmission system on the fly will not be cheap, and companies that understand the need and can provide solutions will do well, not only in the United States but in developing countries as well.

The key is identifying economic megatrends, some of which may be obvious by simply listening and looking around. What is hot now? What is getting a lot of attention and is on the verge of becoming a mainstream industry? We've all thought about putting solar panels on our roof or buying a hybrid vehicle, and as the economics start to make more sense, *voila!*, it goes mainstream. Someday you'll be able to buy solar panels at Home Depot and install them yourself in a weekend. We're not there yet, but wouldn't you like to be invested in photovoltaic (PV) technologies when that happens?

Here are a few tailwind industries we've already identified:

- Security and surveillance
- Semiconductors and LED lighting
- Business information technology
- "Cloud" computing infrastructure
- Semiconductor manufacturing products

Many of our *100 Best Technology* stocks come from these industries.

Buy Like You're Buying a Business

For those of you readers who also read our *100 Best Stocks You Can Buy*, this and the next few sections will sound familiar. These principles apply to any investment strategy, but are worth emphasizing in the technology investment world, as many people seem to lose track of the numbers when they become enamored with a favorite tech.

Earlier in this introduction, we laid out one of the key tenets of our framework (and frame of mind, really)—that while this book is about growth investing, we still emphasize and use a value approach. The implied principle, of course, is that growth is part of the value equation. But that's not all—here are a few more components of our value thought process.

As with any value investing approach, you must think of buying shares in a company as buying the company itself, that is, buying the business. Particularly with emerging growth companies, you should put yourself in an entrepreneurial frame of mind well beyond a simple investing frame of mind. Would you want to own that business? Why or why not? That's the first and biggest question you must answer.

Fundamentally, whether or not you want to own the business depends on two factors: first, the returns you expect to receive on your investment in the near and long-term future and second, the risk you'll take in generating those returns. Fortunately, the third factor the prospective entrepreneur must consider—"do I have the time for this?"—isn't typically a consideration, although as we'll point out later on, technology investing may well take more of your time than plain old *100 Best* investing. Things change more and faster.

So you are looking for tangible value—tangible worth—for your precious, scarce, and hard-earned investment capital dollars. That return doesn't have to be immediate in the form of dividends or a share of the assets, as many in the traditional value school suggest. For growth stocks, it will come in the form of enterprise growth for the longer term.

If you realize your return in the form of owning a share of a larger company eventually, that's still a legitimate return. Cash flow received later in the form of a higher share price or a takeover is still a cash return, it is just less certain because of the forces of change that may take place in the interim. It may theoretically be worth less because of the nature of *discounting*—a dollar received tomorrow is worth more than a dollar received twenty years in the future. But future cash returns are what we all seek, and are what may be truly worth waiting for if we pick the right growth stock.

Value also implies safety. The safety comes in two forms. First is the fundamental quality and soundness of the firm's financial fundamentals, that is, income, cash flow, and the balance sheet. Value companies have plenty of reserves, a large enough margin of safety, to weather downturns and unforeseen events in the marketplace; but many typical growth companies do not enjoy such protection. But, second, they can have strong enough intangibles— brands, market position, innovation capability, supply chain strength, etc.— to maintain their position in that marketplace and generate future returns. For example, we feel that Apple and Agilent, among our picks, have strong brands and reputations that have become part of their intrinsic value and add to their safety. These companies are safer than "no-brand" companies trying to compete in the same market.

If you're really practicing value investing principles, you buy these companies at reduced prices, when the markets are down, when the company is out of favor. You're looking for situations where the price is less than what you perceive to be the value, although calculating the value that precisely is elusive. When you buy cheap you provide another margin of safety; that margin makes it less likely that the stock will drop further. It gives you room for error if you turn out to be wrong about a choice. Again, it's much like buying a business of your own—you want to pay as little as possible in case things don't turn out as you'd expect.

Taking a strong "I'm buying this business" approach provides greater confidence and safety and is more likely to get you through today's volatile business and investing cycles.

Focus on Financials, of Course

In *100 Best Stocks*, we called financials the strategic fundamentals that define, or keep score of, a company's success. We've identified eight strategic financial fundamentals below. They are "strategic" because they go beyond the typical revenues, earnings, cash flows, and so forth reported as snapshots of past financial performance; these strategic indicators are designed to tell you what is *really* going on with a company and to be, to an extent, leading indicators of future financial performance.

These eight strategic fundamentals are also found in our mainstream *100 Best Stocks* book. They work the same way with growth/technology stocks, but more emphasis may be placed on some, such as profit margins and the generation of excess capital, and less on others, like dividends. You can use this as a checklist, although it's hard to find a company that shows excellence in all of these areas.

Are Gross and Operating Profit Margins Growing?

We like profitable companies; who doesn't? But what really counts is the size of the profit margin and particularly the growth in that margin, especially with a new or rapidly growing company. If a company has a gross margin (sales minus costs of goods sold) exceeding that of its competitors, that shows that it's doing something right, probably with its customers and/or with its costs. If gross or operating margins are growing rapidly, so much the better—its products are really catching on with customers.

Competitive analysis is elusive because direct apples-to-apples compares are hard to find, and there are no industry standard gross margins, particularly in emerging industries. It is best to look at the company's own history for valid comparisons.

Many innovative technology companies are built based on improved gross margins. If my company's power supply design, for example, is built using the latest highly integrated methods and costs 10 percent less to build than the design you're using now, and your current supply represents 10 percent of your manufacturing cost, my company can add 1 percent to the gross margin of every product you make that uses this design.

While a growing gross margin signals that the company is doing something right, it's not a perfect indicator. The economy as a whole may have moved from boom to bust, and even excellent companies may report declines in gross and especially operating margins (sales – cost of goods sold – operating expenses) as workers are laid off and capacity is reduced. Still, in a steady state environment, it makes sense to favor companies with growing margins. In a declining market, companies that can protect their margins will come out ahead.

Does a Company Produce More Capital Than It Consumes?

Make no mistake about it—we like cash. And pure and simple—we like it when a company produces more cash than it consumes, particularly in the early phases of its growth, when that's particularly hard to do. Cash flow is a particularly sensitive measure for smaller technology companies, where R & D can quickly consume a significant amount of the available capital.

At the end of the day, cash generation is the simplest measure of whether a company is successful, especially over the long term. Sure, if a company buys an airplane or opens a factory or a bunch of stores in a given quarter, it will be cash-flow negative. But that should be a temporary thing; over the long haul, it should produce, not consume cash. Companies that continually have to borrow funds or sell shares to raise enough cash to stay in business are on the wrong track.

How do you determine this? You'll have to become familiar with the statement of cash flows or equivalent in a company's financial reports. Cash flow from operations is usually positive and represents cash booked from sales less cost of goods sold, with adjustments for noncash items like depreciation and for increases or decreases in working capital. In simple terms, is the cash going into the cash register from the business?

Cash used for investing purposes or similar is a bit of a misnomer, and represents net cash used to invest in the business—usually for capital expenditures, but also for short term noncash investments such as securities and a few other smaller items usually beyond the scope of a typical assessment. This figure is typically negative unless the company sells some part of its infrastructure. Over the long haul, cash generated from operations should well exceed cash used to invest in the business.

Companies in growth or expansion mode may not show such a surplus, and that's where cash from financing activities comes in. That's the cash generated from issuing debt or selling securities—or paying off debt or repurchasing shares, if things are going well, and dividends are included here as well. Again, a successful company will produce more cash—capital—from the business than it consumes, just as a successful household does the same, else it goes into debt. Smart investors track this surplus over time.

Again, a company in an extreme growth phase can be expected to consume cash to finance business growth; the less the better, and if a company is self-funded in its early or rapid growth stages, so much the better.

Are Expenses Under Control?

Again, just like your household, company expenses should be under control, and anything else, especially without explanation, is a yellow flag.

The best way to test this is to check whether "selling, general, and administrative" expenses (SG&A) are rising, and more to the point, rising faster than sales. If so, that's a yellow, not necessarily a red, flag. For very rapidly growing companies, expense growth exceeding revenue growth may be tolerable in the very short term, as the company is building for growth, say, by adding a sales force. But if the excess expense growth continues, it suggests that something is out of control, and it will catch up with the company sooner or later. In the recent downturn, companies that were able to reduce their expenses to match revenue declines scored more points, too.

Is Noncash Working Capital Under Control?

Working capital is a hard concept to grasp—even for small entrepreneurs who live with its ups and downs on a daily basis. Insufficient working capital is one of the biggest causes of death for small and growing businesses, and working capital, and especially changes in working capital, can signal success or trouble.

Using a simplistic analogy, working capital is the circulatory lifeblood of the business. Money comes in, money goes out, working capital is what circulates in the veins in between. In its purest sense, it is cash, receivables, and inventory, less short-term debts. It's what you own less what you owe aside from fixed assets such as plants, stores, and equipment.

If receivables are increasing, that sounds like a good thing—more people owe you more money. But if receivables are rising and sales aren't, that suggests that people aren't paying their bills, or worse, the business has to finance more to achieve the same level of sales. Similarly, a rise in inventory without a rise in sales means that it costs the business more money— more working capital—to do the same amount of business. That costs twice, because unless the firm is lucky, more inventory means more obsolescence and potentially more writeoffs down the road, especially in the tech industry where products tend not to live very long.

Such inventory growth in the short term may precede a growth spurt. On the other hand, in the technology sector, obsolescence is a major risk factor due to the rapid pace of development. A quick look at the number of one-year-old products in the bargain bin at any technology store will tell you all you need to know about obsolescence.

So a sharp investor will check to see that major working capital items— receivables and inventory—aren't growing faster than sales; indeed, a company that generates more sales with a decrease in working capital is becoming more productive.

Is Debt in Line with Business Growth?

Like many other fundamentals items, you can tear your hair out looking at debt figures and trying to decide whether they're in line with asset levels, equity levels, and industry norms. A simpler test is to see whether long-term debt is increasing or decreasing, and in particular, whether it is increasing faster than business growth. Gold stars go to companies with little to no debt, and to companies able to grow without issuing mountains of long-term debt.

A sharp-eyed investor might also check out other items, like capital leases, often hard to tease out of financial statements but a financing activity just the same, just not debt in its purest sense.

Is Earnings Growth Steady?

We enter the danger zone here, because the management of many companies has learned to manage earnings to provide a steady improvement, always beating the street by a penny or two. So stability is a good thing for all investors, and companies that can manage toward stability get extra points. It's worth checking for, but with the proverbial grain of salt.

Still, a company that is able to manage its sales, earnings, cash flow, and debt levels more consistently than competitors, and perhaps more consistently than what would be suggested by the ups and downs of the economy—or its competitors—is desirable, or at least more desirable than the alternatives.

Is Return on Equity Steady or Growing?

Return on equity (ROE) is another of those hard-to-grasp concepts, and another subjective measure in valuing assets and earnings. But at the end of the day, it's what all investors really seek; that is, returns on their capital investments.

Like many other figures derived from income statements and balance sheets, a pure number is hard to interpret—does a 26.7 percent ROE mean, in itself, that a company is excellent? The figure sounds healthy, to be sure—it's a heck of a lot better than investing your money in a CD or T-Bill. But because earnings and asset values are subjective, it may not represent true success. In fact, a company can increase ROE simply by borrowing money (yes!) and investing it into the business, even if it isn't invested as productively as other previous funds invested. The math is complicated; we won't go into it here.

So the true test of ROE success is to check whether it is steady or increasing. Increasing—that makes sense. Why steady? Because if a company makes profits in a previous period and reinvests them in the business, that amount of money becomes part of equity (retained earnings). If the company reinvests productively, it will produce more returns, and ROE will at least keep up. If the company can't reinvest those earnings productively, ROE will drop—and perhaps it should be paying the earnings to you as dividends instead of investing them unproductively in the business. So if ROE is steady, the company still has good investments to make, and management is probably doing the right thing.

For very new growth companies, ROE figures may be understated. First, if they have considerable cash on hand from initial financing, that is also part of their equity position. This cash earns little (almost nothing these days) but is being banked for future needs. This cash inflates the denominator and reduces the reported ROE. Similarly, most early-stage companies are financed by equity—stock sales, venture capital, and so forth—and tend to use relatively less debt, again reducing financial leverage, and thus reported ROE.

Does the Company Pay a Dividend?

Those of you coming from *The 100 Best Stocks You Can Buy* recognize dividends as an important investing theme for the mainstream *100 Best* stocks. Aggressively growing companies—those with a good story, anyway—should be able to invest funds in their business with good results, and thus, as an investor, you should want them to do that. For any financially secure company, we like to see dividends as a gesture of appreciation for investors and a bird in the hand to its investors. Similarly, we like to see dividends as payback to investors for growth companies but realize that it might not always make sense. A company with great and well-funded growth prospects and dividends is the best of both worlds and is to be admired, but if a growth company is paying dividends, one is always nagged by the question "if the business is really growing and doing well, why can't these guys (and gals) invest these funds for a greater return than I can get?"

Technology companies, in particular, are less likely to pay dividends than many others. In fact, if you find a technology-heavy company that *is* paying a dividend, you should look twice to see if there's some reason for it. Certainly, huge cash generators like Google, Apple, and Oracle can afford a dividend (they barely know what to do with all the money they've already got), but smaller companies should be putting all of their spare dollars into the company and advancing their innovation agenda.

Bottom line: We like dividends, but in the technology stocks arena, they are not always the thing you really want.

Price-to-Earnings-to-Growth Ratio

Finally, we'll tip our hats to one of the more standard and commonly used financial metrics applied well to growth stocks: the price-to-earnings-to-growth (PEG) ratio. The ratio is comprised of two parts: the conventional and ever-popular price-to-earnings ratio (P/E), and the growth rate, usually measured as the five-year growth rate in earnings per share or something similar. The ratio is obtained by first calculating the P/E, then dividing that figure by the growth rate. The purpose of the ratio, along with its component P/E, is valuation; that is, to determine if a stock's price makes sense related to the level of earnings generated.

So if you have a growth stock with a P/E ratio of 20, that implies a 5 percent return (earnings of, say, $1 on a share price of $20)—a relatively low rate considering the risks involved but not too far out there (recently, the S&P 500 benchmark had a P/E ratio just exceeding 16). But that's not the whole story, especially for a growth stock.

A P/E of 20 is relatively high compared to the market—*if* there is little in the way of growth prospects for the company. Stated differently, the price paid is high relative to the earnings generated, given that there is little growth prospect for the earnings. But if the earnings are growing at 20 percent per year, now what? Without going into the math details, those earnings will double in approximately four years. (If you want to learn the shorthand calculation for this—look up "Rule of 72" in a search engine.)

So now you can think of the P/E as being something closer to 10—in four years; that's pretty good. Or, turned around, if the stock price reflects this growth and the P/E ratio stays constant at 20, the price will be $40 in four years—$2 in earnings times a P/E of 20.

Many investors choose—wisely, we think—to use the PEG ratio to incorporate growth into the valuation exercise. The growth rate determines whether the P/E, and thus the stock price, really makes sense. Our $20 stock with a P/E of 20 and a growth rate of 20 percent would have a PEG ratio of 1. A stock with a $60 price and earnings of $1—P/E of 60 and a growth rate of 20 percent—would have a PEG of 3. The 20 percent growth rate is nice, but it doesn't support a $60 stock price or the P/E of 60 currently experienced by the shareholders.

Generally, a PEG ratio of 1 or less is considered reasonable, but a P/E of 3 is considered too high; that is, the growth rate does not really support the stock price as it is. PEG serves as a good and fast valuation benchmark, but there are two caveats. First, reported earnings may not reflect the true earning potential of the company because of one-time items and accounting tricks. Second, the growth rates, especially for new companies without a track record, may also be fickle and hard to project too far into the future.

Intangibles—Now More Than Ever

Now we will turn our attention beyond the financial statements to those ephemeral, true but hard-to-grasp qualities that make companies great now and in the future—the intangibles. Intangibles are sort of the rest of the story for all stocks, but a big part of the story for growth stocks. Why? Because the right combination of intangibles—the right story—will bring success and ultimately solid financial fundamentals down the road.

Intangibles can be thought of as the secret sauce that makes any company work. If the secret sauce is right, the company will vault past its competition and take full advantage of its growth opportunity. In extreme cases like Apple or Starbucks a few years ago, the secret sauce will create the opportunity; that is, it will define new markets for products customers didn't even know they needed.

Because so many of the stocks in *100 Best Technology Stocks* operate in the world of developing applications, the intangibles can be *the* story to an investor. Many of our companies are working on products for which there is no currently established market. As an example, when the first personal computers hit the market, their sales figures were not earthshaking. Later, when the software started appearing that let people do genuinely useful things with a computer, sales took off. Would we have enjoyed being a Dell investor when people found they could do their own taxes and manage their own finances on a computer? We would.

The nature of technology is to enable what was previously not even considered, so new technology markets develop constantly. Trying to present the business case for the first consumer digital camera was an exercise in total speculation—there were no hard numbers to go on, just a lot of cost figures and projected market share capture rates. But it turned out to be a great story, even without an established market or a product.

A Hundred Billion to Spend

When you look at any company, perhaps the bottom-line question follows the Buffett wisdom: If you had a hundred billion to spend (and we'll assume, the genius intellect to spend it right), could you re-create that company?

If the answer is "yes," it may still be a great company, but it may not be great enough to fend off competition and keep its customers forever. If the answer is "no," the company truly has something unique to offer in the marketplace, difficult to duplicate at any cost. That distinctive competence, that sustainable, competitive edge—whatever it is, a brand, a trade secret, a lock on distribution or supply channels—may be worth more than all the factories and high-rise office buildings and cash in the bank it could ever have. Buffett often used this example to describe the value of the Coca-Cola Company, but we think it now fits Apple perfectly.

The intangibles are the "soft" factors that make companies unique, the factors that add up to more than the sum of their parts, the factors that ultimately drive future revenues. Intangibles not only define excellence, they define the future, while most financial fundamentals mainly define the past. Following are seven key intangible categories to think about in any company or industry.

Does the Company Have a Moat?

A business "moat" performs much the same role as the medieval castle equivalent—it protects the business from competition. The factors that create the moat (some discussed to follow) are ultimately the factors that prevent you, with your $100 billion, from taking their business. Moats are usually a combination of brand, product technology, design, marketing and distribution channels, and customer loyalty all working together to protect a company. A moat doesn't just protect the existence of a company, it helps it command higher prices and earn higher profits now and in the future.

Moats are a particularly important concept for growth companies. They can be very dynamic and even fleeting, and even more difficult to assess. A new company in a new industry, say, LED lighting, may have a moat right out of the gate, because it came into the market, as Civil War General Nathan Bedford Forrest famously said, "firstest with the mostest." It enjoys initial success because of its "first mover" advantage, but this advantage quickly dissipates as other competitors—some with new and better technologies or manufacturing processes or marketing channels, etc.—hit the market. The moat can dry up, so to speak, so determining the *permanence* of the moat becomes imperative.

Other companies may come into a market with no moat at all—but they acquire one because they have a better way of doing something. Dell, which we'll come back to in a second—might qualify here.

Whether a company has a "narrow" moat, a "wide" moat, or none at all is a subjective assessment for you to make. You can get some help at Morningstar (*www.morningstar.com*), whose stock ratings include an assessment of a company's moat.

Coca-Cola has a moat because of the sheer impossibility of surpassing its brand and brand recognition worldwide. Dell *built* a moat when they entered the already crowded PC market with a direct-to-consumer sales model that supported customization and fast shipping. They were able to capture the vast majority of the sales channel costs, which put them far ahead of all the players who sold their products at retail. While this model has been duplicated at many of its competitors, Dell had a clear five-year head start on the field. As with our *100 Best Stocks* book, we have a "Moat Stars" list to identify the Top 10 stocks with a solid and sustainable competitive advantage—see Table 6 to follow.

Does the Company Have an Excellent Brand?

It's hard to say enough about brand, especially in today's fast-moving, highly packaged, highly national and international culture. A strong brand means consistency and a promise to consumers, and consumers sold on a brand will prefer it over any other, almost regardless of price. People still buy Tide, and although there's been a slowdown lately, Starbucks is still synonymous with high quality and ambience.

Good brands command higher prices, and foster loyalty and identity and even customer "love." Consider Apple again. Do people line up around the block to buy a new computer from HP or Acer? Not even close. In China recently there were a dozen or so fake Apple stores closed by the government after complaints from the real company. Is anyone setting up fake Gateway Country stores in China? We very much doubt it. Most PC manufacturers have to take out expensive ads in print and broadcast media just to get people to look at their products. Apple, on the other hand, can issue a three-sentence press release and turn the tech world upside down overnight. Once a company has created a dominant brand in the marketplace, aside from some major faux pas, it will endure and continue to create value for shareholders for years to come; a good brand is one of the most valuable (yet hard to value) long-term assets around.

Consumer brand loyalty is easy to spot and understand. On the commercial side, it's a bit more subtle, but it still exists. Engineers develop a strong affinity and preference for a certain set of design tools or a certain manufacturer's components. IT organizations are fiercely loyal to suppliers that support their products and solve problems on a timely basis. Ask yourself if a company has a sought-after brand, a brand customers would pay extra to buy or align with, a brand that would be difficult to duplicate at any cost. Would customers rather fight than switch?

See Table 9 for our list of Brand Stars.

Is the Company a Market Leader?

Market leadership usually—but not always—goes hand in hand with brand. The trick is to decide whether a company really leads in its industry. Often—but not always—that's a factor of size. The market leader usually has the highest market share, and the important point is that it calls the shots with regards to price, technology, marketing message, and so forth—other companies must play catch-up and often discount their prices to keep up. Apple is a market leader in digital music, Intel is the market leader in microprocessors, and Toyota is emerging as the market leader in automobiles.

Market leaders may be leaders in smaller, or niche, markets—it still works. Mentor Graphics is the leader in electronic design automation, Autoliv is the leader in automotive passive restraints, and Cree leads the way in LED lighting and components.

Excellent companies tend to be market leaders, and market leaders tend to be excellent companies. But this relationship doesn't always hold true—sometimes the nimble but smaller competitor is the excellent company—and will likely assume market leadership eventually. Examples of smaller companies with market-leading products like 8x8, Digi, Ormat, and Riverbed can be found on our list.

Does the Company Have Channel Excellence?

Channels in business parlance refers to the chain of players engaged to sell and distribute a company's products. These players might be stores, they might be other industrial companies, or they might be independent sales forces or distributors. If a company is considered a top supplier in a particular channel or a company has especially good relations with its channel, that's a plus.

Excellent companies develop solid channel relationships and become the preferred supplier in those channels. Companies such as Flextronics, First Solar, Power-One, and Stryker all have excellent relationships with the channels through which they sell their product. Or they might *be* the channel, as is the case with Arrow Electronics, Avnet, or Insight, and simply do it better than anyone else.

Does the Company Have Supply Chain Excellence?

Like distribution channels, excellent companies develop excellent and low-cost supply channels. They are seldom caught off guard by supply shortages and tend to get favorable and stable prices for whatever they buy. This is often not an easy assessment unless you know something about a particular industry. Companies like Dell, Celestica, and Sanmina-SCI succeed because they manage their supply chains well. Large volume manufacturers in low-margin businesses are scrupulous about their supply chain processes and are often the models that others follow.

Does the Company Have Excellent Management?

Well, it's not hard to grasp what happens if a company doesn't have good management; performance fails, and few inside or outside the company respect the company. It's not easy for an investor to determine if a management team does a good job or acts in shareholder interests.

Clues can include candor and honesty and the ability of company management to speak in accessible, easily understood terms about the company and company performance (it's worth listening to conference calls as a resource). A management team that admits errors and eschews other forms of arrogance and entitlement (i.e., luxury perks, office suites, aircraft) is probably tilting their interests toward shareholders, as is the management team that is financially prudent and refrains from excess expenditure or temptation arising from an abundance of early cash invested in the business.

This may be the most subjective and elusive assessment of all, as few investors work with these folks on a daily basis. Technology companies, many of which are very young, may still be run by founders who have not had time to hone their business skills. Some may still be run by the original technical development team who had little in the way of management skills to begin with. Or they can be run by a founder like Steve Jobs, and you know what that has meant. Look closely at the executive team and see if they have a track record of business successes, not just technical achievement.

Is the Company an Excellent Innovator?

This question seems pretty obvious, especially for tech companies. Innovation, and the effective management of innovation, is key to new or emerging companies, and even re-emerging companies, building their market presence. *Innovation*—as differentiated from its oft-interchanged word *invention*—implies not only the creative capacity and effort to create new products—but also to *bring them to market* in a way to satisfy or delight *customers*. The italicized parts of the last sentence are key to determining the quality and value of a company's innovation. Innovations must be about things customers want or need or even about a better customer experience, and they must be real and available in the marketplace to succeed.

Innovation is not just about the products that a company sells. Innovative companies don't wait for a market to develop and then compete with a half dozen other companies to address it. A truly innovative company recognizes an unmet need well before others and produces a product that is both first to market and best to market. Apple has taught the consumer electronics industry how to innovate by releasing products that define an entire category, like the iPod, iPad, and iPhone.

Be Streetwise

One savvy guiding principle advanced through the years, especially by Fidelity Magellan fund manager and investing guru Peter Lynch, but also by Buffett and others, is to observe what's happening on the street to gain an investing advantage.

In the view of Lynch, Buffett, and others (including ourselves) it is important to acquire a sense of the business before investing in it. Again, it's like buying the whole business for yourself—why would you do it if you didn't understand it? The principle goes further: You can often gain the best insight into a business simply by watching what goes on on the street.

Stop, Look, and Listen

We're talking Main Street here, not Wall Street. Watching a business in person means watching customers go in and out, engaging with the business yourself, or if they make high-tech 3D vision components for integrated circuit manufacturing, something you wouldn't normally be able to see on the street, find out more by reading about it or networking with those who do see it.

The idea is to gain a real, on-the-ground understanding of the marketplace, and how the company performs in it. Is the customer experience right? Do customers respond well? Does the business seem to be growing, and managing its growth effectively? When we see three Home Depots within three miles of each other, we start wondering whether management really sees through to customer needs and operational costs at the ground level or if decisions are being made on some other basis.

We advise watching, listening, reading, networking, and gaining personal experiences with a company wherever possible. Buffett once watched the number of railroad tank cars being switched in and out of a chemical company to get some investing insight. You may or may not wish to go this far, but if you like coffee anyway, why not go to a Starbucks at least once in a while to gauge activity, customer service, and customer response? If you're investing in technology, take a small survey of your own experiences with the technology you use and see on a daily basis. Is there one vendor or brand that constantly impresses you with either their products or service? Or, is there an industry that, for the life of you, makes no sense as a business proposition? As an intelligent investor, you trust what you see and discount what you cannot confirm. Watch the financial press and especially the trade press on these industries to get the best data you can.

Keep It Simple . . .

A corollary principle, again spearheaded by Buffett, is to follow and invest in what you know and understand. With technology stocks, this principle may break down a bit as many new technologies defy thorough knowledge, especially by those individuals outside the industry. Buffett might have trouble with technology stock investing, at least the way we approach it, because it is doubtful that he, nor very many other people, would be able to *thoroughly* understand the technologies and businesses built around them.

As a result, you can choose to find some creative ways to stay on board, again through networks or industry journals and such, or you can choose to stay away from the more esoteric businesses altogether. There are plenty of "simple" businesses even in the technology space.

Manage Risk with a Tiered Portfolio

Although *The 100 Best Technology Stocks You Can Buy* is designed to help you pick the best of the best growth stocks to buy, investing by nature goes well beyond simply buying stocks, just like owning an automobile goes far beyond buying it. Just as clearly, this book isn't about investing strategy or about the personal financial strategies necessary to ensure retirement or a prosperous future. That said, we think a few words are in order.

We find that a lot of investors lose the forest in the trees, spending all of their energy trying to find individual stocks or funds without putting enough consideration into their overall investing framework. If they look at the big picture at all, they look at the formulaic covenants of asset allocation, a favorite subject of the financial planning and advisory community, as though the difference between 50 percent equities and 60 percent equities makes all the difference in the world. Sure, it might in the world of pension funds and other institutional investments, where a 10 percent adjustment could move millions into or out of a particular asset class and more or less toward safety, but what about a $100,000 portfolio? Does $10,000 more or less in stocks, bonds, or cash make that much difference?

Perhaps not. And of course there's more to that story—doesn't it matter more which equities you invest in than just the fact that you're 60 percent in equities? While asset allocation models make for nice pie charts, we prefer to approach big-picture portfolio constructs differently.

Moreover, in connecting *100 Best* with *100 Best Technology* stocks, the question becomes what percentage of your portfolio should be allocated to each (as well as other assets, like fixed income, real estate, gold, etc.). Rather than make hard-and-fast rules, like "Twenty percent of your portfolio should be in technology (or utilities, or health care) stocks," it makes sense to put some thought into your overall portfolio and the *components* of that portfolio, and how they all fit together.

Start with a Portfolio in Mind

First, we'll make an assumption: You are not a professional investor. You have other things to do with your time, and time is of the essence. You cannot spend forty, fifty, or sixty hours a week glued to a computer screen analyzing your investments.

To that assumption, we'll add another: that, as an individual investor, you're looking to beat the market. Not by a ton—20 percent sustained returns simply aren't possible *for your entire portfolio* without taking outlandish risks. But perhaps if the market is up 4 percent in a year, you'd like to achieve 6, perhaps 7 or 8 percent, without taking excessive risks. Or if the market is down 20 percent, perhaps you cut your losses at 5 or 10 percent. You're looking to do *somewhat better* than the market.

Because of time constraints, and owing to your objective to do slightly better than averages, and because you have *The 100 Best Technology Stocks You Can Buy* already at your fingertips, we suggest taking a tiered approach to your portfolio. The tiers aren't based on the type of assets; they're based on the amount of activity and attention you want to pay to different parts of your portfolio. It's a strategic portfolio approach you would probably take if you were managing a small business—put most of your focus on the products and customers who might bring the greatest new return to your business; let the rest of your slow, steady customer base function as it has for the long term.

To do this, we suggest breaking your portfolio into three tiers, or segments: the Foundation Portfolio, the Rotational Portfolio, and the Opportunistic Portfolio.

The Foundation Portfolio

In this construct, each investor defines and manages a cornerstone foundation portfolio, which is long-term in nature and requires relatively less active management. Frequently the foundation portfolio consists of retirement accounts (the paradigmatic long-term investment) and may include your personal residence or other long-lived personal or family assets, such as trusts, collectibles, and so forth.

The typical foundation portfolio is invested to achieve at least average market returns through index funds, quality mutual funds, and some income-producing assets such as bonds held to maturity. A foundation portfolio may contain some long-term plays in commodities or real estate to defend against inflation, particularly in such commodities as energy, precious metals, and real estate trusts. The foundation portfolio is largely left alone, although as with all investments it is important to check at least once in a while to make sure performance—and managers, if involved—are keeping up with expectations.

The stock selections in our sister book, *The 100 Best Stocks You Can Buy*, are generally well suited for this portfolio segment—although they can be used to populate all three portfolio segments at times.

The Rotational Portfolio

The second segment, the rotational portfolio, is managed fairly actively to keep up with changes in business cycles and conditions. It is likely in a set of stocks or funds that might be rotated or remixed occasionally to reflect business conditions or to get a little more offensive or defensive.

More than the other portfolios, this portfolio follows the rotation of market preference among different kinds of businesses and business assets. The portfolio is managed to redeploy assets among market or business sectors, between aggressive and defensive business assets, from large-cap to small-cap companies, from companies with international exposure to those with little of the same, from companies in favor versus out of favor, from stocks to bonds to commodities, and so forth. Sector-specific exchange-traded funds are a favorite component of these portfolios, as are cyclical and commodity-based stocks like gold mining stocks. As we indicated in our section on cyclicality, the semi-conductor sector is a perfect component for the rotational portfolio.

Is this about market timing? Let's call it intelligent or educated market timing. Studies that have been around for years tell us that it is impossible to effectively time market moves. It is impossible to catch highs and lows in particular investments, market sectors, or even the market as a whole. Nobody can find exact tops or bottoms. But by watching economic indicators and taking the pulse of business and the marketplace, long-term market performance can be boosted by well-rationalized and timely sector rotation. The key word is *timely*. The agile active investor has enough of a finger on the pulse to see the signs and invest accordingly.

While the idea isn't new, the advent of low-friction exchange-traded funds and other index portfolios makes it a lot more practical for individual investors. What does *low-friction* mean? They trade like a single stock—one order, one discounted commission. You don't have to liquidate or acquire a whole basket full of investments on your own to follow a sector. We should note that it's been possible to rotate assets in mutual fund families for years with a single phone call, but most funds in these families are less pure plays in their sector, and most fund families do not cover all sectors.

See the fourth and newest book in our series, *The 100 Best Exchange-Traded Funds You Can Buy 2012*, for more on exchange-traded funds.

The Opportunistic Portfolio

Here is where this book, *The 100 Best Technology Stocks You Can Buy*, is most likely to find a home.

The opportunistic portfolio is the most actively traded portion of an active, self-directed investor's total portfolio. The opportunistic portfolio looks for stocks or other investments that seem to be notably under- or overvalued at a particular time, or for more technology plays to boost the returns of the overall portfolio. Many technology stocks tend to go out of favor for no reason other than the fact that other technology stocks are out of favor. A broad-brush approach is used far more often than one might think—how else to explain upside surprises in revenue or earnings reports? As we said before, technology stocks can be difficult to understand, but this is what creates opportunity for those willing to do just a little bit of digging. Or reading. By the way, is that a book on technology stocks in your hand?

The opportunistic portfolio may be used to generate short-term income or cash, through short-term trading, or swing trading, or through short-term equity option strategies. Both topics are beyond scope here. And this part of the portfolio—or if you prefer to look at it as two separate twin peaks on your investing mountain—can also be used to layer in some technology plays. Perhaps you allocate 20 percent of your portfolio to technology stock plays, to be held onto for a year to a few years, and another 10 percent to short-term swing trades to be held onto for a few days or a few weeks. It depends on the investing styles you're comfortable with, and how much time you have to manage your investments.

ARE RETIREMENT ACCOUNTS ALWAYS PART OF THE FOUNDATION?

The long-term objectives and nature of retirement accounts suggest normal inclusion as part of the foundation portfolio. In fact, retirement assets can be deployed as part of either the rotational or opportunistic portfolio. And in fact, it might make a lot of sense. Why? Because returns generated are tax free, at least until withdrawn. Tax-free returns can compound much faster. Because of the importance of these assets, one should only commit a small portion to an actively managed opportunistic portfolio, but it can be a good way to juice the growth of this important asset base.

Make the Time Commitment

This final investing principle refers more to personal strategy than investing strategy. Many otherwise-savvy investors lose it because they simply don't have the time to do the homework, the investing due diligence, to manage their portfolios, especially with the rapid changes in business and investing sentiment inherent in today's markets.

We've said all along that buying a stock is like buying a business. Anyone who owns their own business knows about the time commitment involved to manage *one* business, let alone several. The good news, though, is that you have professional management teams in place to manage each of the businesses in your portfolio. Thank goodness.

Still, now you're in the position of a Warren Buffett or some other manager of a collection of businesses or a conglomerate. You must devote some time to each. You must keep track of what each is up to, and you must be able to, usually on a moment's notice, decide whether to invest more in that business or to liquidate some or all of that business. You must keep track of all that *changes* in that business, and all that changes in the marketplace that business operates in.

That's not a simple task if you own, say, twenty different businesses in ten different industries. You'll need to put your time into it. You'll need to segment your time strategically, too—to spend the most time watching the businesses that change the most and the most time selecting new businesses to "acquire"—while letting the stable parts of your business portfolio ride. But don't let them ride too long; we all know what can happen.

We can't give you a precise formula for how much time to spend on what. But we can tell you that most investors don't spend enough time managing their portfolios. They don't evaluate companies as though they plan to buy them or own them, and they don't come back to the trough often enough to see what has changed. If this sounds scary, it's why a lot of investors throw their investing over the wall to professionals and fund managers. You may choose to do this for part of your portfolio as well.

Most who seek professional help will throw their foundational portfolio components over the wall or simply buy index funds or ETFs. But you may also choose to let professionals manage your opportunistic portfolio—your technology portfolio, too. Just be aware that professionals in this space charge more, and that their "follow the crowd" tendencies can really hurt in this arena.

In producing *The 100 Best Technology Stocks You Can Buy*, we hope to save you enough time to continue to manage this part of your investing portfolio yourself.

Selecting the 2012 List

So now the moment you all have been waiting for. Drumroll, please. What are the *100 Best Technology Stocks You Can Buy*, and how did we come up with the list?

You've read a lot of philosophy and explanation of our thought process. But now, how do we turn those more abstract principles and thought processes into actual stock picks? How do we come up with a list of *100 Best Technology* stocks out of the 10,000-plus names to choose from?

If you're looking for an instantly replicable formula or list of selection criteria, you're out of luck. Stock picking simply defies fixed formulas. As we've already discussed, companies aren't just about numbers, and the factors beyond numbers create synergies for the present and future far beyond the capability of any black box model to analyze. If that were not the case, we'd all be buying QuickStocks or some other PC software program, and we'd all be investing in the same stocks—and a lot of fund managers and other investment professionals would be looking for jobs.

We do use some quantitative tools to narrow down the choices for further research. Then, we simply dive into all the company, industry, and marketplace information we can get. Sure, we start with the financials. But the real test is whether or not the rest of the story shouts out "Winner!" to us. There is no way we can precisely describe to you what makes that happen. Winners have great stories. The whole is greater than the sum of the parts. Many or most of the strategic financials and strategic intangibles are positive. Beyond that, there is nothing else to say.

Stock Screens: Ya Gotta Start Somewhere

Stock screeners serve as useful filters to narrow down the list for further research. Despite the increased complexity and scope (number of variables) available with today's screeners, they will never be suitable for final picks. They will, however, whittle down 10,000 companies to 200 or 300 to look more closely at. Suffice it to say, this book would be next to impossible without them.

We used Fidelity's stock screener (the more advanced one, which you can get to if you have an account). But there are others out there in the Yahoo! and Google financial portals, among others. We also made use of Value Line's excellent Investment Survey and Investment Analyzer products. We rely on them for most, if not all of the hard numbers provided in each company's review.

We ran several screens—some of the canned screens like GARP (growth at a reasonable price) and "Mo Plus Grow." We also made up a few of our own. By way of illustration, here are a few of our favorite criteria:

- Sector: Technology
- Market Cap > $200M
- Share price > $5

- Daily volume > 50,000 shares
- Cash Flow Growth Rate: highest 20 percent of selected group
- EPS Growth Rate, projected current year vs. last year: highest 20 percent of group, or > 15 percent
- EPS Growth Rate, projected next five years: highest 20 percent of group, or > 15 percent
- Price Earnings to Growth (PEG) ratio < 2.0

These criteria were run in various combinations with each other and with certain other criteria, to build a master list for further research.

Incorporating Investing Themes

Remember the tailwind principle we laid out earlier? We identified a few megatrends and industries likely to benefit from them—business IT services, security and software services, cloud computing infrastructure, semiconductors, and semiconductor and LED manufacturing products.

From this list, we either knew of or could identify one or two companies in each of these industries. To build a list of companies in an industry, we used tools such as Google Finance. Google Finance (*www.finance.google.com*) gives a list of ten "Related Companies"; from that list, we could build a list of companies in more or less the same business. Where it made sense, we also used trade publications, articles, and various searches to fill in industry players. In some cases, like alternative energy, we had to build a few subgroups; e.g., solar, wind, and battery technology.

It would have been nice if all of our theme companies also happened to be picked up by the screeners, but that only happened occasionally. Obviously, if a stock fit a theme and met the screening criteria, it is a bright prospect. Beyond that, we added some (not all, in most cases) theme stocks to our list for further analysis.

▼ **Table 2: Investing Themes**

THEME: ALTERNATIVE ENERGY/ENERGY CONSERVATION

Company	Ticker	Sector	Industry	Business
Advanced Energy Industries	AEIS	Utilities	Electronic Instruments and Controls	Power inverters and plasma sources
Digi International	DGII	Technology	Computer Hardware	Remote monitoring and control systems, smart meters
First Solar	FSLR	Utilities	Semiconductors	Thin film PV solar modules
GT Advanced Technologies	GTAT	Technology	Semiconductors	PV manufacturing services and materials for solar
Ormat Technologies	ORA	Utilities	Electric Utilities	Geothermal power plants
Power-One	PWER	Technology	Electronic Instruments and Controls	Energy-efficient power management solutions
Suntech Power ADS	STP	Utilities	Electronic Instruments and Controls	Solar panel manufacturing

THEME: SECURITY AND SURVEILLANCE

Company	Ticker	Sector	Industry	Business
AeroVironment	AVAV	Defense	Aerospace	Unmanned reconnaissance vehicles
CACI Inc.	CACI	Government	Software and Services	Software and systems integration for government
Digi International	DGII	Technology	Telecommunications	Remote monitoring and control systems, smart meters
Esterline Technologies	ESL	Defense	Electronic Instruments and Controls	Avionics, sensors and systems for defense
L-3 Communications	LLL	Defense	Electronic Instruments and Controls	Sensors, controls, communication gear for defense
ManTech Intl.	MANT	Government	Software and Services	IT services for the intelligence community

THEME: SEMICONDUCTOR MANUFACTURING PRODUCTS

Company	Ticker	Sector	Industry	Business
Brooks Automation	BRKS	Technology	Semiconductor Equipment	Semiconductor, LED manufacturing capital equipment
KLA-Tencor	KLAC	Technology	Semiconductor equipment	Inspection and wafer process control
Kulicke & Soffa	KLIC	Technology	Semiconductor Equipment	Assembly and test, bonding equipment
Lam Research	LRCX	Technology	Semiconductor Equipment	Etchers and clears for wafer fabrication
Novellus	NVLS	Technology	Semiconductor Equipment	Deposition, etching, polishing
Photronics	PLAB	Technology	Semiconductor Equipment	Photomasks for all processes
Ultratech	UTEK	Technology	Semiconductors	Equipment for specialty manufacture—LEDs, nanotech

THEME: BUSINESS INFORMATION TECHNOLOGY

Company	Ticker	Sector	Industry	Business
BMC Software	BMC	Technology	Software and Services	Business systems management middleware
Computer Sciences Corp	CSC	Technology	Software and Services	Business systems management and consulting
IBM Corp	IBM	Technology	Software and Services	Computer and systems management, consulting
Itron	ITRI	Technology	Electronic Instruments and Controls	Metering, data collection, and software for utilities
Intuit	INTU	Services	Software and Services	Financial management software
Manhattan Associates	MANH	Services	Software and Services	Supply chain management software and consulting
MICROS Systems	MCRS	Services	Software and Services	Enterprise software for hospitality industry
Oracle Corp	ORCL	Technology	Software and Services	Database management and middleware, consulting

THEME: BUSINESS INFORMATION TECHNOLOGY—*continued*

Company	Ticker	Sector	Industry	Business
Tech Data Corp	TECD	Technology	Software and Services	IT Products distributor and VAR
VMWare	VMW	Technology	Software and Services	Virtualization software and tools

THEME: CLOUD COMPUTING

Company	Ticker	Sector	Industry	Business
8x8	EGHT	Services	Communications Services	IP telephony, video, web-based conferencing
Apple	AAPL	Technology	Computer Hardware	Personal computers, mobile and digital music devices
Arris Group	ARRS	Technology	Telecommunications	Network backbone hardware and services
Google	GOOG	Technology	Computer Services	Online search and advertising, mobile operating system
Insight Enterprises	NSIT	Technology	Computer Hardware	IT services provider, outsourcing
JDS Uniphase	JDSU	Technology	Telecommunications	Fiberoptic interfaces and infrastructure
NetApp	NTAP	Technology	Computer Storage Devices	Enterprise network storage and data management
QLogic	QLGC	Technology	Computer Storage Devices	Interfaces for data storage, switches, and routers
Radware	RDWR	Technology	Communications Equipment	Network management solutions, security
Riverbed	RVBD	Technology	Communications Equipment	Distributed computing, cloud products
Teradata Corp	TDC	Technology	Computer Storage Devices	Enterprise data warehousing
VMware	VMW	Technology	Software and Services	Virtualization solutions, cloud applications

THEME: SEMICONDUCTORS AND LED LIGHTING

Company	Ticker	Sector	Industry	Business
Analog Devices	ADI	Technology	Integrated Circuits	Analog and mixed-signal components
Atmel Corp	ATML	Technology	Integrated Circuits	Microcontrollers and human interface
Cirrus Logic	CRUS	Technology	Integrated Circuits	Develops ICs for most audio and video products
Cree	CREE	Technology	Semiconductors	LED components, chips, lighting, RF products
Cypress Semiconductor	CY	Technology	Integrated Circuits	Mixed signal and human interface chips
Fairchild Semiconductor	FCS	Technology	Semiconductors	Broad-line analog and power management chips
Integrated Device Technology	IDT	Technology	Integrated Circuits	Wireless and mixed-signal products
Intel	INTC	Technology	Integrated Circuits	Processors, logic, and memory products
International Rectifier	IRF	Technology	Semiconductors	Power and power management, discretes
Linear Technology	LLTC	Technology	Integrated Circuits	Analog components for power and communications
Marvell Technology	MRVL	Technology	Integrated Circuits	Analog and mixed-signal for wireless, networking
ON Semiconductor	ONNN	Technology	Semiconductors	Discretes, signal, and power management
PMC-Sierra	PMCS	Technology	Integrated Circuits	Networking and communications chips
Power Integrations	POWI	Technology	Integrated Circuits	Power supply specialist, fixed function parts
Semtech	SMTC	Technology	Integrated Circuits	Communications and power management
STMicroelectronics	STM	Technology	Integrated Circuits	Analog and mixed-signal for consumer, automotive
TSMC	TSM	Technology	Integrated Circuits	Contract foundry and packaging

Testing, Testing

Using the combined list as a starting point, we researched each company further. We looked at financials, company communications (press releases, annual and quarterly reports, etc.), company websites, conference call transcripts, analyst commentary, comments on forums, and trade press materials where available. We looked at research reports from Value Line, Reuters, and others. There is no real process here except that we usually started by reading research reports from the Value Line Investing Survey where available.

We examined items on our strategic financials list and used the various media mentioned above to get a sense of the intangibles. We looked for sustainable success and sustainable competitive advantages throughout. We looked for that certain something, a special quality that sets the company apart from the others. All through the process, we asked ourselves whether we'd want to own the company.

About the List

Here are some further breakdowns of the list.

Sectors and Industries

▼ **Table 3: Sector Analysis**

Sector	No. of companies
Technology	70
Manufacturing	7
Basic Materials	3
Distribution	4
Government/Defense	4
Health Care	6
Energy	6

Industries

▼ Table 4: Top 5 Industries

Industry	# of companies
Semiconductors	20
Software and services	12
Electronic instruments/controls	11
Semiconductor equipment	6
Telecommunications	5

Crossover with 100 Best Stocks

▼ Table 5: Crossovers: Companies Also on 2012 *100 Best Stocks* List

Company	Symbol	Sector	Business
Apple	AAPL	Technology	Computer hardware
Becton, Dickinson	BDX	Technology	Biotechnology and drugs
Google	GOOG	Technology	Computer services
IBM	IBM	Technology	Hardware, software, services
Oracle	ORCL	Technology	Software and programming
Stryker	SYK	Health Care	Biotechnology and drugs

The Brightest Stars in the Sky

Moat Stars

▼ Table 6: Top Technology Stocks for Sustainable Competitive Advantage

Company	Symbol	Sector	Industry	Business
Apple	AAPL	Technology	Computer Hardware	Personal computers, mobile and digital music devices
Corning	GLW	Technology	Fiber Optics	Optical cable, catalyst cores
Cree	CREE	Technology	Semiconductors	LED lighting
Google	GOOG	Technology	Internet	Internet search and advertising
Intel	INTC	Technology	Semiconductors	Processors and logic chips
Oracle	ORCL	Technology	Software and Services	Database management and tools

Niche Stars

▼ **Table 7: Top Technology Stocks for Niche Strength**

Company	Symbol	Sector	Industry	Business
Adobe	ADBE	Technology	Software and Programming	Content management and development software
Aerovironment	AVAV	Technology	Aerospace	Unmanned aircraft
Autoliv	ALV	Manufacturing	Automotive	Passive restraints and safety systems
Cree	CREE	Technology	Semiconductors	LED components, chips, lighting, RF products
Electronics For Imaging	EFII	Technology	Hardware and Services	Large format printers and controllers
Mentor Graphics	MENT	Technology	Software and Programming	Hardware and software electronics design systems
MICROS Systems	MCRS	Services	Hospitality	Management software for hospitality industry
Ormat Technologies	ORA	Utilities	Electric Utilities	Geothermal power plants

Innovation Stars

▼ **Table 8: Top Technology Stocks for Innovation Excellence or Market Disruption**

Company	Symbol	Sector	Industry	Business
8x8	EGHT	Technology	Telecommunications	VOIP services for small businesses
Accuray	ARAY	Healthcare	Medical Equipment and Supplies	Oncology and radiology
Apple	AAPL	Technology	Computer Hardware	Personal computers, mobile and digital music devices
Exact Sciences	EXAS	Health Care	Biotechnology and Drugs	Molecular diagnostics for colorectal cancer detection
Google	GOOG	Technology	Computer Services	Online search and advertising, mobile operating system
Greatbatch, Inc.	GB	Health Care	Medical Equipment and Supplies	Implantable devices and surgical tools

Company	Symbol	Sector	Industry	Business
Orbotech	ORBK	Technology	PCB Manufacturing	Design and manufacturing tools for printed circuit boards
Riverbed Technology	RVBD	Technology	Communications Equipment	Distributed computing, cloud products
VMWare	VMW	Technology	Software	Virtualization software and tools

Brand Stars

▼ **Table 9: Top Technology Stocks for Brand Recognition and Advantage**

Company	Symbol	Sector	Industry	Business
Adobe	ADBE	Technology	Software and Programming	Content management and development software
Agilent	A	Technology	Electronic Instruments	Test equipment and instruments
Apple	AAPL	Technology	Computer Hardware	Personal computers, mobile and digital music devices
Corning	GLW	Technology	Fiber Optics	Optical cable, catalyst cores
Google	GOOG	Technology	Computer Services	Online search and advertising, mobile operating system
IBM	IBM	Technology	Computer Hardware	Hardware, software, consulting services
Intuit	INTU	Technology	Software and Programming	Financial software and consulting
Microsoft	MSFT	Technology	Software and Programming	Operating systems and office productivity
Oracle	ORCL	Technology	Software and Services	Database management and tools
Trimble Navigation	TRMB	Technology	Electronic Instruments	Positioning and geolocation products

And Now, Presenting . . .

▼ **Table 10: 100 Best Technology Stocks**

Company	Ticker	Industry	Business
8x8	EGHT	Communications Services	IP telephony, video, web-based conferencing
Accuray	ARAY	Medical Equipment and Supplies	Oncology and radiology
Adobe	ADBE	Software and Programming	Content management and development software
Advanced Energy Industries	AEIS	Electronic Instruments and Controls	Power supplies and inverters for solar industry
AeroVironment	AVAV	Aerospace	Produces unmanned reconaissance aircraft
Affymetrix	AFFX	Scientific and Technical Instruments	Genetic analysis systems
Agilent	A	Electronic Instruments and Controls	Electronic test and production equipment
Analog Devices	ADI	Semiconductors	Analog/mixed/digital signal processing ICs
Apple	AAPL	Computer Hardware	Personal computers, mobile and digital music devices
Arris Group	ARRS	Communications	Cable infrastructure and equipment
Arrow Electronics	ARW	Electronics Distribution	Electronic components distributor
Atmel	ATML	Semiconductors	Semiconductor mfg. capital equipment
Autoliv	ALV	Auto and Truck Parts	Automotive safety systems, airbag components
Avnet	AVT	Electronics	Computer systems and components distributor
AVX	AVX	Manufacturing	Passive electronic components
Becton, Dickinson	BDX	Medical Equipment and Supplies	Manufactures medical equipment and consumables
BMC Software	BMC	Software and Programming	Property, power, and infrastructure asset manager
Brooks Automation	BRKS	Semiconductors	Develops business middleware platforms
CACI	CACI	Software and Programming	Software and services, federal agencies

Company	Ticker	Industry	Business
Celestica	CLS	Electronic Instruments and Controls	Contract electronics manufacturer
Cirrus Logic	CRUS	Semiconductors	Application specific circuits for audio and energy markets
Coherent	COHR	Semiconductors	Lasers, photonics products and components
Computer Sciences	CSC	Software and Programming	Software and services, large governmental agencies
Corning	GLW	Communications	Fiber optics and catalytic converters
Cree	CREE	Semiconductors	LED components, chips, lighting, RF products
Cypress Semiconductor	CY	Semiconductors	Semiconductor design and manufacturing
Dell	DELL	Computer Hardware	Personal computers, servers, and related technology
Digi International	DGII	Computer Hardware	Remote monitoring and control systems, smart meters
DTS	DTSI	Electronic Instruments and Controls	Develops hardware and software for audio
Eastman Chemical	EMN	Chemicals—Plastics and Rubber	Plastics, inks, polymers, coatings, adhesives
Electronics For Imaging	EFII	Electronic Instruments and Controls	Large format printers and controllers
Esterline Technologies	ESL	Electronic Instruments and Controls	Avionics, controls, structures for aircraft
Exact Sciences	EXAS	Biotechnology and Drugs	Molecular diagnostics for colorectal cancer detection
Fairchild Semiconductor	FCS	Semiconductors	Semiconductors for power, mobile, communications
Faro Technologies, Inc.	FARO	Scientific and Technical Instruments	Three-dimensional measurement, imaging systems
First Solar	FSLR	Semiconductors	Thin film PV solar modules
Flextronics	FLEX	Electronic Instruments and Controls	Contract electronics manufacturer
Flow Int.	FLOW	Misc. Capital Goods	Water jet cutting, cleaning, surface prep solutions
Google	GOOG	Computer Services	Online search and advertising, mobile operating systems

Company	Ticker	Industry	Business
Greatbatch	GB	Medical Equipment and Supplies	Medical implants, passive and powered
GT Advanced Technologies	GTAT	Semiconductors	PV manufacturing services and materials for solar
IBM	IBM	Computers	Computer hardware, software, and services
Insight Enterprises	NSIT	Computer Hardware	IT services provider, outsourcing
Integrated Device Technology	IDTI	Semiconductors	Analog/mixed/digital signal processing ICs
Intel	INTC	Semiconductors	CPU, memory, and logic for computing
International Rectifier	IRF	Semiconductors	Analog and power devices
Intuit	INTU	Software and Programming	Accounting and tax software for small businesses, consumers
Itron	ITRI	Electronic Instruments and Controls	Metering, data collection, and software for utilities
Jabil Circuit	JBL	Electronic Instrumentsand Controls	Contract electronics manufacturer
JDS Uniphase	JDSU	Electronic Instruments and Controls	Fiberoptic telecommunications equipment
KLA-Tencor	KLAC	Semiconductors	Semiconductor capital equipment
Kulicke & Soffa	KLIC	Semiconductors	Semiconductor capital equipment
L-3 Communications	LLL	Electronic Instruments and Controls	Communications and surveillance equipment
Lam Research	LRCX	Semiconductors	Semiconductor capital equipment
Linear Technology	LLTC	Semiconductors	Analog, power, and communications semiconductors
Manhattan Associates	MANH	Software and Programming	Software for logistics management
ManTech	MANT	IT Services	Technology services for U.S. government
Marvell Technology	MRVL	Semiconductors	Communications and networking semiconductors
Mentor Graphics	MENT	Software and Programming	Hardware and software electronics design systems
MICROS Systems	MCRS	Software and Programming	Platform software for hospitality industry
Microsoft	MSFT	Software and Programming	Operating systems and office software

Company	Ticker	Industry	Business
Molex	MOLX	Electronic Components	Connectors, cabling, and hardware
Motorola Mobility	MMI	Communications Equipment	Wireless handsets, accessories, entertainment devices
NetApp	NTAP	Computer Storage Devices	Enterprise network storage and data management
Newport	NEWP	Electronic Instruments and Controls	Manufacturer of optical equipment and lasers
Novellus Systems	NVLS	Semiconductors	Semiconductor capital equipment
ON Semiconductor	ONNN	Semiconductors	Discrete semiconductor devices
Oracle	ORCL	Software and Programming	Enterprise database and application software, systems
Orbotech	ORBK	PCB Manufacturing	Design and manufacturing tools for printed circuit boards
Ormat Technologies	ORA	Electric Utilities	Geothermal power plants
Photronics	PLAB	Semiconductors	Manufacturer of photomasks
PMC-Sierra	PMCS	Semiconductors	Fabless semiconductor, analog, comm, and SOC
Power Integrations	POWI	Semiconductors	High voltage ICs for power supplies
Power-One	PWER	Electronic Instruments and Controls	Energy-efficient power management solutions
Powerwave Technologies	PWAV	Communications Equipment	Wireless communications network devices
QLogic	QLGC	Computer Storage Devices	Interfaces for data storage, switches and routers
Radware	RDWR	Communications Equipment	Network management solutions, security
Red Hat	RHT	Software and Programming	Linux operating system services
Riverbed Technology	RVBD	Communications Equipment	Distributed computing, cloud products
SanDisk	SNDK	Computer Storage Devices	Storage devices, memory cards
Sanmina-SCI	SANM	Electronic Instruments and Controls	Contract electronics manufacturer
Semtech	SMTC	Semiconductors	Fabless semiconductor, analog and mixed-signal
Solutia	SOA	Chemicals—Plastics and Rubber	Reinforcement material for tires and glass

Company	Ticker	Industry	Business
STMicroelectronics	STM	Semiconductors	Semiconductor manufacturer, broad range
Stryker	SYK	Medical Equipment and Supplies	Surgical tool and implants
Suntech Power ADS	STP	Energy	Solar panel manufacturing
TE Connectivity	TEL	Electronic Components	Engineered components, cable, connectors
Tech Data	TECD	IT Services	IT services, logistics management
TECHNE	TECH	Biotechnology and Drugs	Proteins and diagnostic assay kits
Teradata	TDC	IT Services	Data warehousing and access
Trimble	TRMB	Electronic Instruments and Controls	GPS and motion control devices for industry
Triumph Group	TGI	Aerospace	Engineered structures and components
TSMC	TSM	Semiconductors	Semiconductor foundry services
TTM Technologies	TTMI	Electronic Instruments and Controls	Specialty printed circuit boards for defense, others
Ultratech	UTEK	Semiconductors	Equipment for specialty manufacture—LEDs, nanotech
Vicor	VICR	Electronic Instruments and Controls	Electric power systems and components
Vishay Intertechnology	VSH	Electronic Components	Passives and diodes
VMware	VMW	Software and Programming	Virtualization solutions, cloud applications
Western Digital	WDC	Computer Storage Devices	Computer, digital video hard drives
Zygo	ZIGO	Electronic Instruments and Controls	Metrology products and optical components

Part II

THE 100 BEST TECHNOLOGY STOCKS YOU CAN BUY

8x8, Inc.

Ticker symbol: EGHT (NASDAQ) ▫ S&P rating: NA ▫ Value Line financial strength rating: NA ▫ Current yield: Nil

Who Are They?

Pronounced "Eight by eight," it is a relatively small company with an unusual name. It provides point-to-point and cloud-based telephony, Internet-based video communications, and IT services to consumers and (generally smaller) businesses. It has been around longer than one might assume, given its size (242 employees) and revenues ($70 million in 2010). Founded in 1987, the company went public in 1997, and has been unprofitable until FY2010, when it earned $4 million.

The company originally was established as a supplier of IP telephone services back when Skype, Vonage, and others were also just getting started. At the time, voice-over-IP (VoIP) was competing mainly with POTS (plain-old-telephone-service) providers and so the list of features was fairly Spartan. 8x8's telephony product line now, however, is broad and deep with very sophisticated functionality. Its target market is still the small/medium business, but the services available are well beyond what was available even ten years ago.

By the way, the name 8x8 refers to a technical aspect of video data compression (as if you didn't already know).

Why Should I Care?

For most of 8x8's history as a public company, it was supplying chips and software to the VoIP market. It later entered the consumer VoIP market with a service called Packet8. This entire market turned into a race to the bottom with the entry of a number of large players, most notably Skype (now owned by Microsoft). Recently the company has focused its efforts on the small-to-medium business market and has found real opportunity, to say nothing of some earnings. As the company exits the residential market, some of the losses in residential are masking earnings in the commercial market. We see that the commercial gains are becoming more apparent, and comparisons to Vonage's residential business tend to show 8x8 in a more favorable light. 8x8 spends $825 to acquire each subscriber but collects $200 per month, for a four-month payback. The corresponding numbers at

Vonage show an eight-month payback. 8x8 has also bettered Vonage's operating margins: Where both companies had 65 percent operating margins in 2009, 8x8's most recent four quarters have produced a 68 percent margin, where Vonage is still at 65 percent. 8x8 exited 2011 in the black and has turned in record earnings in the first quarter of 2012, whereas Vonage has yet to make a profit.

Key to the company's success are the net neutrality discussions taking place in the halls of the FCC and elsewhere. "Net neutrality" refers to a condition wherein the operators of a particular branch of the Internet infrastructure allows all traffic to pass without impediment, regardless of the type of traffic, its source, or destination. Smaller service providers like 8x8 compete directly with companies like AT&T, who also happen to operate large portions of the Internet, including the critical "last mile," the length of wire between the customer and the branch exchange. If an ISP such as AT&T is permitted to block, throttle, or apply fees to time-critical data (such as telephony), the consequences for smaller competitors such as 8x8 could be dire. In the two major court cases that have touched on this issue, the rulings have been in favor of a neutral approach.

How's Business?
Good. The company ended FY2011 with close to $6.5 million in earnings on just more than $70 million in revenue. This represents a 67 percent increase in earnings for a 10 percent bump in revenue—pretty good leverage. Earnings for the first quarter of 2012 were up 91 percent on a 10 percent increase in revenue, reflecting the positive effects of exiting an unprofitable segment. Its client base increased approximately 15 percent during 2010 and churn (cancellation divided by client base) fell half a percent to 2.2 percent.

Upside
- Positive earnings momentum
- Exiting costly consumer market
- Superior small business offerings

Downside
- Nearest competitor is ten times its size
- Regulatory uncertainty risk
- Downside to the volume sensitivity of earnings

Just the Facts

SECTOR: **Communications**
BETA COEFFICIENT: **1.60**
5-YEAR COMPOUND EARNINGS-PER-SHARE GROWTH: **NA**

	2007	**2008**	**2009**	**2010**	**2011**
Revenues (Mil)	53.1	61.7	64.7	63.4	70.1
Net Income (Mil)	(9.93)	0.03	(2.5)	3.88	6.49
Price: high	1.67	1.26	1.60	3.15	5.23
low	0.86	0.42	0.45	1.17	3.15

8x8, Inc.
810 Maude Avenue
Sunnyvale, CA 94085
(408) 727-1885
Website: *www.8x8.com*

BIOTECH

Accuray Inc.

Ticker symbol: ARAY (NASDAQ) ❏ S&P rating: NA ❏ Value Line financial strength rating: NA ❏ Current yield: Nil

Who Are They?

Accuray is a technology leader in the radiation therapy market, specifically in the area of radiosurgery. Its products provide a noninvasive, nonsurgical treatment option for cancers and other tumors in areas that may be difficult to treat surgically. Accuray's flagship product, the CyberKnife system, destroys targeted tissues through the application of energetic particles (electrons, in this case) from a device outside the patient's body. No surgery or anesthetic is required for the procedure (although you might need a drink or two when you get the bill), and recovery time is negligible.

The company was founded by a team of Stanford researchers in 1990. The first approval for the system's use was in Japan in 1996; FDA approval came in 1999. The company completed its IPO in 2007.

Why Should I Care?

Once used almost exclusively for cranial procedures (brain tumors, basically), the CyberKnife system is now approved for the treatment of tumors anywhere in the body, including the spine, lung, prostate, liver, and pancreas. These "extra-cranial" applications represent over half of all CyberKnife procedures and are the fastest-growing area for the current installed base of more than 200 machines.

There are other radiation treatment products on the market, most of them made by much larger companies. What sets the CyberKnife product apart is its positioning system, which relies on radiological data to initially map the tumor and then to compensate in real-time for any movement of the tumor due to the patient's breathing or pulse. The robotic positioning system is unique in that it allows the electron source to be moved into almost any position with respect to the patient.

The accuracy of the positioning is critical to the success of the procedure. Most radiation treatments have to use a relatively low dosage in order to minimize damage to adjacent healthy structures. The accuracy of the CyberKnife's positioning system allows for the application of a much higher and far more effective dosage. Because each dosage is so much higher, the CyberKnife procedure typically requires just one to five separate treatments, whereas conventional radiation procedures can require thirty to forty separate patient visits. And whereas most radiation treatments are used as a follow-up or an adjunct to surgery, the CyberKnife procedure can often be used to completely replace conventional surgery.

How's Business?

The results from the third quarter 2011 were encouraging. Gross margins are improving, and although earnings disappointed somewhat, the company reaffirmed its revenue outlook for $210–$225 million for the fiscal year. Operating expenses have declined significantly under a new board and CEO, and the company is managing its cash well. In March, the company bought TomoTherapy (another radiation oncology provider, 2010 revenues of $180 million) for $277 million in cash and stock, a move that should improve service revenues and add to the bottom line in 2012. Associated with the purchase, the company has announced plans to issue $100 million in notes at attractive rates. And, despite the company's continued delays in shipment of some core systems, orders remain healthy.

Upside
- R & D is well funded
- Book/bill a healthy 1.4
- Profitable

Downside
- Aging backlog
- TomoTherapy purchase could be burdensome
- Barely profitable

Just the Facts

SECTOR: **Health Care**
BETA COEFFICIENT: **1.10**
5-YEAR COMPOUND EARNINGS-PER-SHARE GROWTH: **NA**

	2007	2008	2009	2010	2011
Revenues (Mil)	141	210	234	222	215
Net Income (Mil)	(5.6)	5.4	0.6	2.84	3.0
Price: high	29.3	17.8	8.0	7.5	11.0
low	13.2	4.1	4.1	5.9	6.3

Accuray, Inc.
1310 Chesapeake Terrace
Sunnyvale, CA 94089
(408) 716-4600
Website: *www.accuray.com*

SOFTWARE/SERVICES

Adobe Systems, Inc.

Ticker symbol: ADBE (NASDAQ) ▫ S&P rating: BBB+ ▫ Value Line financial strength rating: A+
▫ Current yield: Nil

Who Are They?

Adobe Systems develops computer software used for the creation and printing of images and documents. It also develops tools to assist in the creation
and support of websites of all sizes and types. Its products are used on desktops, servers, and mobile devices by developers, consumers, and enterprises
for creating, managing, and delivering content across multiple operating
systems, devices, and media.

Its products include the Creative Suite, for the production of print and
web-based designs, websites, and high-end video; the Acrobat line, for the
creation and editing of cross-platform, visually complex documents; the
Photoshop family, used in the production and manipulation of still and
video images; the Online Marketing suite, which allows users to track and
characterize the performance and usage patterns of a monitored Internet
website; and Flash, an application programming interface that allows for the
delivery of content across multiple platforms with one content development
effort.

Adobe's products are sold through its own sales channel and through a
network of independent retailers, OEMs, VARs, and system integrators. Its
software is also licensed through hardware manufacturers, software developers, and service providers.

Why Should I Care?

You have to acknowledge any company whose product name has become
a verb. *Xerox*, *FedEx*, and now *Photoshop* are all part of our daily lexicon as
legitimate substitutes for "copy," "send," and, "Dude, make me look like
George Clooney." Several of Adobe's products, in fact, have achieved ubiquity
in our modern technical life. Photoshop is the most popular image processing software in the world; Flash is the most widely used multimedia platform
for personal computers; Acrobat is the most widely used document viewing
platform for personal computers; and Adobe's PDF format is by far the most
widely used document distribution and printing format in the world.

Adobe has been around so long and has been so successful at what it does that many people no longer associate the products with the company but rather assume that PDF and Flash just "are" (in fact, PDF has recently moved into the public domain and is now an ISO standard). Adobe has taken pains in recent years to make sure its brand is closely associated with the products it develops and supports (such as the name change from Acrobat Reader to Adobe Reader), and it's a move we applaud.

As a software company, Adobe's incremental revenues are highly leveraged. In the first quarter of FY2011, for example, revenues increased a modest 9 percent over the previous year. Earnings for the same period, however, grew 45 percent with no extraordinary financial events skewing the results. This is a very good ratio on incremental revenues, and the second quarter of 2011 is on track to produce even more dramatic results.

How's Business?
The company's first quarter of 2011 showed real strength in revenue growth, less so in earnings. The top line gained 20 percent versus the year-ago quarter, but hiring expenses and weakness from the Japanese market (anticipated, due to the disaster recovery there) cut into margins somewhat. The continued weak recovery in the United States has taken a toll as well, but we like Adobe's financial strength during this period compared to smaller, more highly leveraged businesses in this sector. Adobe's rocket-ship growth days are behind it, but there is still significant upside in the shares.

Upside
- Recent acquisitions contributing quickly
- Good financials for more acquisitions
- Highly regarded products

Downside
- Dominant market share reduces potential for growth
- Creative Suite may be overdue for a refresh
- No native support for Flash on iPhone

Just the Facts

SECTOR: **Software**
BETA COEFFICIENT: **1.20**
5-YEAR COMPOUND EARNINGS-PER-SHARE GROWTH: **8.0%**

	2007	2008	2009	2010	2011
Revenues (Mil)	3,158	3,580	2,946	3,800	4,120
Net Income (Mil)	724	872	387	775	920
Price: high	48.5	46.4	38.2	37.8	35.9
low	37.2	19.5	15.7	25.5	25.9

Adobe Systems, Inc.
345 Park Avenue
San Jose, CA 95110–2704
(408) 536-6000
Website: *www.adobe.com*

SEMICONDUCTOR EQUIPMENT/ENERGY

Advanced Energy Industries, Inc.

Ticker symbol: AEIS (NASDAQ) ❑ S&P rating: NA ❑ Value Line financial strength rating: B ❑ Current yield: Nil

Who Are They?

Here's an interesting little company. It has two product lines, Thin Film and Renewables. The Thin Film line has no thin film products in it, but the Renewables line does involve renewable energy. Thin Films is a line of power supplies and plasma sources used in the production of thin-film solar panels. The Renewables line is a series of small, medium, large, and *really* large inverters used to convert the DC output of . . . wait for it . . . solar panels into usable and grid-compatible AC power.

Why Should I Care?

The company has done quite well as of late. It was hit hard by the recession and had consecutive unprofitable years but recovered nicely in 2010 with strong sales and good operating margin. The company is debt free and has adequate cash on hand. We also like its business model; providing tools for the producers of solar panel equipment (applied materials accounts for 25 percent of its sales) gives them exposure to the market while spreading out the risk. On the other end of the value chain, the inverter business has a fair amount of synergy with the power supply operation and allows the company to remain agnostic on solar technology. Inverters don't particularly care whether the panel is thin film, poly, or monocrystalline, so AEIS's Renewables line has no bets on that race, hedging the Thin Film business.

How's Business?

Now we get to the sticky part. During a reasonable first quarter of 2011, the company offered revenue guidance on the second quarter in line with previous estimates of $148–$160 million. Then, in early July, the company lowered second quarter guidance to $137–$140 million, with EPS expected at the low end of the previous range of $.36–$.44. Soft orders led to other problems as the company grew inventory well ahead of shippable orders and ended up with a pile of parts rather than a pile of cash. Compounding that problem is AEIS's spotty cash generation, although it appears to be holding steady through the magic of accelerating receivables.

The actuals for the second quarter came in at $138.5 million in revenue, which was expected, but with earnings of only $.31/share, which was no bueno. Management felt that a combination of market factors led to the lower-than-expected numbers. In the Q2 announcement, we see that those factors must still be in place, as guidance has been lowered for Q3 as well. Sales for Q3 are anticipated to be $130–$145 million, with earnings expectations of $.20 to $.30 per share. Assuming a third quarter of $.25 per share and a fourth quarter of 5 percent growth in earnings, we're at $1.26–1.28 for the year, against expectations of $1.85 to start FY2011. With no aces up its sleeve, we can't yet recommend AEIS to any but the gamblers. We do like this stock's potential, but we'd wait for at least one quarter of improved orders before committing our hard-earned winnings. We think you'll be able to get in cheap, but wait and see.

Upside
- Good leverage in solar
- Strong incremental earnings
- Well capitalized

Downside
- Little inventory issue
- CEO retiring, worth watching
- Soft orders at the moment

Just the Facts

SECTOR: **Technology**
BETA COEFFICIENT: **1.45**
5-YEAR COMPOUND EARNINGS-PER-SHARE GROWTH: **NA**

	2007	2008	2009	2010	2011
Revenues (Mil)	385	329	186	459	550
Net Income (Mil)	34.4	(1.8)	(34.7)	53.6	65.0
Price: high	26.0	17.0	15.3	18.5	16.8
low	12.2	5.7	5.4	10.9	8.7

Advanced Energy Industries, Incorporated
1625 Sharp Point Drive
Fort Collins, CO 80525
(970) 221-4670
Website: *www.advanced-energy.com*

AEROSPACE

AeroVironment, Inc.

Ticker symbol: AVAV (NASDAQ) □ S&P rating: NA □ Value Line financial strength rating: B++ □
Current yield: Nil

Who Are They?

AeroVironment was founded in 1971 by the late Dr. Paul MacCready, known as the father of human-powered flight. His aircraft designs were the first to achieve sustained, controlled flight powered only by human muscle, and the first to cross the English Channel, again powered only by human effort. In 1981, AeroVironment created the Solar Challenger, which flew from Paris to England (163 miles) at an altitude of 11,000 feet, powered solely by sunlight (via photovoltaic cells). In 2001, a solar-powered Aero-Vironment design with a 250-foot wingspan flew to more than 96,000 feet and sustained flight at that altitude. The service ceiling of the SR-71 Black-bird, by comparison, is 85,000 feet.

AeroVironment now produces three very small, very sophisticated air-craft and one very large, very sophisticated aircraft for various unmanned applications, typically reconnaissance. The company's background in the production of ultralight and ultra-efficient airframes is extremely valuable in this work. This business accounts for 85 percent of its revenue.

It also produces electric vehicle recharging stations for commercial and consumer use. This business is just getting started, but the company has won several development and early production contracts.

Why Should I Care?

One of the real success stories in the Defense Department's ongoing chal-lenge to get more from less has to be its entire unmanned aircraft systems (UAS) program. UAS technology, at a fraction of the cost of manned aircraft, has performed well in every role and theater in which it's been deployed. Surveillance missions are now conducted around the clock by multiple air-craft, at a lower cost and lower risk than a single manned craft, which is limited in its time-on-station. Strike missions are managed remotely, often with superior penetration and effect, leaving manned craft free to engage the fast targets. There are many, many examples of how effective (and cost effective) these devices have been. There are competitors in the military mar-ket, but most are used in an offensive capacity, whereas the AeroVironment units are used in intelligence, reconnaissance, and surveillance (IRS) applications. They're quite small and can be deployed from a soldier's pack while in the field. They're extremely cost effective and have proven their worth over and over again in hazardous areas and otherwise inaccessible locations. Technology like this also has broad civilian applications. Besides the obvious public safety applications in Homeland Security and police activities, there are general commercial applications, such as meteorology, aerial surveying, mapping, pipeline inspection, traffic monitoring, crop management, forest management, and fire reconnaissance. Almost any application that currently uses an airborne human observer can be done far more efficiently with one or more UAS devices.

How's Business?

Despite its beginnings as "provers of the impractical," AeroVironment is not a bunch of well-paid dreamers. This is a well-run company with a solid business plan. Since going public in 2005, it has never lost money and has turned in 8–10 percent net year after year. There's no debt, plenty of cash, and we don't think it'll be affected at all by any budget cutbacks at the DoD. In fact, as we wrote this, the company announced a $65 million deal to supply the army with Puma aircraft.

Upside

- R & D well funded
- More commercial applications soon?
- Chargers making good progress

Downside

- Larger contractors may crowd airspace
- Charger program probably not profitable
- Military reducing field profile

Just the Facts

SECTOR: **Defense**

BETA COEFFICIENT: **0.70**

5-YEAR COMPOUND EARNINGS-PER-SHARE GROWTH: **NA**

	2007	2008	2009	2010	2011
Revenues (Mil)	174	216	248	250	293
Net Income (Mil)	20.7	21.4	24.2	20.7	25.9
Price: high	26.9	38.7	41.2	35.4	36.3
low	18.0	18.4	18.5	20.7	24.2

AeroVironment, Incorporated

181 West Huntington Drive, Suite 202

Monrovia, CA 91016

(626) 357-9983

Website: *www.avinc.com*

BIOTECH

Affymetrix

Ticker symbol: AFFX (NASDAQ) ❑ S&P rating: NA ❑ Value Line financial strength rating: B ❑ Current yield: Nil

Who Are They?

Affymetrix develops, manufactures, and markets consumables and systems for genetic analysis in the life sciences and clinical health care markets. It also sells analysis services using its own equipment. The company's GeneChip system and related microarray technology is used to acquire, analyze, and manage complex genetic information. These products are used mainly as tools to better understand the role of genetic factors in disease and the effectiveness and safety of therapies.

The GeneChip system cleverly integrates semiconductor fabrication techniques and common laboratory chemical processes to produce a single "chip" with as many as 500,000 test sites on its surface. This chip (not an electronic device, but rather an array of chemical structures), which is a consumable in the diagnostic process, is the company's revenue mainstay, consistently accounting for more than 80 percent of its annual sales.

The company sells its products directly to pharmaceutical, biotechnology, agrichemical, diagnostics, and consumer products companies as well as academic research centers, government research laboratories, private foundation laboratories, and clinical reference laboratories in North America and Europe. The company also sells some of its products through authorized distributors in Latin America, India, the Middle East, and the Asia-Pacific regions, including China.

Why Should I Care?

Affymetrix was once one of the shining stars of the genomics research market, but fell on hard times and has been languishing as rivals like Illumina have grown to many times Affymetrix's size. So why is Affymetrix in this book and not one of the other players? Well, for one thing, Affymetrix isn't trading at multiples approaching 100, like some of its rivals. Yes, it is losing money at the moment, but 2011 has proven to be profitable, and its share price is in the mid-single digits. In Q1 of 2012, it announced some weaker-than-expected revenues and was taken once again to the digital woodshed by traders, but the earnings are beginning to show the effect of structural improvements put in place by the new CEO. And this is one of the reasons we like it—Affymetrix looks like a company that has turned itself around and has demonstrated a plan for success.

Affymetrix's plan includes the development of new markets, such as the personal DNA scanning market. In this business, individuals pay up to $1,000 each for a DNA scan for various genetic markers indicative of hereditary diseases. This service has been doing well as of late, and Affymetrix has already signed up a screening customer for its hardware. Another area of focus is the routine testing and validation businesses, which management feels will grow faster than the overall research market in 2012. The company is also expanding its product line into cancer assays, with new tools for pathologists and oncologists.

Lastly, the company has retired significant portions of its debt and has reduced expenses and manufacturing costs for its highest volume products.

How's Business?

The company's first quarter 2011 was encouraging. Revenues were down 10 percent versus 2010, but cost of goods sold fell 18 percent, leading to a bump in gross margins from 61 percent to 65 percent. Expenses fell 13 percent, as well. As we said, the second quarter revenues were disappointing, but further cost cutting will continue to alleviate pressure on margins, and several new products show promise.

Upside

- Share price is fully laundered
- Improved expense profile
- New products in pipeline despite downturn

Downside

- Earnings surprise in Q2
- Fair level of revenue tied to governmental/public funding
- Chasing the market technology leaders

Just the Facts

SECTOR: **Technology**
BETA COEFFICIENT: **1.40**
5-YEAR COMPOUND EARNINGS-PER-SHARE GROWTH: —

	2007	**2008**	**2009**	**2010**	**2011**
Revenues (Mil)	371	320	327	311	310
Net Income (Mil)	24.5	(32.2)	(23.9)	(10.2)	4.0
Price: high	32.0	23.8	10.1	8.4	8.1
low	20.0	2.0	1.8	3.8	4.6

Affymetrix, Inc.
3420 Central Expressway
Santa Clara, CA 95051
(408) 731-5000
Website: *www.affymetrix.com*

Agilent Technologies

Ticker symbol: A (NYSE) ❑ S&P rating: BBB- ❑ Value Line financial strength rating: B+ ❑ Current yield: Nil

Who Are They?

Agilent began as the instrument and test business of Hewlett-Packard before being spun off in 1999 in what was at the time the largest IPO in the history of the industry ($2.1 billion). It now calls itself "the world's premier measurement company," and we'd have a hard time disputing that claim. Its product lines cover a broad range of disciplines in chemical analysis, life sciences, and electronic measurement with hundreds of test platforms in each segment. The company is well known for the high performance and reliability of its products, all of which are backed up with first-rate service.

The first few years of operation after the spinoff were complicated by the end of the tech bubble and the need to shed a great many marginal product lines. Sales from 2001 to 2006 fell some 40 percent, and the company lost more than $3 billion in three years. Beginning in 2004, Agilent started making money, and operating margins grew quickly even as revenues were still on the way down. Since then (absent the 2009 recession year), the company has been solidly profitable with good cash generation.

Why Should I Care?

The electronic measurement segment is doing very well. Cost structures since the recession have been addressed, and the product line has better focus. The growth in its target markets, coupled with the improved operations, has made for solid results. Orders from the industrial segments remain strong, and a dynamic consumer device market should persist through 2012.

On the operations side, Agilent's gross margins have been remarkably steady in the face of shifting revenue sources. In each of the last eight quarters, gross margin has been consistently in the mid-50 percent range. This is a good indication of both the strength of the core business and an active management that stays on top of the basics of matching spending to revenue. Many of the assets acquired in the Varian acquisition, for example, were not cost-effective and have been restructured and re-aligned with Agilent's improved cost structure.

Agilent has a history of innovation and understands that technical leadership is critical to margins. Although the restructuring efforts have not been easy and have had an impact on the balance sheet, the company has retained its commitment to R & D, with an average of 10–11 percent of annual revenues set aside for research. As a result, the company has continued to provide leading-edge products to its traditional markets. Agilent also has announced plans to serve the growing need for specialized instruments in the surveillance and nanotechnology areas.

Agilent has done well with its acquisition strategy. It typically targets smaller companies with niche expertise to complement or fill out a product line. Consequently, integration issues have been minimal. The Varian acquisition ($1.5 billion cash) was a big move to expand the bio-analytical measurement segment, which is an area of strong focus for Agilent. The purchase added $800 million in revenue in the first year, and management expects to create $100 million in net savings over the next three years.

How's Business?

The 2011 fiscal year will close on a high note for Agilent, and the year overall has been very good in terms of growth in earnings and cash flow, both up nearly 50 percent. The outlook for 2012 is not quite as strong, but the recent pull-back in share price will create a good entry point for this quality issue.

Upside
- Strong presence in China
- Solid execution
- High-margin markets

Downside
- Semiconductor capital expenditure slowing
- Varian acquisition still dragging op margin
- Manageable debt, but still net negative

Just the Facts

SECTOR: **Technology**
BETA COEFFICIENT: **1.10**
5-YEAR COMPOUND EARNINGS-PER-SHARE GROWTH: **NA**

	2007	2008	2009	2010	2011
Revenues (Mil)	5,420	5,774	4,481	5,444	6,650
Net Income (Mil)	610	693	(31.0)	624	960
Price: high	40.4	38.0	31.8	42.1	52.4
low	30.3	14.8	12.0	26.7	30.5

Agilent Technologies, Inc.
5301 Stevens Creek Blvd
Santa Clara, CA 94306
(877) 424-4536
Website: *www.agilent.com*

SEMICONDUCTORS

Analog Devices, Inc.

Ticker symbol: ADI (NYSE) ❑ S&P rating: A- ❑ Value Line financial strength rating: A+ ❑ Current yield: 2.6%

Who Are They?

Analog Devices designs, manufactures, and markets high-performance analog, mixed-signal, and digital signal processing chips used in a multitude of electronic equipment. It does not make large-scale microprocessors, discrete digital logic, or memory, but concentrates instead in the area of real-time signal processing (both analog and digital), front-end signal acquisition, conversion, and amplification. Its high value-add components find their way into products such as medical imaging equipment, cellular base stations, digital cameras and televisions, industrial process controls, defense electronics, factory automation systems, and automobiles. In all, the company derives nearly half its revenue from the industrial market, with communications, automotive, and consumer markets accounting for the other half. The company has a small and declining business in the computer market. It makes thousands of products, with the ten highest-revenue products in total accounting for just below 9 percent of revenues.

The company makes many of its own analog parts at either of its two fabs, located in Massachusetts and Limerick, Ireland. ADI also employs third-party suppliers (primarily TSMC in Taiwan) for fabrication of its submicron CMOS die. The company closed its wafer fabrication facility in Massachusetts at the end of fiscal 2009 and now sources its blank wafers from third parties.

Why Should I Care?

Analog chip suppliers tend to hold design wins for the life of a customer's product. In critical circuits, in particular, products are often designed with the characteristics of a particular supplier's components in mind, and a change of suppliers for those key components often necessitates a redesign or a re-spec of the final product. For this reason, ADI's earnings are quite a bit more reliable than that of the suppliers of commodity ICs.

Fab ownership is a double-edged sword. If the fab is not fully utilized during a down cycle in the economy, the higher fixed costs lead to lower operating margins. As someone once said, "It's like owning a bunch of elephants—you can get a lot of work done, but they have to eat." During an up cycle, however, you're paying yourself rather than someone else to build your dies, effectively capturing what would have gone out the door to a vendor. In the end, fabs are nearly always a net positive if kept fully utilized. Owning the fab also means you can control and modify its operation very specifically to get the most out of your product designs. This is a real benefit to a maker of analog parts, as fab tuning for analog processes tends to be as much art as it is science and competency there is often a critical differentiator.

How's Business?

ADI's second-quarter 2011 earnings were up 36 percent over prior year, surprising analysts with strong revenue growth across all segments. The company recently announced the offering of $375 million in notes at 3 percent, with payments representing roughly 8 percent of 2011 cash flow through 2016. Although a divided bump of 16 percent was recently announced, the company has very little debt and the share base has already declined by 20 percent over the last five years, so we think it's safe to assume ADI is going shopping. Likely targets might include companies with unique high-voltage IP for the energy management field.

Upside

- Strong margins
- Healthier automotive sector
- Captive fab capacity

Downside

- Communications sector still in recovery
- Top-line growth only moderate
- TI purchase of NatSemi bodes ill for ADI bargain hunters

Just the Facts

SECTOR: Technology
BETA COEFFICIENT: 0.90
5-YEAR COMPOUND EARNINGS-PER-SHARE GROWTH: 7.5%

	2007	2008	2009	2010	2011
Revenues (Mil)	2,511	2,583	2,015	2,762	3,100
Net Income (Mil)	474	525	285	712	870
Price: high	41.5	41.1	36.3	31.9	42.6
low	26.1	30.2	15.3	17.8	31.5

Analog Devices, Inc.
One Technology Way
Norwood, MA 02062–9106
(781) 329-4700
Website: *www.analog.com*

Apple Inc.

Ticker symbol: AAPL (NASDAQ) ❏ S&P rating: not rated ❏ Value Line financial strength rating: A++ ❏ Current yield: NA

Who Are They?

Apple Inc. designs, manufactures, and markets personal computers, portable music players, cell phones, and related software, peripherals, and services. It sells these products through its retail stores, online stores, and third-party and value-added resellers. The company also sells a variety of third-party compatible products such as printers, storage devices, and other accessories through its online and retail stores, and digital content through its iTunes store.

The company's products have become household names: the iPad, iPhone, iPod, and MacBook are just some of the company's hardware products. And while the software may be less well known, iTunes, QuickTime, and OSX are important segments of the business, each with their own revenue streams.

The company was incorporated in 1977 as Apple Computer but has since changed its name to simply Apple Inc. The name change in 2007 was the last step in a ten-year retooling that had already changed the company from a personal computer also-ran into one of the most recognizable and profitable consumer electronics brands in the world.

Why Should I Care?

It's hard to imagine the current consumer tech landscape without Apple's presence at the top of the heap. Its iconic products have become so successful and its marketing so ubiquitous that if it didn't exist, we would have to invent something very much like it to fill in the void. Its product line, while comparatively narrow, is focused on areas where the user interface is highly valued. Apple has leveraged this focus on the user experience into a business that is far and away the most profitable in the industry.

Enhancing the user experience is the industrial design. The Apple design ethic is extraordinarily well executed and is a large part of the value proposition for every product they release. Many of its customers are uncomfortable with any tech product not designed around Apple's common content management interface. This overall focus on the user experience has been instrumental in creating an extremely loyal customer base and a brand cachet unequaled in the consumer electronics business. Apple was able to weather the downturn in consumer spending so well in part because many of its customers will forgo other expenditures in order to afford their next Apple purchase.

How's Business?

For the past five years, Apple has been the 800-pound gorilla of the consumer electronics space. Scratch that—it's been King Kong. Since 2006, revenues have more than tripled and profit has increased over sevenfold. While we here at *100 Best* tend to look favorably on a company that increases its margin by 20–30 basis points per year, Apple, over the five-year period, has increased its net margin by more than 1,250 basis points (an average of 250 points per year).

How is it doing this? Let's take a look at the cell phone market and see what we can learn. The iPhone launched in mid-2006 and has grown market share at a fairly steady pace, to the point where it now constitutes 3 percent of the total market unit share. And what does this rather modest market share contribute to the bottom line? Merely 65 percent of all handset profits worldwide. That's right—with only 3 percent of the market, the iPhone's EBIT dollars exceed the entire rest of the market by nearly a factor of two.

It would be hard to believe this sort of performance could possibly continue, except that Apple's market share for its computer products is at a similarly modest 5 percent, which leaves enormous potential for growth. Its computer products are not as profitable as its other lines, but it is still the leader in its segment. The iPad, a product that virtually created its own segment, remains backordered nearly a year after its introduction even as the cost of its core components is declining. That's the power of user-centric design. Given how ingrained this design ethic is at Apple, and given the company's unique and envied culture, we don't see the passing of Steve Jobs having an immediate effect on the company's performance. Many Apple employees remember all too well the days of Gil Amelio and have no desire to return.

Just the Facts

SECTOR: **Consumer Electronics**
BETA COEFFICIENT: **1.05**
5-YEAR COMPOUND EARNINGS-PER-SHARE GROWTH: **70%**

	2007	2008	2009	2010	2011
Revenues (Mil)	24,006	32,479	36,537	65,225	103,000
Net Income (Mil)	3,496	4,834	5,704	14,013	22,500
Price: high	203	200.3	214	326.7	403.4
low	81.9	79.1	78.2	190.3	315.3

Apple Inc.
1 Infinite Loop
Cupertino, CA 95014
(408) 996-1010
Website: *www.apple.com*

Arris Group

Ticker symbol: ARRS (NYSE) ❑ S&P rating: NA ❑ Value Line financial strength rating: B+ ❑ Current yield: Nil

Who Are They?

Arris provides a variety of telecommunications equipment and services used by cable and fiber system operators for the implementation of high-speed networks. Its platforms are used to deliver broadband services such as telephony, video-on-demand, advertising, and high-speed data. The company's products are also used to help operators make the most of their existing infrastructure through minimum-investment upgrades and market-specific technology.

Why Should I Care?

Ignoring for the moment the fits and starts of all the local cable and broadband providers in this country in their efforts to bring high-speed services to consumers, the longer view shows that this market is slowly coming around. Local broadcasters are losing their leverage in the nationwide conversation over media outlets, and local governments are looking at broadband as a business opportunity rather than an annoyance. In addition, broadband providers in the United States are finally starting to Get It. People actually want this stuff. And they're willing to pay for it, if someone can just figure out how to make it happen.

One way to make it happen is to employ the people at Arris group to upgrade your existing infrastructure with their DOCSIS 3.0–compliant CMTS headend. Assuming your downline equipment is up to snuff, you can start offering your customers 160Mbps service to their cable modems. If their cable modems are typical of what most operators in the country offer, not to worry, Arris sells compliant versions of those, as well.

The company also makes a very interesting "convergence" product. Called a Mobility Application Server, it allows cable operators to offload 30–40 percent of mobile voice and data traffic to underutilized landline infrastructure. This is a concept that no other company is currently exploring, one that makes sense for a variety of environments, particularly in the developing economies.

This broadband issue has been very much that same chicken/egg problem that DSL was in the 1990s. No one wanted to upgrade their infrastructure until they sensed the demand was there, but the demand wasn't going to materialize until people could see what the bandwidth provided, and people couldn't see what the bandwidth provided until there was content that took advantage of the bandwidth, and content providers weren't interested until the infrastructure was in place. As we said, though, the market is finally starting to move forward, largely due to pressure from competing technologies (FiOS, for one) from other suppliers. We would expect the growth to come from communities with younger, well-educated populations and then gather momentum in more densely populated areas. Whatever the reason, the provisioning of more high-bandwidth service will be good for Arris. The company has been an investor darling on the cusp of a breakout for some time now, and we are beginning to see the signs of an upward turn in its market. A little rain, a little fertilizer, and if it catches a break here and there, an investment in Arris could bear fruit in 2012.

How's Business?

Pricing pressure on its higher volume products cut into earnings a bit last year, but 2012 should bring some relief in the form of higher volumes. The company has always been able to turn a buck, with a very steady near–10 percent net for the past six years and adequate cash flow.

Upside

- This could be the year
- If it's not, then 2013
- They'll do well regardless

Downside

- Competition at price points
- Lethargic customers
- Risk-averse market

Just the Facts

SECTOR: **Communications**
BETA COEFFICIENT: **1.30**
5-YEAR COMPOUND EARNINGS-PER-SHARE GROWTH: **NA**

	2007	2008	2009	2010	2011
Revenues (Mil)	992	1,147	1,108	1,088	1,110
Net Income (Mil)	89.3	96.6	129	109	110
Price: high	17.9	10.4	13.8	13.0	13.7
low	9.5	4.5	5.8	8.2	9.7

Arris Group, Inc.
3871 Lakefield Drive
Suwanee, GA 30024
(678) 473-2000
Website: *www.arrisi.com*

Arrow Electronics

Ticker symbol: ARW (NYSE) ❑ S&P rating: BBB- ❑ Value Line financial strength rating: B+ ❑ Current yield: Nil

Who Are They?

New York–based Arrow Electronics is one of the world's largest distributors of electronics components and computing products. The company sources products from more than 1,200 suppliers and distributes them to over 115,000 customers through its 340 locations across fifty-two countries and territories. Arrow also employs sales representatives who sell in the field and by telephone. The customer base includes original equipment manufacturers (OEMs), contract manufacturers (CMs), value-added resellers (VARs), and other commercial users. The company's products are primarily targeted at the industrial sector; typically, companies manufacturing computing, telecom, automotive, aerospace, and scientific and medical devices. ARW has a broad customer base, with no single customer generating more than 2 percent of the total sales. Competition comes from other electronics product distributors such as Avnet, Bell Microproducts, AVX Corporation, and Future Electronics.

Arrow operates two business segments, differentiated by product type: electronics components and enterprise computing solutions. The electronics components segment supplies all of the lower-level components used to build circuits, to build circuits into assemblies, and to build assemblies into products. It also sells tools, test equipment, and embedded solutions for integrated products. The enterprise computing solutions segment supplies computing hardware, software, training, and other services directed at the IT professional, and the software and systems development markets.

In 2010, approximately half the company's products were sold into the Americas, with the components segment accounting for 70 percent of sales. Supporting these sales is a sophisticated global inventory system that the company claims provides real-time visibility to inventory levels at any location, anywhere in the world.

Why Should I Care?

As a supplier to such a broad market with a very large customer base, Arrow is a reliable bellwether for the industrial sector as a whole. When Arrow is selling, everyone is building. Consequently, Arrow tends not to have one or two good quarters in a row, but rather several good years in a row as industrial growth cycles ramp up, sustain, and wind down over longer periods of time.

Since April of 2010, Arrow has acquired no fewer than eleven companies in North America, Europe, and Asia. All of these acquisitions are supplementary to its current businesses; acquisition is a very common practice in the distribution business, and Arrow's growth plans often require a purchase in order to get access to specific lines, geographies, or customers. The resources the company can bring to bear in down market cycles should not be discounted—Arrow can spread like wildfire, particularly when the smaller firms are gasping for air.

The company's most recent acquisitions have been higher value-add, service-based companies, but which still provide opportunities for sell-through of Arrow's lines. We like this move as a business multiplier and as a way to improve the quality of the cash flow.

How's Business?

Arrow's second quarter 2011 results were very encouraging, with a second consecutive quarter of record-setting sales and earnings. The company produced income of $1.35 per share and on sales of $5.54 billion, compared with $.07 per share and $4.61 billion in the second quarter of 2010. Cash flow growth has been very strong, which should give the company a substantial cushion for future acquisitions. The company has also added another $100 million to its share repurchase pool. The company is well positioned for both acquisitions and organic growth over the next two years.

Upside
- Recovery on track at Arrow
- Shares are still reasonably priced
- Big fish in a big pond

Downside
- Growth for second half of 2011 likely to taper
- Attractive takeover target
- Price could move up quickly

Just the Facts

SECTOR: **Technology**
BETA COEFFICIENT: **1.15**
5-YEAR COMPOUND EARNINGS-PER-SHARE GROWTH: **12.5%**

	2007	2008	2009	2010	2011
Revenues (Mil)	15,985	16,761	14,684	18,745	22,625
Net Income (Mil)	408	356	202	494	630
Price: high	44.9	39.4	30.1	35.0	46.5
low	32.0	11.7	15.0	21.8	27.9

Arrow Electronics, Inc.
50 Marcus Drive
Melville, NY 11747
(631) 847-2000
Website: *www.arrow.com*

Atmel

Ticker symbol: ATML (NASDAQ) ❑ S&P rating: NA ❑ Value Line financial strength rating: B ❑
Current yield: Nil

Who Are They?

Atmel, founded in San Jose in 1984, is a designer and manufacturer of integrated circuits, specializing in microcontrollers and human-interface applications. Its products are used primarily as enablers for human control of electronic devices. If you build automobiles and you need speed control of wipers, brightness control for lights, monitoring and warning circuits for safety items . . . Atmel makes the parts you need. These same sorts of devices are easily adapted to nonautomotive applications, so Atmel also makes devices for building and industrial automation. In fact, many of the functions that used to be performed by electro-mechanical devices and expensive passive components can now be handled by microcontrollers at a reduced cost. Additionally, features that were not possible before are now implemented reliably and inexpensively, such as GPS and hybrid battery charging control.

Atmel's other major line is its capacitive controllers for touchscreen devices such as smartphones and tablets. They make controllers for large array screens and for smaller surface device configurations such as sliders and wheels.

Why Should I Care?

Over the past several years we've seen touchscreen interfaces show up in so many products that it's hard to count them all: automobiles, refrigerators, washing machines, security systems, sprinkler controls(!), and of course the ubiquitous smartphones, e-book readers, and tablets. There appears to be no end to the potential applications for these devices. The drivers for this trend are several: a higher level of internal product functionality; the rising cost of the increasing number of buttons, switches, and dials needed to control this functionality; the growing amount of front-panel real estate required to accommodate the buttons/switches/dials; and the rapidly falling cost of display technology and the intelligence behind it.

So let's talk about being in the right place at the right time. Atmel has been producing and perfecting its microcontrollers and touchscreen interfaces for many years, and the market seems to have finally caught up with them. It'll net more revenue in 2011 from its microcontrollers alone than it did from its entire product line in 2009. Its touchscreen expertise and libraries are widely used. It has solid financials and has gotten leaner through a couple of recent de-acquisitions. Given all that, the next couple of years hold tremendous promise for this niche player in the semiconductor market. It has a unique product line, a happy and engaged customer base, and what looks to be an enormous market that is just starting to show its potential. This is one of the few tech stocks we'd hold onto for at least three years, even if there are significant gains after just three or four quarters.

How's Business?

Atmel's most recent quarter (second quarter FY2011) was the company's ninth consecutive quarter of sequential revenue growth, and it is not exactly giving away the store to get those results. Gross margins hit 51.8 percent, the company's highest ever. Seven new smartphones using Atmel's controllers began shipping this quarter, as well as a new tablet and two new tablet reference designs from Qualcomm and TI. The company also began volume shipments of four new touchscreen controllers.

Upside
- Touchscreen this, touchscreen that . . .
- Customers' increased expectations for product intelligence
- Very profitable at the *start* of its market's growth

Downside
- The competition is robust, but not as nimble
- Success will call attention
- Touch feedback products needed, but not yet available

Just the Facts

SECTOR: **Semiconductor**
BETA COEFFICIENT: **0.85**
5-YEAR COMPOUND EARNINGS-PER-SHARE GROWTH: —

	2007	2008	2009	2010	2011
Revenues (Mil)	1,639	1,567	1,217	1,644	1,940
Net Income (Mil)	40.7	40.6	3.1	224	375
Price: high	6.5	4.7	4.8	12.7	16.3
low	4.3	2.5	2.9	4.3	9.3

Atmel Corporation
2325 Orchard Parkway
San Jose, CA 95131
(408) 441-0311
Website: *www.atmel.com*

Autoliv, Inc.

Ticker symbol: ALV (NYSE) ❏ S&P rating: BBB+ ❏ Value Line financial strength rating: B++ ❏ Current yield: 2.5%

Who Are They?

Autoliv, Inc., is the world leader in automotive safety systems. It develops and builds systems in-house for all the major automotive manufacturers. Together with its joint ventures, Autoliv has eighty facilities with nearly 43,000 employees in twenty-eight vehicle-producing countries. The company also has ten technical centers and twenty-one test tracks in nine countries around the world.

The company produces passenger safety devices such as seat belts, airbags, steering, and night vision systems, in addition to equipment for specialized applications. The bulk of its production is in restraints (seatbelts and airbags), where it is far and away the leading supplier, with just over one-third of this $18 billion market. Autoliv invented the side airbag and still has 40 percent of this market worldwide. Europe and North America are its two largest markets, followed by Japan and China. Its top five customers account for just over half of 2010 sales, with the rest going to more than two dozen customers.

Why Should I Care?

Frontal airbags reduce driver and passenger deaths impacts by 20–30 percent and have been mandated in many markets where they're in use. These volumes are not going away as long as there's demand for automobiles, and their volumes reduce the costs for follow-on products such as side curtain and rear-passenger airbags. Customer demand for airbags has increased significantly; in 2005, the average number of airbags per vehicle was just over one, but in 2013 it is expected to be 2.8 per vehicle, and total airbag demand for 2013 will be five times higher than that of 2008.

Automobile and truck production in the rest of the world (outside of North America, Europe, and Japan) now makes up 18 percent of the global market. Autoliv has been well positioned there and as a result has seen its shipments increase 300 percent to the region. It expects further growth in market share in the region as its two major rivals (TRW and Takata) have a minor presence there. In 2010, the company grew sales 60 percent in China and began construction of a completely new manufacturing facility, doubling the size of the older plant that it replaces.

Autoliv supports its customers with local supply; the company builds components for its products in a number of centralized locations, shipping lower-level components for stocking at local assembly facilities. When needed, finished products are assembled and delivered to customers. In this scenario, Autoliv can provide two-to-five hour delivery on customer orders, keeping the customer's just in time (JIT) manufacturing process on schedule.

How's Business?

For the second quarter of 2011, the company reported sales and earnings slightly lower than the prior quarter but still up year over year. The decline was due almost entirely to lower light vehicle production because of the recent events in Japan. Even so, net sales were up 14 percent over the prior year, though per-share net fell 4 percent due to higher raw material costs and volume-based cost drivers. Organic sales were up 5 percent, even as global light vehicle production declined 1 percent. Autoliv is growing market share and protecting margins at the same time, not an easy thing to do. The numbers would have been better had it not been for the effects of the earthquake and tsunami in Japan, where light vehicle production was down 36 percent.

Upside

- Pricing power in several markets
- Leading technology
- Four consecutive blockbuster quarters

Downside

- Japanese downturn will last at least another quarter
- Heavy R & D spend on new "active safety" products
- Two top competitors

Just the Facts

SECTOR: **Automotive**
BETA COEFFICIENT: **1.25**
5-YEAR COMPOUND EARNINGS-PER-SHARE GROWTH: **2.0%**

	2007	2008	2009	2010	2011
Revenues (Mil)	6,769	6,473	5,120	7,171	8,250
Net Income (Mil)	308	214	108	591	630
Price: high	65.1	62.6	44.5	82.0	83.5
low	51.3	14.5	12.0	40.3	50.2

Autoliv, Inc.
World Trade Center, Klarabergsviadukten 70
Section E, SE-107 24, Stockholm, Sweden
46-8-587-20-600
Website: *www.autoliv.com*

DISTRIBUTION

Avnet, Inc.

Ticker symbol: AVT (NYSE) ❑ S&P rating: BBB- ❑ Value Line financial strength rating: B+ ❑
Current yield: Nil

Who Are They?

Founded in 1921, Avnet has grown with the electronics industry from its
inception to become the largest (in terms of revenue) distributor of electronic
parts, computing, and storage products in the world. Avnet and a few of its
competitors (Arrow, for one, another of our recommendations) occupy a special place in the electronics distribution segment. Although all of these companies have a main line as a supplier of parts to electronics manufacturers,
Avnet and Arrow also are significant distributors of IT hardware and software.
Avnet's line card includes seventy-five of the largest companies in the IT market, including HP, Dell, IBM, Microsoft, Cisco, NetApp, and others. The
company's revenue is split roughly 60/40 between electronics marketing (the
parts business) and technology solutions (hardware/software distribution).
Avnet also happens to be Oracle's and AMD's largest distributor.

Distributors fill a vital role in the electronics parts business, just as they
do in the automotive, construction, or plumbing businesses. Among other
things, they're the warehouse for most of the small businesses in this country. Linear Technology, for example, with its catalog of more than 100,000
different parts, does not maintain inventory on each of those parts. If you
need one, call Avnet. If they don't have it, it'll find out who does and get it
for you.

Why Should I Care?

Avnet, because of their position in the industry as both buyer and supplier,
with connections to nearly every electronics manufacturer on the planet, is
often viewed as a bellwether stock for the technology sector. Does this mean
you should own it? We think so. The trend in the sector for the next few
years is for sustained growth, and Avnet does well in these periods. It has
issued solid guidance for the next year, and has backed it up with a new plan
to buy back nearly 12 percent of the company's stock.

And why not buy back this stock? The shares are trading at the lowest
multiple in the past fifteen years (6.32 P/E as we write this). Avnet's shares
normally trade with multiples in the range of 17–19, making anything

below 10 attractive. Operating and net margins have been growing steadily over the past three years, and there are no red flags on the balance sheet. Given the company's expansion into mainland China and Latin America (and its financial strength to support the moves), we like the prospects here. Put AVT on your short list.

How's Business?

Revenue grew 39 percent and earnings 57 percent over the prior year, both to record levels. Organic growth was quite a bit less, as Avnet went shopping in 2010–2011, making eleven acquisitions (not at all uncommon in the distribution business) that in total accounted for nearly 20 percent of its FY2011 revenue. Organic revenue growth was a more modest 17 percent, but 2011 was still a very good year in the Avnet world and leverage should improve in 2012 as these operations are fully integrated into Avnet's infrastructure.

Upside

- First stop for most customers
- Growth in highest-margin lines
- Global coverage reduces risk

Downside

- Book/bill at EM on the decline
- Buying growth can be expensive
- Exposed to higher fuel costs

Just the Facts

SECTOR: **Industrials**
BETA COEFFICIENT: **1.2**
5-YEAR COMPOUND EARNINGS-PER-SHARE GROWTH: **37.5%**

	2007	2008	2009	2010	2011
Revenues (Mil)	15,681	17,953	16,230	19,160	26,534
Net Income (Mil)	413	484	289	424	667
Price: high	44.7	36.8	30.8	34.1	37.8
low	25.5	11.9	14.5	22.4	24.2

Avnet, Incorporated
2211 South 47th Street
Phoenix, Arizona 85034
(480) 643-2000
Website: *www.avnet.com*

SEMICONDUCTORS

AVX Corporation

Ticker symbol: AVX (NYSE) ◻ S&P rating: NA ◻ Value Line financial strength rating: B++ ◻
Current yield: 1.5%

Who Are They?

AVX is a manufacturer of what are known in electronics as "passive" components. Passives are some of the most basic devices in the designer's palette and include resistors, capacitors, inductors, and diodes (they're called passive because, unlike "active" components such as transistors, they cannot produce power gain). Passives are not considered particularly sexy and don't get a lot of respect, at least not until you need to protect a $10,000 solid-state drive from a ten-thousand volt static discharge—then Mister Forty-cent Transient Suppressor is pretty darn cool.

AVX products are sold into various markets, including consumer, commercial, automotive, medical, and military. Its products are often found in extreme operating environments, as the company specializes in high-reliability designs, but its parts are also found in consumer equipment such as tablets, smartphones, and televisions. Its line is very broad and includes not only the devices named above but also ceramic transducers, surface acoustic wave devices, sensors, and connectors.

Kyocera of Japan, a manufacturer of advanced materials for the electronics industry, has majority ownership of AVX, and AVX is the manufacturing and distribution arm of Kyocera in the United States for certain of Kyocera's products.

Why Should I Care?

AVX's business over the past ten years had shown steady, if unremarkable growth, at least until FY2009. At that time, the company began a series of cost-reduction initiatives that have resulted in a significant improvement in the operating margin. For FY2011, AVX is expecting an operating margin over 26 percent, compared to the typical 13 percent of just three years ago. The effect on the bottom line has been dramatic, with per-share earnings more than doubling on similar revenues. Many of AVX's products require raw materials such as tantalum, gold, silver, and palladium for their construction. Obviously, there are pricing issues with these materials, but tantalum in particular has been subject to large swings in price (up over 400 percent in the past five years). AVX's management of these costs, evidenced by the greatly improved operating margin, has been impressive. The company has said that there is still room for improvement on the cost-management front and expects further gains there.

In general, AVX's products are used where there are needs for power storage, conversion, or filtering. Starting a few years ago, the consumer and commercial electronics manufacturers began to get very serious about improving the energy efficiency of their products, both in order to comply with new standards and to improve the performance of their products in the marketplace with regard to battery life and size. AVX's product line is very well positioned to benefit from these industry initiatives toward efficiency. Its products occupy a number of performance and form-factor niches that are available only to a manufacturer with AVX's advanced technology and advanced materials. AVX components have typically been priced at the top of the market but were able to support the price with their higher performance and/or niche positioning. With its leaner cost model, however, AVX may well be able to compete on price and win on performance, which could lead to a significant increase in volumes. The next few quarters for AVX could be interesting to watch in this regard.

How's Business?

As noted, the company has had two consecutive knockout years, with structural changes driving greatly improved profitability. Look for more of the same in 2012, and keep a close eye on shipments—it may start swapping unit margins for volume.

Upside

- Steady volumes with potential upside
- Recent improved profitability
- Catalog is broadening

Downside

- Raw materials' cost volatility
- Japanese market still depressed
- Automotive still in recovery

Just the Facts

SECTOR: **Industrials**

BETA COEFFICIENT: **0.9**

5-YEAR COMPOUND EARNINGS-PER-SHARE GROWTH: **19.4%**

	2007	2008	2009	2010	2011
Revenues (Mil)	1,619	1,390	1,305	1,653	1,790
Net Income (Mil)	150	108	143	244	265
Price: high	18.4	14.0	13.0	15.8	16.5
low	13.0	7.1	7.3	11.7	11.4

AVX Corporation

801 17th Avenue South

Myrtle Beach, SC 29577

(803) 448-9411

Website: *www.avxcorp.com*

BIOTECHNOLOGY

Becton, Dickinson & Co.

Ticker symbol: BDX (NYSE) ❑ S&P rating: AA- ❑ Value Line financial strength rating: A++ ❑ Current yield: 2.0%

Who Are They?

Becton, Dickinson is a medical technology company and a supplier to health care institutions, life science researchers, clinical laboratories, industry, and the general public. BD designs and manufactures a broad range of medical supplies, devices, laboratory equipment, and diagnostic products.

The company operates in three worldwide business segments: Medical, Biosciences, and Diagnostics. BD Medical produces hypodermic needles and syringes, infusion therapy devices, insulin injection systems, and prefillable drug-delivery systems for pharmaceutical companies. BD Diagnostics offers systems for collecting, identifying, and transporting specimens, as well as instrumentation for analyzing specimens. The business also provides customer training and business management services. BD Biosciences provides research tools and reagents to accelerate the pace of biomedical discovery. Clinicians and researchers use BD Biosciences' tools to study genes, proteins, and cells to understand disease, improve technologies for diagnosis and disease management, and facilitate the discovery and development of new therapeutics.

In addition to the development work done in the product segments, BD maintains a separate R & D center with its own business development charter. BD Technologies licenses its research to other companies and institutions and provides resources for companies looking to outsource portions of their own R & D. Co-development agreements are not uncommon in the biomedical segment, particularly during phases driven by regulatory-compliance processes.

Why Should I Care?

BD stock has been one of the most reliable issues from any company on any market over the past decade. The stock is characterized by remarkably steady sales and earnings increases and, absent the effects of the recession, steady growth in the share price. The company's operating margin, averaging in the mid-20s for the past ten years, hasn't varied up or down by more than 3 percent over the period, even during the recession. It's very unusual to see this sort of performance from any stock, to say nothing of shares in a technology-driven company. Growth in the share price has tapered somewhat in the past year, even as net margin continues to grow, and that's one of the reasons we're recommending it here. For the first time in a long time, BD is trading at a "discount" to forward earnings, with a forward multiple 40 percent below the stock's long-term average. There hasn't been a bad time to own BD stock over the past ten years, but now is a better time than most to actually buy it.

This is a cornerstone stock—the pasta on which you put your pesto, Alfredo, or Bolognese, as you see fit. You will lose no sleep owning this stock. Earnings growth is just part of the story; the company's dividend, now at 2 percent, has kept pace with (or even slightly outgrown) the price of the stock, growing 15 percent per year over the past ten years. Also, over the same period, the company has repurchased 20 percent of the outstanding shares.

How's Business?

Earnings for FY2012 will continue to increase at their long-term rate, or slightly above. Full-year growth should come in at 12–13 percent above FY2011's numbers, with similarly significant growth in cash flow.

Upside
- Earnings reliability
- Excellent management
- Good product pipeline

Downside
- Low volatility works both ways
- Minor exposure to currencies
- We don't own enough of it

Just the Facts

SECTOR: **Health Care**
BETA COEFFICIENT: **0.65**
5-YEAR COMPOUND EARNINGS-PER-SHARE GROWTH: **NA**

	2007	2008	2009	2010	2011
Revenues (Mil)	6,360	7,156	7,161	7,372	7,810
Net Income (Mil)	978	1,128	1,220	1,185	1,245
Price: high	85.9	93.2	80.0	85.5	89.7
low	69.3	58.1	60.4	66.5	76.4

Becton, Dickinson & Co
One Becton Drive
Franklin Lakes, New Jersey 07417
(201) 847-6800
Website: ***www.bd.com***

SOFTWARE/SERVICES

BMC Software, Inc.

Ticker symbol: BMC (NASDAQ) ❏ S&P rating: NA ❏ Value Line financial strength rating: A ❏ Current yield: Nil

Who Are They?

BMC is a large developer of a particular class of business software, the type typically known as "middleware." Its products are used not by the typical end user of a corporate application, nor does it develop operating systems or operating environments. Its products are used in the realm of what's come to be known as business systems management (BSM). The goal of BSM software is to reduce cost and risk by making distributed software environments easier to run and manage.

The idea is that by considering the entire business as a user and then taking user-centric approaches to service provisioning, the focus on the technology and the hardware that makes up a system is removed and the focus becomes the services provided to the business. In addition to providing a better alignment between user needs and the services provisioned, this approach also provides for a better pathway to service-oriented architectures, virtualization, and cloud implementations.

Why Should I Care?

The BMC tools and methods are coming along at a time when the IT community is very receptive to the idea of everything being a service. In this setting, "data storage" should not conjure up images of racks and racks of drives, but rather a data archival and retrieval process that could be implemented locally, remotely, in a distributed fashion, developed and supported in-house, or provided completely by a third-party. In this approach, it doesn't matter where the storage is physically, how it's implemented, or who owns it—the point is that it provides a service, and the service is what you want to manage and not necessarily its underpinnings. Scaling this concept up, BSM attempts to complement the business process management methods by integrating common processes with common services to make for a more efficient IT environment. The company's basic pitch, though, is in helping enterprises build flexible, growth-friendly IT infrastructures.

The company provides software that allows IT departments to efficiently manage processes such as Service Desk, Capacity Optimization,

Mainframe Automation, Financial Planning and Budgeting, Storage Management, Business Analytics, Supplier Management, and many more. These are all traditional IT functions, and their inclusion in a company's product checklist is not surprising. What is unusual, though, is to find as many functions and services provided in one integrated package that the company claims (and customers seem to agree) makes sense *as* an integrated package.

The company's business reports through two segments, their Mainframe Service Management (MSM) segment and their Enterprise Service Management (ESM) segment. Although ESM (the larger of the two segments) has seen some weakness in booking, the MSM segment (the more profitable of the two) is doing well, growing some 15 percent through FY2011.

How's Business?

BMC feels 2011 was a transition year in which it went from strong, moderate growth to a model of sustained, accelerating growth. We'll see about that, but it did post some record numbers. Bookings for the year reached $2.2 billion, up 13 percent over the previous year, while cash flow was up 20 percent to $765 million. The company entered FY2012 with $1.96 billion in backlog, an increase of 8 percent over FY2010.

Upside
- Earnings reliability
- Price stability
- Growing customer base

Downside
- Bumping into the Big Boys (HP, IBM, etc.)
- Europe to be flat for a few quarters
- Price stability

Just the Facts

SECTOR: **Technology**

BETA COEFFICIENT: **0.85**

5-YEAR COMPOUND EARNINGS-PER-SHARE GROWTH: **NA**

	2007	**2008**	**2009**	**2010**	**2011**
Revenues (Mil)	1,732	1,872	1,911	1,065	2,240
Net Income (Mil)	314	288	376	399	420
Price: high	37.1	40.9	40.7	49.1	56.5
low	24.8	20.6	24.8	34.2	37.5

BMC Software, Inc.

2101 CityWest Boulevard

Houston, TX 77042–2827

(713) 918-8800

Website: *www.bmc.com*

Brooks Automation, Inc.

Ticker symbol: BRKS (NASDAQ) ◻ S&P rating: NA ◻ Value Line financial strength rating: C++ ◻ Current yield: Nil

Who Are They?

When we think of semiconductor equipment manufacturing, we tend to think of the very large and expensive machines from companies such as Applied Materials and Lam Research. But there are also many smaller pieces of gear required for the production of semiconductors. Brooks, founded in 1978, is one of the companies with the skills and experience to survive in this very competitive business, supplying equipment such as automated wafer handlers, cryogenic refrigeration systems, and work-in-progress tracking tools. The company's customer base includes semiconductor manufacturers such as Intel and TSMC, and system integrators that assemble solutions and then sell to manufacturers.

The company reports in three segments: the critical solutions group, which produces the bulk of the company's mainline products; the systems solutions group, which provides a range of engineering and manufacturing services, mainly for the purpose of developing custom solutions for a particular application of customer; and global customer operations, the company's training and support services operation. The company typically derives about half of its revenue from outside the United States.

Why Should I Care?

If you wanted a case study for the boom/bust cycles in the semiconductor business, you could do worse than look at Brooks. It's generally feast or famine with all of the smaller players in this industry (and with many of the big ones as well). Fortunately for Brooks and investment guide writers, we're in the middle of a boom cycle. Normally this would not be the best time to hop on the bandwagon in Chelmsford, as by now most of the investors will have bid the stock way up beyond the point where a late arriver could expect a decent return. But we like the recent news from Brooks and its efforts at diversifying its customer base. We think there's a bit more growth in the up cycle and a bit less contraction in the down cycle than in the past. The cycles have traditionally had two main drivers: consumer spending and technology shifts. Now, however, we're seeing some smoothing effects coming from solar panel and LED production. These two products are on their own schedules, outside Brooks's traditional, highly cyclical markets, and are driving significant volumes of wafers. Just last year twenty-four new LED fabs started up, and there are another half a dozen expected to start this year. Brooks is moving aggressively into those markets, as well as the microelectromechanical systems market.

Intel, TSMC, and Global Foundries plan to let orders for more than $22 billion in new equipment in 2011 alone. The entire semiconductor sector should be up 9 percent in 2011 and another 6 percent annually through 2015. If these numbers hold up, then companies such as Lam Research, one of Brooks's biggest customers, will be very busy.

The company recently placed a dozen new design wins, two of which displaced competitors and eight of which were for lateral markets where it was not competing previously. Geographically, Brooks is expanding its markets in both Japan and China.

How's Business?

In 2010 the systems solution group experienced a 310 percent increase in revenue. The extended factory business, which is an operation providing critical manufacturing support for semiconductor OEMs, was responsible for the bulk of that growth. This bodes well for future revenue growth. The company recently acquired an automation supplier to the pharmaceutical industries, growing laterally into a new supplier base. This will bear watching, as it expects significant growth in this market over the next few years.

Upside
- The harvest is in
- In good financial shape, despite a horrific 2009
- Still trading fairly cheap (7–8 P/E)

Downside
- For portfolios with adult supervision
- Unreliable earnings
- Much speculative interest

Just the Facts

SECTOR: **Technology**
BETA COEFFICIENT: **1.50**
5-YEAR COMPOUND EARNINGS-PER-SHARE GROWTH: —

	2007	2008	2009	2010	2011
Revenues (Mil)	743	526	219	593	700
Net Income (Mil)	54.3	(25.8)	(129.2)	50.1	94
Price: high	20.1	13.4	9.1	10.8	14.3
low	11.7	2.5	3.3	5.5	8.2

Brooks Automation, Inc.
15 Elizabeth Drive
Chelmsford, MA 01824
(978) 262-2400
Website: *www.brooks.com*

CACI International Inc.

Ticker symbol: CACI (NYSE) ❑ S&P rating: NA ❑ Value Line financial strength rating: B++ ❑ Current yield: Nil

Who Are They?

CACI (previously Consolidated Analysis Centers, Incorporated) is a software developer and systems integrator that provides professional services and IT solutions to the federal government and its agencies. The bulk of its work is in the areas of defense, intelligence, homeland security, and logistics. But before you get the wrong idea, these are not a bunch of guys who go to work in balaclavas and walk around saying "Roger that" and so forth. Yes, there are a lot of classified programs at CACI, but the work it does tends to be in the infrastructure of the agencies just mentioned. Although 80 percent of its revenues for FY2010 was for the Department of Defense, its principal service areas are business systems, data and information management, enterprise IT and network services, health care IT, and logistics. It does some field work, and there is a good deal of activity in the areas of cyber security and secure communications, but generally the work is the usual mix of IT services. It's just being done by people with high-level clearances. Got it? Okay. Now if you would, please, just look into this little flashy thing here . . . .

Founded in 1961 by two friends as a software company with one product, the company grew fairly quickly into a $1 million business and now has close to 14,000 employees working in more than 120 locations in the United States and Europe. Its revenues have doubled over the past five years and have increased 600 percent over the past decade, largely through acquisition but also via significant organic growth.

Why Should I Care?

The United States has been engaged in active military conflict pretty much full time since the 9/11 attacks. With what appears to be an imminent winding-down of activities in both Iraq and Afghanistan, many defense contractors are expecting a parallel downturn in government spending and thus, their business. Not CACI, though. There will be some reduction in its real-time activities, but the bulk of its business will actually grow as the military continues to recognize and address the growing threat of cyber attacks. Data and communications security are already a big part of CACI's business, and this will only expand as the need for protection against state- and nonstate-sponsored attacks increases.

The larger part of CACI's business—infrastructure and general IT support for DoD programs—will remain largely unaffected by any reduction in conflicts. Revenues are expected to increase 20 percent over the next two years, and profitability is expected to improve as well. In fact, the company recently announced improved earnings guidance for 2012, up 4 percent. The company also announced its plans to repurchase 12 percent of its outstanding shares over the next eighteen months.

How's Business?

CACI closed the 2011 fiscal year on a high note, posting per-share earnings of $4.61, up 33 percent year over year and beating most estimates of FY2011 earnings by 5 percent. Revenues have been increasing steadily over the past few years, and the company recently announced a number of key acquisitions, including one of the largest players in the data security field. Also in 2011, the company won prime seats on at least five major programs with a total value of nearly $50 billion over an average of eight years.

Upside

- Steady growth
- Solid backlog
- Low exposure to conflict reduction

Downside

- Long, indefinite sales cycles
- Defense spending at some risk in budget debates
- Visible litigation still pending

Just the Facts

SECTOR: Defense
BETA COEFFICIENT: 0.8
5-YEAR COMPOUND EARNINGS-PER-SHARE GROWTH: 7.5%

	2007	2008	2009	2010	2011
Revenues (Mil)	1,938	2,421	2,730	3,149	3,578
Net Income (Mil)	78.5	83.3	95.5	107	138
Price: high	57.6	54.0	49.9	54.1	65.8
low	42.0	36.0	33.9	40.0	47.4

CACI International, Inc.
1100 North Glebe Road
Arlington, VA 22201
(703) 841-7800
Website: *www.caci.com*

SERVICES

Celestica, Inc.

Ticker symbol: CLS (NYSE) ❑ S&P rating: BB ❑ Value Line financial strength rating: B ❑ Current yield: Nil

Who Are They?

Celestica is an electronics manufacturing services (EMS) operation. If you're a company such as Apple, Sun, IBM, etc., then you most likely use Celestica (among others) to build the hardware that goes into your products. You also might use Celestica to design, manufacture, deliver, and support the entire product throughout its life cycle. Celestica provides many levels of service and support, including design, assembly, test, quality assurance, agency certification, and supply-chain management with facilities in dozens of countries around the world.

Celestica is one of the mid-tier players in the EMS game. There's only one player in the top tier, and that's Foxconn, with a market cap approximately sixty times that of Celestica. Flextronics and Jabil Circuits are about twice the size of CLS, and there are many companies smaller than CLS.

Why Should I Care?

Celestica, Foxconn, Flextronics . . . these guys carry the lunch buckets in the global electronics business. They build the products that most of us use many times throughout the day. The PC you work on, the radio you listen to, the television you watch, and all the servers you connect to while browsing the web—all of them, whatever the brand on the outside of the product, were built entirely or in part by one or more of these companies, and that business is not going away anytime soon.

The EMS business is not glamorous. Margins, even for some of the most successful of them, are *desperately* thin. In its very best year, Celestica generated a 5.7 percent operating margin. Its average year is closer to 4 percent, and that's operating margin. Pay the R & D; selling, general, and administrative expense; marketing; and taxes, and you're looking at an average net margin in the 2 percent range. You won't find another company in this book that does $8 billion in sales and makes this little money. So you might be asking yourself at this point "What kind of an endorsement is this?"

As it turns out, Celestica has made some changes recently that should accelerate bottom-line growth even if revenues do not grow as quickly as expected in the economic recovery. The company has reduced its fixed costs over the past five years and is now sized appropriately for the level of antici-pated business. It has eliminated its long-term debt entirely and in 2010 retired 7 percent of its shares. Even with revenues at just 75 percent of their peak, the company is turning in record net margins. The company is now in great financial shape for the anticipated turnaround in the EMS busi-ness, which is expected to grow to $400 billion in revenues in 2014 (from $270 billion), with operating margins expected to more than double for the sector. So there is a silver lining in this EMS business if you're a competent player and a savvy investor.

How's Business?

The second quarter was a very good one for Celestica, with new business awards driving a 250 percent increase in earnings compared to the first quarter. Revenues were up 16 percent over the prior year. The company re-affirmed their projection for the year of 10–15 percent revenue growth, providing encouragement for an optimistic outlook on earnings for the year. Second-quarter 2011 earnings per share of $0.21 were driven by revenue growth of 19 percent. For the first half, the company saw revenues grow 17 percent with an 88 percent increase in earnings over the prior year.

Upside

- Rising tide, with more business coming from Apple
- Inexpensive—trading at a 10 multiple
- Company is much leaner than even three years ago

Downside

- Inventory prices will rise during growth cycle
- Recent Sanmina EPS warning
- Business remains concentrated in fairly small customer base

Just the Facts

SECTOR: Manufacturing
BETA COEFFICIENT: 1.25
5-YEAR COMPOUND EARNINGS-PER-SHARE GROWTH: 25.0%

	2007	2008	2009	2010	2011
Revenues (Mil)	8,070	7,678	6,092	6,526	7,525
Net Income (Mil)	52.8	188	142	196	160
Price: high	8.1	9.9	10.1	11.3	12.0
low	5.2	3.2	2.6	7.4	7.3

Celestica, Inc.
844 Don Mills Road
Toronto, Ontario, Canada M3C 1V7
(416) 448-5800
Website: *www.celestica.com*

Cirrus Logic, Inc.

Ticker symbol: CRUS (NASDAQ) ❑ S&P rating: B ❑ Value Line financial strength rating: C++ ❑ Current yield: Nil

Who Are They?

Cirrus Logic is a designer and marketer of semiconductors targeted at the audio and energy markets. It is one of the largest suppliers in the audio semiconductor market, providing solutions for applications throughout the audio chain to manufacturers such as Apple, Sony, and most (if not all) of the other largest players in the business. Its top-of-the-line products are considered to be among the best available. The energy product line is broadly defined and includes power management circuits, ADCs and DACs, linear amplifiers, products for seismic applications, and power amplifier modules. The bulk of Cirrus's approximately 700 products are proprietary, but the catalog includes many industry-standard commodity designs as well. The revenues in 2010 were split 70/30 between audio and energy.

It does not own a fabrication facility but it has broad expertise in the various semiconductor processes required to build its products. Fab capacity has not been an issue for them in the past and would not appear to be so going forward.

Why Should I Care?

The electronic product markets that have seen the largest growth in the past twenty years have without a doubt been those associated with the computer (PC and server) market. The advancement of the technology in the processor and memory fields are well known and closely followed as bellwethers of the health of the overall semiconductor market. The investment market's focus on the core suppliers of digital functionality for PCs and servers tends to leave players like Cirrus out of the conversation, but in many ways its position gets more and more attractive even as Intel and AMD gobble up the bulk of the system value-add.

The concentration of digital functionality in three parts—the CPU, the north bridge, and memory—has led to the decline of the margin players like SiS, Cyrix, and many others. Cirrus and other suppliers of analog and mixed-signal parts, on the other hand, are relatively safe from the encroachment of the digital giants. Their business relies on the fact that many digital processing streams either begin or end with an analog signal; Cirrus specializes in the conversion of the signal between the two domains and in the specialized processing of analog signals as a "front-end" to the general-purpose CPU.

Its recent growth is due in main to its focus on the special applications of portable audio. Every portable music player and smartphone on the planet, regardless of generation or the underlying CPU or OS, is a potential seat for Cirrus silicon. Cirrus has capitalized by reducing both the chip count and footprint of not only their parts but the associated passive components as well. Cirrus's expertise is not just in product design but also in the chip manufacturing process. This expertise is vital in getting the performance from analog parts—unlike in the digital world, performance in analog does not always improve as geometries shrink, and knowing how to optimize a fabrication process is a big advantage when optimizing functionality of the final chip.

How's Business?

The close association with Apple has Cirrus whistling a happy tune. Cirrus provides the core audio silicon for both the iPad2 and the iPhone4, which, as you may know, are fairly popular products. Both operating margin and net margin doubled in 2010. The company has no debt and is well capitalized; we would not be surprised to see Cirrus pick up one or two smaller players during the year.

Upside
- Strong relationship with Apple
- Good product direction
- Strong finances

Downside
- Not much rockin' in pro audio market
- Revenue growth flattening
- Capacity/costs bear watching

Just the Facts

SECTOR: **Technology**

BETA COEFFICIENT: **1.05**

5-YEAR COMPOUND EARNINGS-PER-SHARE GROWTH: **28.1%**

	2007	**2008**	**2009**	**2010**	**2011**
Revenues (Mil)	182	175	221	360	405
Net Income (Mil)	24.1	17.9	28.6	90.0	85.0
Price: high	9.4	7.6	6.9	21.2	25.2
low	4.5	2.3	2.2	6.2	12.8

Cirrus Logic, Inc.

2901 Via Fortuna

Austin, TX 78746

(512) 851-4000

Website: *www.cirrus.com*

INSTRUMENTS

Coherent, Inc.

Ticker symbol: COHR (NASDAQ) ❑ S&P rating: NA ❑ Value Line financial strength rating: B+ ❑ Current yield: Nil

Who Are They?

Coherent is one of the world's leading suppliers of lasers for commercial, industrial, and scientific applications. It also supplies tools for laser measurement and control, and accessories for use with lasers in laboratory and production environments. In addition to standalone lasers, the company also supplies fully integrated shop-floor laser machining cells and work cells customized for the solar panel industry.

Why Should I Care?

Photonics has come into its own. The technology base has been growing steadily over the past few decades, supported mainly by industrial and military users. Now there are mainstream tools and applications that hadn't even been dreamed of as little as thirty years ago. The unique properties of laser light, which had made lasers irreplaceable as laboratory tools, now make them equally valuable in commercial products as mundane as a $5 laser pointer and as exotic as the excimer laser used to perform eye surgery (a procedure that, to show how far the technology has come, is now also considered fairly mundane).

Coherent supports the broad commercialization of the technology with a product line that covers all existing laser technologies and most high-value applications. Applications in the microelectronics and semiconductor industries have been growing rapidly as device geometries are shrinking beyond the point where standard wide-band optical techniques operate effectively. A monochromatic, coherent light source is ideal for detection of sub-micron faults in silicon wafers and in the semiconductor device itself, for example. Lasers are used in the wafer cutting and die separation processes, leading to higher yield and fewer defects when compared to traditional diamond saw methods. In addition, lasers are used to produce many of the fine geometries in special materials employed in LCD and plasma flat panel displays, and lasers are the only tool capable of creating the inner-layer connections in the tiny circuit boards used in densely packed handheld devices such as cell phones and music players. Finally, lasers have found new applications recently in the processing of raw silicon and the production of LEDs. These new applications have yielded significant improvements in LED brightness and efficiency, two properties of very high value to flat panel display manufacturers.

How's Business?

With the advent of some high-volume, cutting-edge applications, Coherent has been recognized as a growth opportunity, and the shares have been bid up accordingly. Still the company is trading at just over two times book value, in part due to its rather bleak operating margins (roughly 8 percent in 2011). With a high-mix, low-volume production model, ten separate R & D facilities, thirteen separate manufacturing facilities, and expensive/exotic raw material, it's not surprising that COGS is a high 57 percent. This is a problem that is partially mitigated by higher volumes, but Coherent will be saddled with these costs for some time. The company plans to buy back $75 million in stock. While we wish there were higher-leverage opportunities for the cash, it does represent nearly 5 percent of the outstanding shares, which is not bad for comps going forward.

Upside
- Momentum with higher volume customers
- Intriguing new applications
- Market share leader

Downside
- Poor cost structure
- Shares won't be cheap
- Perhaps better as a longer-term play

Just the Facts

SECTOR: **Technology**
BETA COEFFICIENT: **0.9**
5-YEAR COMPOUND EARNINGS-PER-SHARE GROWTH: **4.5%**

	2007	2008	2009	2010	2011
Revenues (Mil)	601	599	436	605	800
Net Income (Mil)	16.2	34.3	(16.0)	36.9	63.0
Price: high	33.4	38.5	30.2	47.3	63.8
low	24.6	20.0	14.3	25.9	41.2

Coherent, Inc.
5100 Patrick Henry Drive
Santa Clara, CA 95054
(408) 764-4000
Website: *www.coherent.com*

SOFTWARE/SERVICES

Computer Sciences Corp.

Ticker symbol: CSC (NYSE) ❑ S&P rating: A- ❑ Value Line financial strength rating: A ❑ Current yield: 2.5%

Who Are They?

Computer Sciences is one of the bigger players in the systems consulting business. With nearly 91,000 employees, it is the largest independent outsourcing vendor headquartered in the United States. It has a great deal of business with the U.S. government, and its client list includes organizations such as NASA, Jet Propulsion Laboratories, the Atomic Energy Commission, and the U.S. Navy. CSC's clients also include foreign governments and commercial enterprises that rely on information services and systems for their operations. The company's business strategy is based on helping these clients remain competitive in their businesses and maintain a high level of service to their customers. CSC's service offerings include IT and business process outsourcing, emerging services such as cloud computing and cyber security protection, and a variety of other IT and professional services.

The company reports in three segments: the North American public sector (NPS), the managed services sector (MSS), and the business solutions and services (BSS) sector.

- The NPS business provides IT services to the federal government and its agencies, including most civil departments and branches of the military.
- The MSS business provides public companies with information systems outsourcing services, handling standard processes for clients in dozens of different industries.
- The BSS business is the private sector project operations, where one-off programs to provide industry-specific solutions are completed to a customer's specification.

Why Should I Care?

The NPS business, which represents 37 percent of CSC's revenue, is the segment that has some question marks surrounding it. The federal government has begun to address the budget deficit with announced cutbacks in spending over the next ten years, and a new process that will automatically increase the size of these cuts if an agreement on the budget cannot be reached by those "in charge." Obviously, we can't predict what the actual outcome of this process will be, but we don't anticipate that it will significantly impact revenue to NPS. The type of jobs being done by NPS is the day-to-day work of government and programs that are intended to actually *improve* the efficiency of government operations. De-staffing either of these types of programs runs counter to the notion of making government work better.

In fact, CSC received for 2012 contract awards for NPS of $5.5 billion. In total, the company received contract awards of $14 billion, and the company exited the year with a total backlog of $36 billion. This is down from 2010's exit backlog of $43.2 billion, but the business atmosphere in 2011 has been far more cautious than in 2010, and we do not expect that this environment will persist long into 2012. In any case, the company's business model provides for a base of revenue in any given year when contract awards may slow or the market for services softens.

How's Business?

Compared to FY2010, FY2011 revenues increased 0.8 percent, while operating income fell 12.8 percent to $1,217 million and operating income margins decreased to 7.6 percent from 8.8 percent. Net income of $759 million was down $75 million or 9.0 percent. Earnings per share of $4.73 were down $0.55, or 10.4 percent. Not a great year on the books, but we feel the numbers are fully baked into the price of the shares at this point, and any turnaround in the economy will provide a significant boost to the stock.

Upside

- Good backlog, with more than $11 billion deliverable in 2012
- Steady revenue growth, even in slow economy
- Dividend and buyback initiated to placate large shareholders

Downside

- ADHD Congress
- Defense business will be affected somewhat
- Contract season can't come soon enough

Just the Facts

SECTOR: **Technology**
BETA COEFFICIENT: **0.95**
5-YEAR COMPOUND EARNINGS-PER-SHARE GROWTH: **10.5%**

	2007	2008	2009	2010	2011
Revenues (Mil)	16,500	16,740	16,128	16,042	16,550
Net Income (Mil)	653	621	817	706	735
Price: high	63.8	50.5	58.4	58.1	56.5
low	46.9	23.9	31.1	39.6	26.9

Computer Sciences Corporation
3170 Fairview Park Drive
Falls Church, Virginia 22042
(703) 876-1000
Website: *www.csc.com*

MATERIALS

Corning, Inc.

Ticker symbol: GLW (NYSE) ❑ S&P rating: BBB+ ❑ Value Line financial strength rating: B+ ❑ Current yield: 1.1%

Who Are They?

Corning, incorporated way back in 1936, is perhaps still best known for its Pyrex brand of glass cookware for the home. The company divested its consumer products division in 1998 (though retaining the brand) and today derives only a small percent of its revenues from Pyrex-branded laboratory equipment. In 2010, more than 70 percent of its revenues were from the sale of glass panels for liquid crystal displays and optical fiber. Corning also makes the core ceramic component of the automotive catalytic converter and the diesel particulate filter. The company's five business segments are all technology-based, and R & D spending accounts for more than 9 percent of sales. The specialty materials segment has its own markets and revenue but also provides a critical feeder research role in the company in the development of leading-edge materials and new applications.

Why Should I Care?

Tech watchers have had an eye on Corning's stock for some time, waiting for the moment when U.S.-based Internet service providers finally commit to large-scale fiber service delivery. What's happened instead is a slow, measured, cautious rollout from Verizon and AT&T, while back-end infrastructures are built up only in the densest and most profitable markets. Needless to say, this has led to a lot of disappointment on the part of GLW investors, to say nothing of Corning itself. We see the pace picking up moderately, but no major changes in the ISP's minimum-risk strategy are apparent.

Corning's second-quarter results brought out some high and low points. TV demand is down, and the company has had to lower its expectations for total glass demand, including the demand for Gorilla Glass. The computing market did better, with most projections showing tablet market growth benefiting Corning. Other areas were in line with expectations, and with the results from Japan being better than anticipated (both glass and automotive), long-term growth seems to be on pace. Hopes remain high for a successful television holiday season, so buy a few shares of Corning and go buy that sixty-inch screen!

The Gorilla Glass product looks very interesting from an applications perspective, as it opens up design possibilities unique to that product—the best way in the world to get sole sourced. Providing improved impact resistance, scratch resistance, and higher toughness even with thinner geometries, Gorilla looks to be the best product available both for mobile devices and traditional displays. Even in existing applications, the business should grow well over the next couple of years. Used in more than 280 devices from twenty brands, Gorilla is found in touchscreen devices ranging from the iPhone to high-end smartphones made by Samsung. The product is already boosting earnings from the materials group, and higher volumes and manufacturing efficiencies have already improved margins in this business. As the company's investment in this product increases, costs will rise and the bottom line will feel the pinch, but we think if they build it, the revenue will come.

How's Business?
For the second quarter of 2011, Corning reported revenue of $2 billion, which was up 4.3 percent sequentially and 17.1 percent year over year. Corning stated that the supply chain was looking more cautious ahead of the 2011 holiday season and build rates at this time of the year were lower than may be considered typical. Looking ahead, all the major LCD TV makers (Samsung, LGE, Sony, Sharp, others), as well as the less-familiar Chinese makers have lowered their build plans from December 2010 to June 2011.

Upside
- Gorilla Glass—the 800–pound product?
- Fiber rollouts proceeding
- Diesel filters cleaning up

Downside
- Some panel business flattening
- Softening TV market
- Revenue concentrated in two markets

Just the Facts

SECTOR: **Technology**
BETA COEFFICIENT: **1.25**
5-YEAR COMPOUND EARNINGS-PER-SHARE GROWTH: **28.5%**

	2007	2008	2009	2010	2011
Revenues (Mil)	5,860	5,948	5,395	6,632	8,160
Net Income (Mil)	2,267	2,424	2,114	3,275	3,240
Price: high	27.3	28.1	19.5	21.1	23.4
low	18.1	7.4	9.0	15.5	13.2

Corning, Inc.
One Riverfront Plaza
Corning, NY 14831
(607) 974-9000
Website: *www.corning.com*

Cree, Inc.

Ticker symbol: CREE (NASDAQ) ◻ S&P rating: NA ◻ Value Line financial strength rating: B+ ◻
Current yield: Nil

Who Are They?

Cree, Inc., is a manufacturer of semiconductor devices and materials. Recently it has moved into the packaged lighting and fixtures business, using its internally developed LED products as a core. Founded in 1987 in Durham, North Carolina, the company has grown to 4,300 employees and more than $850 million in revenue, with manufacturing facilities in North Carolina and China. The bulk of its revenues are derived from products based on light-emitting diode (LED) technology. Recently, it has also developed a new line of power-switching products based on its silicon carbide process expertise. It also is one of the largest providers of gallium nitride semiconductor devices, used primarily in low- to medium-power LEDs.

Why Should I Care?

Cree is the leader in the development of light-emitting diodes based on silicon carbide processes. Both silicon carbide and gallium nitride provide specific benefits when compared to the more common doped silicon semiconductors that have been used since the early 1960s in nearly every electronic product in the world. These benefits are leveraged primarily for applications requiring the efficient production of light and efficient high-speed switching of power devices. The company's ability to leverage these formerly niche technologies into a near-$1 billion business is the story of the LED and Haitz's Law.

When they were first introduced in 1962, LEDs were not very bright, limited to one color (red), and horribly expensive. Since the mid-1960s, however, LED brightness has improved by a factor of two every three years or so, a trend that has come to be known as Haitz's Law (similar to Moore's Law for computing devices). The result is that now we have LEDs that can produce more than 200 lumens per watt, or nearly fifteen times the specific output of an incandescent bulb. Cree's business is about leveraging these improvements into product applications as they become practical and producing the enabling devices. Some of the more easily identifiable applications include automotive lighting, household lighting, and flashlights. Others include fiber-optic sources, signage, and telecommunications.

Further progress along the Haitz trend line will bring into play even more applications and lower costs for existing uses. Next in line will be automotive headlamps, cost-effective interior lighting, and the (potential) elimination of all but a few specialty uses for incandescent and fluorescent lamps. Cree is out in front of all these uses, with product designs that ease the conversion from older technology to LEDs that it supplies.

The company also recently introduced a new class of devices, a MOS-FET based on silicon carbide technology that enables a dramatically more efficient mode of operation for power switching equipment. The device's function may be the most ubiquitous technology you've never heard of; the company claims the market for this single device is close to $4 billion today, and I have no reason to doubt it. If it can produce this device in quantity with reliability, it can charge a healthy premium for it, as it's a potential game changer in many high-volume applications.

How's Business?

Cree lit all the lights in FY2010, with profits nearly as high as the previous four years combined. This is the classic semiconductor model, where the marginal income curve gets very steep as volumes rise above critical levels. Profitability growth in FY2011 will taper significantly as the company has run into heavy price-cutting from its Asian competition in the raw LED market. Also, the company's move into packaged goods (where earning, long-term, could be more attractive) has coincided with reduced consumer and commercial spending. Time will tell on the timing of this move, but at the moment investors seem skeptical. Share price has fallen considerable from its peak, but we feel this is a buying opportunity on a quality, if somewhat speculative issue. The company carries no debt and is sitting on over a billion in cash. Acquisitions or a stock buyback would not be out of the question.

Upside
- Technology leader
- Well-funded R & D
- Enormous displacement potential

Downside
- Somewhat speculative
- Better tech is always possible
- Slow adoption from traditional industries

Just the Facts

SECTOR: Technology
BETA COEFFICIENT: 1.15
5-YEAR COMPOUND EARNINGS-PER-SHARE GROWTH: 2.5%

	2007	2008	2009	2010	2011
Revenues (Mil)	394	493	567	867	980
Net Income (Mil)	26.3	31.8	59.3	179.2	205
Price: high	34.9	35.5	57.3	83.4	69.2
low	15.3	12.6	15.6	47.3	26.7

Cree, Inc.
4600 Silicon Drive
Durham, NC 27703
(919) 313-5300
Website: *www.cree.com*

SEMICONDUCTORS

Cypress Semiconductor

Ticker symbol: CY (NASDAQ) ❑ S&P rating: NA ❑ Value Line financial strength rating: B ❑ Current yield: 1.8%

Who Are They?

Cypress Semiconductor is a chip design and manufacturing company based in San Jose, California. Founded by former AMD CEO T. J. Rogers and others in 1982, Cypress has built a thriving business around an acquisition model, picking up promising niche players and providing them captive fab capacity and ready access to capital. The company is still run as a confederation of start-ups, and the company's history is an interesting study in alternative business models. Cypress's businesses are acquired or developed internally, then either internalized, sold, spun off, or "spun-in," with the employees of the business unit rewarded as though they were part of a separate company, each with its own financing and share values. Mr. Rogers's book title—*No Excuses Management*—says all you need to know about his style, and Cypress is very much a reflection of his personality. If you a run small, independent design house and you have any part of your ego tied up in your company, think twice about picking up the phone if T. J. calls.

Why Should I Care?

We'll be honest with you. One of the challenging things about doing this sort of analysis—looking hard at a company's fundamentals and its near-to-mid-term business prospects—is that the places you have to go to get this information are often the places that are blasting news of the current stock market panic of the day. Trying to find a sober disclosure of data can be difficult. A case in point: As we write this, HP has announced they will discontinue the production of WebOS devices, one of which (the OuchPad, er . . . TouchPad) used the touch controller from Cypress. Now we see a lot of analysts overreacting to the move and its impact on Cypress, but it's been known for a while that restock orders from HP were just not going to happen, what with 90 percent of HP's initial run still unsold two months after release. Cypress's TrueTouch system is a great product and has found seats in many high-volume Android-based phones. No reason for CY shareholders to panic. HP, on the other hand . . . .

Getting back to Cypress, we see that it is sitting on record backlog with a book/bill floating around 1.1, which is the sort of data that matters and is why we're recommending Cypress as a strong momentum play in the current semiconductor market. This stock *will* require adult supervision and should not be purchased after taking nonprescription medications, but right now it's available cheap and is backed by as strong a product portfolio as it's had in quite some time.

How's Business?

The company has beaten the street in its earnings performance for eight quarters in a row. This kind of trend often has as much to do with underpromising as it does with overdelivering, but in the case of Cypress there's a fair amount of both going on. Its history has been to project conservatively and execute like crazy, which is another thing we like about it. Negative surprises in the semiconductor business are not soon forgotten in the market. Witness Cypress's 4Q2008.

Upside

- Cash flow back to prerecession levels
- Record operating margin
- Timely product mix

Downside

- Small setback regarding HP
- Natural volatility of semi market
- Fab not fully utilized

Just the Facts

SECTOR: Technology

BETA COEFFICIENT: 0.95

5-YEAR COMPOUND EARNINGS-PER-SHARE GROWTH: 26%

	2007	2008	2009	2010	2011
Revenues (Mil)	1,596	766	668	878	1,040
Net Income (Mil)	140	30.1	1.0	179	245
Price: high	66.8	54.8	39.3	53.0	68.2
low	39.1	17.9	18.2	31.8	41.9

Cypress Semiconductor

198 Champion Court

San Jose, CA 95134

(408) 943-2600

Website: *www.cypress.com*

COMPUTERS
Dell, Inc.

Ticker symbol: DELL (NASDAQ) ❏ S&P rating: A- ❏ Value Line financial strength rating: A ❏
Current yield: Nil

Who Are They?

Dell is one of the largest computing equipment and services suppliers in the world. It designs, manufactures, and markets personal computers, servers, networking equipment, storage subsystems, and computer peripherals. Its consumer division also resells Dell-branded and third-party equipment and accessories such as televisions, printers, monitors, memory, and storage. The company markets through its direct sales teams to corporate and institutional customers and sells direct via catalog, retail outlets, and the Internet.

Dell's biggest impact on the PC market may have been its original direct-to-the-consumer order fulfillment model. Rather than being forced to choose among prebundled configurations, Dell customers were able to configure systems as they liked. In the process, Dell was able to capture the retail markup while still offering products at a competitive price. This consumer-direct model was unique for its time and was the core of Dell's profit model. HP, IBM, Sony, and others had nothing like this and were forced to rely on the retail channel for the bulk of their sales. Since then, Dell has added conventional retail channels, while its competitors have been quick to add direct models for their highest-volume configurations.

Why Should I Care?

Dell, which many would say perhaps more than any other company characterized the bullish 1990s market, may look like the most boring stock in this book. Most view the company as a "me, too" seller of consumer-grade personal computers, a low-margin business that IBM had the good sense to depart when it sold its PC division to Lenovo in 2004. As it turned out, IBM's timing couldn't have been better; Dell's stock peaked in late 2004 and has been on a steady decline ever since.

In reality, though, Dell's consumer business represents only 20 percent of revenue, while PCs overall account for only 55 percent. In 2010, its enterprise business brought in 30 percent of revenue at record margin levels. And even though the consumer segment revenue fell 8 percent in 2010, the company nearly doubled its earnings overall, as the server and storage businesses averaged 21 percent growth year over year. Dell is clearly not driven by the consumer PC business and certainly isn't the company that most people think it is.

Dell was famous in its heyday for its supply-chain management. Because it was so efficient at turning inventory (for several years it averaged fifty-four inventory turns per year) it was essentially running with negative inventory cost; it got paid on a Monday for products whose parts it was not planning to buy until Friday. Given the "value rot" aspect of computer inventory, this expertise is priceless. And Dell has not lost its touch; in 2009 it was still carrying less than eight days of inventory and was ranked behind only Apple in the overall quality of its supply-chain management.

How's Business?

Talk about a rebound year. Dell's 2010 pulled them out of the recession with significant advances in margins, particularly in the final quarter. Dell's fourth quarter produced $.53 per share in earnings, against a consensus expectation of $.37, and gross margins of 21.5 percent versus a consensus of 18.7 percent. Sales to small, medium, and large businesses were all up 12 percent, with the bulk of the gains coming in storage and services. The rebound has continued in 2011 with significant margin expansion, thanks in large part to the aforementioned supply-chain leadership. The remainder of 2011 looks promising, with a seasonality revenue tailwind and lower operating costs that together should provide for a 25 percent per-share earnings bump for the year overall.

Upside

- No longer reliant on the PC business
- Retail presence fills a void
- Still managing the basics well

Downside

- A bit late to the services party
- PCs have to figure out how to make money
- Direct model no longer a big advantage

Just the Facts

SECTOR: **Technology**

BETA COEFFICIENT: **0.95**

5-YEAR COMPOUND EARNINGS-PER-SHARE GROWTH: **-3.0%**

	2007	2008	2009	2010	2011
Revenues (Bil)	61.1	61.1	52.9	61.5	63.8
Net Income (Bil)	2.95	2.48	1.43	2.64	3.25
Price: high	30.8	26.0	17.3	17.5	17.5
low	21.6	8.7	7.8	11.3	13.2

Dell, Inc.
One Dell Way
Round Rock, TX 78682
(512) 338-4400
Website: *www.dell.com*

COMMUNICATIONS
Digi International, Inc.

Ticker symbol: DGII (NASDAQ) ▫ S&P rating: NA ▫ Value Line financial strength rating: NA ▫
Current yield: Nil

Who Are They?

Digi is one of a number of companies supplying "smart" devices to, among others, operators of alternative energy systems and traditional electric utilities. These devices are designed primarily to monitor and communicate the status of a device's energy consumption, but they are also used for monitoring the operation of mobile equipment such as truck fleets, agricultural equipment, and public safety vehicles. The company's products are also used for remote monitoring of large storage tanks for temperature, capacity, and other valuable data.

The company's strategy is to target the value of the communication link between the device and the grid, rather than the monitor/sensor itself. Digi launched its Drop-in Networking four years ago and plans to focus on this core capability going forward. Drop-in Networking is designed to make nearly any device with a basic data port a wired/wireless Internet Protocol device with specific, customized monitoring features. Digi's belief is that the Internet is a far more robust and flexible communications network than any proprietary network could be (we agree). The company's product line is split roughly 50/50 on a revenue basis between embedded devices (designed into the customer's product) and standalone, external products.

It also provides cloud services (basically, it owns the datacenter) and supplies software tools to integrate desktop and mobile applications that interface with the customer's data.

Why Should I Care?

"You manage what you measure" is an axiom used in many fields. The ability to monitor electricity consumption at the customer's level in real time has profound implications not just for the generating utility but for the individual user as well. A consumer who can see the positive monetary effect of a single change in how he uses electricity is a consumer who's about to change his behavior. This is the thinking behind a number of the incentives the U.S. government is proposing in its vision for a Smart Grid, whereby conservation will become easier and more effective. The Electric Power Research

Institute estimates the implementation of current smart grid tools will save between 4 and 5 percent of all electric use by 2030 (about $20 billion per year in 2012 dollars).

You're driving down a little-used road late at night, and as you make your way the streetlights turn on ahead of your arrival and turn off after you pass by. This is similar in concept to the motion-detection lighting in modern buildings, but it's how approximately 10,000 streetlights work in a Digi-based lighting network in Norway. The system also allows for multiple users to be billed for power consumed by multiple lights attached to the same standard, and for partial dimming in Norway's unique environmental conditions. This particular pilot program has led to a reduction in energy usage of more than 65 percent.

How's Business?

The company had a good turnaround in 2010 in both revenue and earnings, with earnings acceleration in 2010 versus the prior three years. The company recently introduced the industry's first devices that comply with a new data security specification, FIPS 14-2. This new spec is particularly important to users of wireless IP devices and is a requirement for most federal contracts. This is an important certification, assuming the federal government has any money left with which to buy communications hardware.

The second quarter of 2011 was Digi's twenty-ninth consecutive quarter of profitability, with revenues exceeding expectations. Bookings broke into record territory for the second consecutive quarter, and the company has offered increased and bullish guidance going forward.

Upside

- Government incentives of $4 billion to grid industry
- No debt, very good cash flow
- Established technology, new market

Downside

- Trading at a relatively high multiple
- Some negative earnings surprises recently
- Bumpy ride; volume trading by large financials

Just the Facts

SECTOR: **Technology**

BETA COEFFICIENT: **0.74**

5-YEAR COMPOUND EARNINGS-PER-SHARE GROWTH: **(14%)**

	2007	**2008**	**2009**	**2010**	**2011**
Revenues (Mil)	173	185	166	183	207
Net Income (Mil)	19.8	12.4	4.1	8.94	12.1
Price: high	16.5	7.8	10.6	11.8	15.0
low	14.7	13.1	6.8	7.6	9.3

Digi International, Inc.

11001 Bren Road East

Minnetonka, MN 55343

(952) 912-3444

Website: *www.digi.com*

SOFTWARE

DTS, Inc.

Ticker symbol: DTSI (NASDAQ) ❑ S&P rating: NA ❑ Value Line financial strength rating: B++ ❑ Current yield: Nil

Who Are They?

DTS develops audio compression and recovery algorithms used in the motion picture, consumer electronics, and professional audio industries. The company also produces and licenses the hardware and software used in the implementation of this technology to these same customers. The company's products can be found in audio/video receivers, DVD and Blu-Ray players, personal computers, and video game consoles.

Why Should I Care?

Audio compression is useful for a number of reasons. Compression allows the audio signal to be transmitted in digital format, which prevents the degradation that can sometimes occur during transmission. It also allows multiple audio channels (up to eight on some movies now) to be transmitted along one physical wire (if you think your stereo/TV setup looks like a rat's nest now, trust us, it could be worse). Compression also allows the many channels of audio data to fit on lower-capacity media, reducing the delivered cost and greatly simplifying the playback. On the other hand, compression (done badly) can degrade the quality of the sound, and that's how DTS managed to get a solid foothold in the business—twenty years ago, Dolby left the door open just a crack when they were slow to adapt to digital content and the requests from the movie studios for better quality.

DTS had an uphill fight for acceptance, but now its technology is nearly as ubiquitous as Dolby's. Most theatrical releases come with a DTS soundtrack now, as do their DVD and Blu-Ray releases. Console and PC games often use DTS soundtracks as well. Getting the soundtracks supported is the key, because once the content is there, you've got the key to selling the decoding hardware and/or algorithms to the platform builder. Yes, it's the Dolby model all over again, but look at how well it worked for Dolby.

So why is DTS a buy now? Three reasons:

1. The technology has grown in scope, improved in quality, and is spreading more quickly. It's even showing up in smartphones.

2. Dolby took a hit from Redmond. Microsoft's Windows 8 product will not come with a Dolby license, so any Dolby-encoded content played back on a Windows machine will require a separate license, typically provided by the hardware supplier. This is neither here nor there for the end user, but it cuts nearly 20 percent off of Dolby's top line. Ouch.
3. The stock is very much underpriced at the moment due to widespread uncertainty around the consumer market. The shares have shown a steady upward trend (following the market share) over the past six years, interrupted only by the recession and the recent market downturn.

DTS is a company with ubiquitous technology, a known competitive landscape, and a profitable roadmap. Lots to like.

How's Business?
Blu-Ray content (which carries a higher-end DTS license) is driving strong top-line growth at DTS. Blu-Ray–related revenues are up 60 percent so far in 2011, and Blu-Ray devices are showing up in more and more places as the hardware prices fall. The company's margins are growing steadily and cash flow will more than double 2009's total.

Upside
■ Market share appears to be at critical mass
■ Profitable growth
■ Still room to grow

Downside
■ Dolby is no slouch
■ It's the consumer market
■ Have theater revenues seen their peak?

Just the Facts

SECTOR: **Technology**

BETA COEFFICIENT: **1.15**

5-YEAR COMPOUND EARNINGS-PER-SHARE GROWTH: **14%**

	2007	**2008**	**2009**	**2010**	**2011**
Revenues (Mil)	53.1	60.2	77.7	87.1	105
Net Income (Mil)	9.6	9.4	10.6	16.0	24.0
Price: high	34.1	36.0	35.1	50.0	50.2
low	20.4	12.6	13.4	26.0	24.7

DTS, Incorporated

5171 Clareton Drive

Agoura Hills, CA

(818) 706-3525

Website: *www.dts.com*

Eastman Chemical Company

Ticker symbol: EMN (NYSE) ❑ S&P rating: BBB ❑ Value Line financial strength rating: B++ ❑
Current yield: 2.1%

Who Are They?

If you're old enough to be reading this book, you might remember the original Eastman Kodak. That company's cameras and especially its process for creating roll film made Kodak (a name invented in 1888 by George Eastman) the world's leading photography brand. The chemicals used in the production of that film were made by Eastman Chemical. In 1993, Eastman Chemical was spun off from Kodak and became a separate company engaged in the business of manufacturing plastics, chemicals, and fiber products. That company now has a market cap of about ten times that of its old parent Kodak, and by the time this goes to print, Kodak itself may be on the auction block.

Please excuse the trip down memory lane—we're both photographers who started out shooting on Kodak Tri-X black and white film.

Back on topic, Eastman Chemical is not only no longer tied to the photography business, it is not tied to any particular business. It is pretty much everywhere. Its broad product line includes basic materials like yarns, water treatment, adhesives, wood preservatives, inks, polymers, paints, resins, acetate fiber . . . the list goes on and on. Its products are used extensively in packaging, medical equipment and supplies, agriculture, industrial goods, apparel, consumer and durable goods, and even consumables like, yes, photographic film.

Why Should I Care?

Eastman Chemical produces many of the basic ingredients of industry. Its products are key raw materials, integrated directly into other products or are used as part of the production process. When industry grows, Eastman grows and is one of the first companies to get paid. Not surprisingly, it has been getting paid a lot as of late. Its top line is not yet back to prerecession levels, but the recovery has been very good to sales so far, and it looks to be well-positioned for further growth. It has sold off an underperforming plastics operation and added significant capacity in their high-margin olefins feedstock unit. Debt is quite low, and there's adequate cash on hand for acquisitions.

The real story of the past year, however, has been the growth in the bottom line. It has been beating earnings estimates in each of the past four quarters. Over the past two years, earnings have more than doubled. Cash flow is up more than 60 percent over the same period. Earnings estimates for 2012 keep rising, but as of right now they're at $8.82, which would predict a share price in the $140–$150 range at recent multiples. Rising cigarette sales, particularly in the Far East, has given Eastman's fibers unit a big boost. The company has a new acetate operation in South Korea and plans to build another in China in 2013 to further serve this market.

How's Business?

As we mentioned, Eastman had a monster 2010. Even with the rise in petroleum prices, operating margins increased significantly. This bodes extremely well for performance over the next few years, given the recent political uncertainty and the speculative nature of that market. The earnings picture for 2011 appears clear, as all four of its operating segments continue to perform at record levels. A full-year EPS increase of 33 percent is realistic. A previously idled plant has been restarted to meet anticipated demands, and the company is eyeing acquisitions similar to the recent Dynaloy and Sterling Chemicals. Currently trading in the low 80s, this stock carries a meager 7.7 multiple. There's real value here, and this stock deserves a position at the core of any portfolio.

Upside
- Good production capacity
- Innovative company
- Fair amount of pricing power

Downside
- Shares could get pricey in a hurry
- Petroleum a major feedstock
- Foreign currency exposure in largest segments

Just the Facts

SECTOR: **Materials**
BETA COEFFICIENT: **1.92**
5-YEAR COMPOUND EARNINGS-PER-SHARE GROWTH: **10%**

	2007	2008	2009	2010	2011
Revenues (Mil)	6,830	6,726	4,396	5,842	7,025
Net Income (Mil)	423	342	266	514	675
Price: high	72.4	78.3	61.9	84.6	108.2
low	57.5	25.9	17.8	51.1	78.1

Eastman Chemical Company
200 South Wilcox Drive
Kingsport, TN 37662
(423) 229-2000
Website: *www.eastman.com*

Electronics For Imaging

Ticker symbol: EFII (NASDAQ) ❑ S&P rating: NA ❑ Value Line financial strength rating: B ❑ Current yield: Nil

Who Are They?

Electronics For Imaging produces large format printers and inks, digital controllers and imaging workstations, and commercial and enterprise printing services. In addition to the printing hardware and imaging software, the company also provides software for workflow management and business management software tailored to the in-house and retail print shop environments. The company's workstations turn the attached copiers and printers into networked print devices accessible from anywhere on the network. They also work with printers supplied by other printer manufacturers, such as Canon, Xerox, Richoh, Oki, and others.

The products are used in many different environments, including advertising agencies, professional photo shops, commercial printers, prepress providers, and print-for-pay operations such as you might find in an OfficeMax or other office support service provider. Applications might include check printing, architectural document production, large-format advertisements such as banners and billboards, general corporate uses, and one-off artistic productions. The company's customers include print-for-pay and small commercial shops; medium and large print shops; display graphics providers; in-plant printing operations; government printing operations; large commercial, publication, and digital print shops; and the packaging industry.

The company plans to expand into larger formats as well. Its newest equipment prints on media as large as five meters wide, useful when the goal is to wrap an entire building with an advertisement or company logo.

Why Should I Care?

Although a mantra in the business world for the past twenty years has been "a paperless environment," there are still a great many needs for a printing solution. This list is far too long to recite here, but it includes such basics as packaging, printed advertising, marketing materials, sales tools, and interior design. Those are just the corporate and general business uses, and don't include the uses for all the other graphics professionals and end users who need larger printed material from time to time. Print uses are actually expanding, thanks to the technology of computer-controlled ink and dye application. Photo-realistic images two meters high were simply not possible twenty years ago, but now you can wallpaper your basement with interior shots of the Taj Mahal. Fetch me my slippers!

Kidding aside, the print business has grown tremendously with the advent of new inks, dyes, and the means with which to apply them accurately. EFI's business will not replace the massive offset machines used to print high volumes of bulk material (such as the book you're currently reading), but EFI and businesses like it have completely taken over the lower-volume and specialty markets, particularly color.

Given the large number of general business applications for EFI's products, the longer-term trend of the stock tends to follow the general business cycle. This tendency is reflected in the stock's beta, which is a measure of the stock price's volatility relative to the market at large. EFI's beta is 1.0, which is exactly the volatility of the overall market. Short-term, there's a fair amount of cyclicality to EFI's stock price, probably due to the cost of the equipment and the budgets where those costs are likely to land. In the corporate world, new fiscal years typically start in March and orders for capital equipment go out soon after. EFI's share price typically starts rising mid-year. It might be worth waiting on this one until May and get in ahead of the move.

How's Business?

EFI has put up a couple of very strong quarters recently and the share price has responded. We feel there's still room to grow, and most estimates have a one-year target price in the mid-$20s. With the stock trading near 14 in the recent pullback, we like the potential. Just watch the timing.

Upside
- Business cycle turning around
- Well-known solution
- Good financials

Downside
- High SG&A
- Executive compensation—'nuff said
- Two customers account for 27 percent of sales

Just the Facts

SECTOR: **Technology**
BETA COEFFICIENT: **1.00**
5-YEAR COMPOUND EARNINGS-PER-SHARE GROWTH: **NA**

	2007	2008	2009	2010	2011
Revenues (Mil)	621	560	401	504	575
Net Income (Mil)	26.8	(12.0)	(53.8)	(2.9)	25.0
Price: high	30.2	22.4	13.1	14.9	18.9
low	20.6	7.6	7.8	9.2	12.9

Electronics For Imaging, Inc.
303 Velocity Way
Foster City, CA 94404
(650) 357-3500
Website: *www.efi.com*

AEROSPACE

Esterline Technologies

Ticker symbol: ESL (NYSE) ❑ S&P rating: BB+ ❑ Value Line financial strength rating: B+ ❑ Current yield: Nil

Who Are They?

Esterline is a company that flies under the radar (literally) of most investors because the majority of its work is for the aerospace and defense markets. The company derives 80 percent of its revenues directly from those contracts, with the other 20 percent coming from the application of its technologies in industrial markets. Its core businesses are avionics and controls, sensors and systems, and advanced materials. It does not make airframes or other vehicle structures, just the advanced systems that allow the military aircraft, vehicles, and ships in which they're installed to operate at the edge of the performance envelope.

Why Should I Care?

The past decade has been a very good one for defense contractors. Since the 9/11 attacks the U.S. defense budget has more than doubled, from $316 billion in 2001 to $708 billion in 2011. Over the same period, defense industry profits are up nearly 300 percent and are now close to $25 billion per year. This year, however, Congress agreed to cut back the country's planned growth in military spending by $350 billion over the next ten years. In response, many defense contractors' stocks have taken a downward turn in recent months as the sector as a whole has fallen out of favor. While Esterline will feel the impact on a few of its active programs, most of its larger contracts should be unaffected by a cutback in current deployments. Its two biggest programs are for avionics for training and refueling aircraft, and those programs should be safe. The company is also a Tier 1 supplier to Boeing, with products in nearly every airframe that Boeing builds.

Another point in ESL's favor is the growth in Homeland Security spending. Many of the programs that populate the Defense budget will fit just as easily under Homeland Security should Defense be unable to support them. Surveillance, communications, night vision, GPS . . . all of these technologies are just as important to protecting domestic borders as they are to supporting the efforts of the deployed military.

As it turns out, Esterline has very little exposure to the highly visible and high-value programs that have landed on the chopping block. The loss of the two major fighter programs and the Navy's proposed DD1000-class destroyer have little if any impact on Esterline's revenue. A de-emphasis on manned aircraft may affect Esterline down the road, but the company's technology is equally applicable to commercial aircraft and vehicles.

The downturn in defense spending will not affect all contractors equally, and we feel Esterline is in better shape than most in this regard. Look for an opportunity to pick up this out-of-favor stock at a discount to its true value.

How's Business?
New orders for the first half of 2011 were $862 million, up 17 percent over the prior year, with backlog rising 7 percent to $1.16 billion. Gross margin improved on the strength of spare parts orders and a retroactive pricing agreement with a customer. The company has raised guidance for 2011 EPS twice (up more than 6 percent), indicating an improved outlook going forward into 2012.

Upside
- Steady long-term contracts support diversification
- Cash for acquisitions
- Recent dip makes for a good buy-in

Downside
- Prospects just got a little dimmer
- Still not exactly cheap—trading near average multiple
- Profits likely tapering until commercial business grows

Just the Facts

SECTOR: **Technology**
BETA COEFFICIENT: **1.2**
5-YEAR COMPOUND EARNINGS-PER-SHARE GROWTH: **19.0%**

	2007	2008	2009	2010	2011
Revenues (Mil)	1,267	1,483	1,425	1,527	1,685
Net Income (Mil)	92.3	114	107	130	165
Price: high	59.2	62.9	44.3	71.3	82.0
low	38.2	25.4	18.9	36.8	62.2

Esterline Technologies
500 108th Avenue NE
Bellevue, Washington 98004
(425) 453-9400
Website: *www.esterline.com*

BIOTECH

Exact Sciences Corporation

Ticker symbol: EXAS (NASDAQ) ❏ S&P rating: NA ❏ Value Line financial strength rating: NA ❏ Current yield: Nil

Who Are They?

Exact Sciences is a biotechnology firm engaged in the development of a methodology for the early detection of human colorectal cancer. Its approach is somewhat unique in that it employs noninvasive, DNA-based stool screening and so can be handled without an office visit or other more expensive procedures. The process is also designed to detect precancerous bodies and can provide earlier screening horizons than most other processes. No special preparations or diet are required, nor are any radioactive materials employed.

Exact Sciences has licensed certain core aspects of the process from the Mayo Clinic and Dr. David Ahlquist. The company will make royalty payments to both parties and will retain the exclusive rights to commercialize additional development that may derive from the license or the collaboration.

Why Should I Care?

There are other screening methods for colorectal cancer that utilize the examination of stool samples, but none are as specific as that proposed and tested by Exact Science. Its method seeks to detect minute traces of DNA that have undergone mutations, correlating these DNA fragments with known markers for precancerous polyp formations in the colon. Other stool sampling approaches require the presence of blood secreted by these precancerous polyps or by active tumors in order to make a positive diagnosis, but these tissues do not secrete blood at all times, reducing the odds of detection. On the other hand, the polyps do shed surface cells on a continual basis, and a percentage of these cells will have DNA that can be detected as cancerous or precancerous in nature. In the largest clinical trial of the approach to date, the Exact Science Cologard method was 64 percent effective at detecting precancerous tissues, while the current competitive nonvisual screening methods were 22 percent, 20 percent, and 12 percent effective. The current gold standard screening method, colonoscopy, was 95 percent effective in the same test, but the cost of a colonoscopy is between three and thirteen times the projected cost of Cologard and requires a significant level of training to perform and interpret in order to achieve that level of effectiveness. The Cologard process, compared to existing stool-based methods, is more sensitive and specific, and appears to be easily automated.

In short, Cologard looks to be a very good candidate to replace all of the current or projected screening methods for colorectal cancer. Since colorectal cancer is far easier to treat when detected early, and since colorectal cancer is the second deadliest form of cancer in the United States, the argument for widespread screening is compelling. The American Cancer Society recommends annual screening for colorectal cancer to everyone over the age of fifty (over 90 million people in the United States) and Exact Sciences estimates the potential market value of their screening process at $1.2 billion annually.

How's Business?

Exact Sciences is not yet profitable, but the prospects are very encouraging. Its burn rate is manageable and it has sufficient capital to see the company through at least 2013, which is when Cologard is expected to be in general availability. It already has over a thousand LabCorp sales reps promoting its current ColoSure product.

Upside
- Solid trial data
- Compelling mortality argument
- Excellent demographics

Downside
- Obvious buyout candidate (not always a bad thing)
- May require an additional stock offering to complete trials
- Important trials results unavailable until late 2012

Just the Facts

SECTOR: **Biotechnology**
BETA COEFFICIENT: **1.27**
5-YEAR COMPOUND EARNINGS-PER-SHARE GROWTH: —

	2007	2008	2009	2010	2011
Revenues (Mil)	2.94	(0.87)	4.76	5.34	4.9
Net Income (Mil)	(12.0)	(9.74)	(9.13)	(11.6)	(21.0)
Price: high	5.4	3.3	4.0	8.8	9.2
low	2.4	0.4	0.6	3.4	5.0

Exact Sciences Corporation
441 Charmany Drive
Madison, WI 53719
(608) 284-5700
Website: *www.exactsciences.com*

Fairchild Semiconductor

Ticker symbol: FCS (NYSE) ❏ S&P rating: BB+ ❏ Value Line financial strength rating: B ❏ Current yield: Nil

Who Are They?

Just so you know, Fairchild was the company that started it all in semiconductors. Beginning in 1957, it invented most of the early devices, led the development of mass-produced semiconductors, and created most of the practices and methods of the initial semiconductor industry. Fairchild today designs, develops, and markets semiconductors of all types: analog, discrete, interface and logic, nonvolatile memory, and optoelectronic. Its focus is on discrete and analog power management and interface products. The company operates in three segments: mobile, computing, consumer, and communications (MCCC); power conversion, industrial, and auto (PCIA); and standard products. Fairchild owns and operates four fabrication plants and three packaging and assembly facilities.

Why Should I Care?

Fairchild's performance coming out of the recession has been encouraging, to say the least. The company's revenues rebounded immediately to prerecession levels with an operating margin well above the previous record highs. The company used the recessionary period to reduce costs and improve efficiency, and this has been reflected in its results. Net margin for 2011 should come in around 12 percent, well above its performance through most of the past decade and well above the current performance of most of its peers. The current price/cash flow is less than 5:1, and in the most recent quarter, the company generated free cash flow of $40 million, continuing the trend of record cash generation begun in 2010. Normally we don't emphasize numbers like these, but these are great for a company that has been considered something of a sleeping dog for the past few years. Results like these tell us that this is not the same company it was before the recession; it is a much leaner operation, and there's some real earnings leverage here.

In our introduction, we talked about companies that don't rely on one or two product lines or markets to make or break a fiscal year. Fairchild is one of those companies. It has a diverse set of customers and a broad product line that provides a lot of insulation from the industry's ups and downs. Yes, it took a beating in the recession, but who didn't? What's important is how you recover, and Fairchild over the past eight quarters is setting a standard.

And lest you think we're downplaying Fairchild's chances in the marketplace, consider this: The 2010 revenue split was 48 percent from industrials and automobile applications and 41 percent from the mobile, communications, and consumer segment. These markets are setting up nicely for recovery through the end of 2011 and all through 2012. Special mention should be made of Fairchild's new line of motor controllers, which provide cost-effective speed control for AC motors of the type often used in consumer appliances. The company claims significant improvements to efficiency and noise, which could very well be a big deal for Fairchild.

How's Business?

The company's current guidance for the rest of 2011 is for very modest growth over 2010's results. Given recent market gyrations, we'll take it. We think FY2012 will be a very good year for Fairchild, however. It is leaner, greener, and it has a couple of product lines that could be real breakouts.

Upside
- Excellent management
- Financial controls that work
- Healthy product line

Downside
- Some bumps in material cost foreseen
- Smart power line may require multiple quarters to develop
- Some consumer spending would be nice

Just the Facts

SECTOR: **Technology**
BETA COEFFICIENT: **1.40**
5-YEAR COMPOUND EARNINGS-PER-SHARE GROWTH: **3.5%**

	2007	**2008**	**2009**	**2010**	**2011**
Revenues (Mil)	1,670	1,574	1,188	1,600	1,700
Net Income (Mil)	113	45.6	(60.2)	153	205
Price: high	20.5	15.3	11.5	16.1	21.0
low	14.2	2.7	2.8	7.7	11.9

Fairchild Semiconductor International
82 Running Hill Road
South Portland, ME 04106
(207) 775-8100
Website: *www.fairchildsemi.com*

INSTRUMENTS

Faro Technologies, Inc.

Ticker symbol: FARO (NASDAQ) ❑ S&P rating: NA ❑ Value Line financial strength rating: B+ ❑
Current yield: Nil

Who Are They?

Faro designs, manufactures, and markets 3D measurement and imaging systems used in manufacturing, construction, industrial, and forensic applications. Its base systems, which consists of a measurement device, its CAM2 imaging software, and a host computer, provide users with fast and accurate dimensioning over a large range of scales—one can measure an object with features as small as five millionths of a meter or the inside of a warehouse 400 feet long. Its systems are used for in-process inspections, reverse engineering, incoming inspection, process characterization, quality monitoring, and many other common industrial requirements. As a measure of the breadth of the applications for Faro's equipment, consider that they have been sold to over 11,000 different customers, from small machine shops to large companies including Boeing, Lockheed, GM, Honda, and General Electric.

Why Should I Care?

There are few things more fundamental to the manufacturing process than measurement. Every object created in a factory is measured in some way before it's shipped off to a customer. In order to measure mechanical dimensions you need tools, an operator (or robot), and a reference. The operator applies the tool to the object, takes a measurement, and based on the comparison of the measurement to the reference, takes some action. This can happen hundreds of times for each object, adding time and labor, thereby increasing the cost of the product. Most of Faro's products are used to significantly reduce the time needed to perform these inspections. Their unique use profile (portable, handheld, multiaxis) sets Faro's products apart from the competitor's, as they can be quickly moved and re-tasked with no tooling changes other than a download of the design files for the part to be inspected.

Faro's tools are also invaluable in the design process. Prototype fabrication is accelerated and first articles are quickly verified. Custom tooling needs are minimized, saving significant time and money, and complete dimensioning of hand-built parts can be accomplished in minutes.

There's still a place for quick and easy measurements to be taken with hand tools such as calipers, hole gauges, micrometers, etc., but these tools do not lend themselves to the measurement of anything even as complex as a simple curve. They cannot automatically record and report process variation data, nor are they capable of automatically updating their inspection criteria to reflect the latest process changes. Faro's tools do all of these things. They're capable of replacing all but the most precise measurement tools available, and they allow even small, low-volume shops to quickly and reliably produce complex, dimensionally accurate products.

How's Business?

Like most of the suppliers of industrial goods, Faro took a beating in 2009, but turned things around in 2010 as orders returned. A revenue uptick of 30 percent brought the company back to profitability, and 2012 looks very promising. The first half results for 2011 show a 29 percent increase in sales and an 82 percent increase in per-share earnings, with improved momentum in the second quarter compared to the prior quarter. New orders in the second quarter were up 42 percent year-to-year, and EPS increased in the second quarter by 127 percent. Production tooling in general is in demand again, and Faro has just one competitor across most of its product lines.

Upside

- Enormous customer base and product appeal
- Global manufacturing
- Powerful IP protection

Downside

- Relatively expensive products—long sales cycle
- Shares can get bid up quickly
- Volumes sold through distribution channels increasing

Just the Facts

SECTOR: **Industrials**

BETA COEFFICIENT: **1.15**

5-YEAR COMPOUND EARNINGS-PER-SHARE GROWTH: **-15%**

	2007	2008	2009	2010	2011
Revenues (Mil)	192	209	148	192	240
Net Income (Mil)	21.4	14.0	(8.0)	11.0	20.5
Price: high	50.3	36.2	22.1	33.5	48.2
low	23.7	10.6	10.8	16.8	29.5

Faro Technologies, Inc.

250 Technology Park

Lake Mary, FL 32746

(407) 333-9911

Website: *www.faro.com*

First Solar, Inc.

Ticker symbol: FSLR (NASDAQ) ❑ S&P rating: NA ❑ Value Line financial strength rating: A ❑ Current yield: Nil

Who Are They?

First Solar is the world's largest manufacturer of thin-film solar panels. It produces panels for sale to integrators, developers, and directly to end users for large-scale programs. The panels produced are typically installed in commercial installations ranging in size from 10kW up to utility-scale projects, the largest of which so far is 80MW on more than a thousand acres.

There are many producers of photovoltaic solar panels, but First Solar's process is a bit different from most others. It does not use wafer silicon and classic semiconductor technologies to produce its products. Instead, it uses standard glass coated on one side with vapor-deposited amorphous silicon and a thin film of cadmium telluride as the collecting material. These panels are much less expensive to manufacture than traditional wafer-based panels and are lighter and more durable, making for a simpler, cheaper, and faster installation process.

The company was founded in 1999 and began production in 2002. Its production capacity in 2012 is expected to be 2.3GW, or the equivalent of two to three modern, full-scale nuclear generation facilities.

Why Should I Care?

The promise of solar energy—nearly free electricity—has been around for a long time, but the economics had been caught in a Catch-22 for decades. The cost of the photovoltaic device had always been comparatively high on a dollars-per-watt basis, and making them less expensive required much R & D and volume manufacturing techniques that could not be economically justified without committed customers. Customers, on the other hand, were unwilling to commit until cost-effective devices were proven and tested in the field. The tipping point came when a number of industrialized countries threw tax incentives at the problem, spurring the development of advanced PV designs and creating a class of customers for PV-generated electricity in the bargain.

China, Inc., has decided to own the market for traditional wafer silicon panels, which have higher conversion efficiency but higher manufacturing costs, while the thin-film business has fallen largely to First Solar and a few smaller players.

GE recently announced its plans to build the country's largest thin-film panel manufacturing plant somewhere in the United States by 2013. While this means that First Solar now has one of the world's largest diversified manufacturers as a competitor, it's also good news in that it will likely expand the market for both company's products. The entry to the market of an industrial bellwether such as GE will draw significant attention and should help to advance the acceptance of solar as a mainstream technology.

How's Business?

The recent rapid growth of the PV industry was due in part to the tax incentives offered by the governments of Germany and France, and those incentives have an uncertain future. Germany had begun to scale back, but the recent events in Japan have led to a complete and rather surprising reversal of public policy in Germany. It has committed to eliminate all of its nuclear generation by 2022, and the country's existing leadership position in the use of solar energy is only expected to increase. Other initiatives based on carbon footprint reduction may supplement the more widespread adoption of solar, but we expect to see First Solar running at capacity for several years to meet existing demand.

The company's share price has fallen 36 percent from the beginning of the year as questions about tax subsidies and the global economic environment persist, but FSLR's position as the lowest-cost supplier is the place to be when pricing pressure is pulling down the entire market, as is the case here.

Upside

- Technological lead
- Cost advantage
- Robust cash flow

Downside

- GE's entry is a concern
- Margins fading somewhat
- Tellurium supply may be constrained

Just the Facts

SECTOR: Energy
BETA COEFFICIENT: **1.40**
5-YEAR COMPOUND EARNINGS-PER-SHARE GROWTH: —

	2007	2008	2009	2010	2011
Revenues (Mil)	504	1,246	2,066	2,564	3,740
Net Income (Mil)	112	348	640	664	815
Price: high	283	317	207.5	153.3	170.8
low	27.5	85.3	100.9	98.7	99.7

First Solar, Inc.
350 West Washington Street, Suite 600
Tempe, Arizona 85281
(602) 414-9300
Website: *www.firstsolar.com*

Flextronics International

Ticker symbol: FLEX (NASDAQ) ❑ S&P rating: BB+ ❑ Value Line financial strength rating: B+ ❑ Current yield: Nil

Who Are They?

Flextronics is the second-largest electronics manufacturing services provider in the world, behind only the mammoth Hon Hai. Like most EMS operations, Flextronics provides clients with an array of capabilities and services. The client may only need to get a lot of printed circuit boards built or have some custom cables fabricated, or they may need to outsource an entire product line, including all of the up-front design, delivery, life-cycle management, and all of the back-end support. As examples of the kind of thing Flextronics does, the company recently completed agreements to design and build televisions in Mexico for the huge Korean manufacturer LG and to build plug-in electric motorcycles in China for a small private company based in Oregon.

Founded in 1969, Flextronics vaulted into the worldwide number-two spot with its $3.6 billion acquisition of Solectron in 2007. The company set up what was at the time one of the first offshore facilities for a U.S. manufacturer, in Singapore. Flextronics moved its headquarters there in 1990 and became one of the big players in the development of Southeast Asia as a manufacturing and logistics hub.

Why Should I Care?

Looking at the EMS industry just in terms of revenue, Flextronics and Jabil Circuit (also in this book) are the clear number-two players. Hon Hai (also known as Foxconn) is approximately twice the size of Flextronics and almost five times the size of Jabil. We mention the relative size of these firms because size plays a big role in this business. These companies are purchasing machines, and the more they can buy at a time the better their landed cost. The margins these companies earn are miniscule in comparison to their revenues. Flextronics, one of the more successful outfits, has never netted more than 6 percent; all of these companies look for every advantage they can possibly get, and purchasing/logistics play a big part in the success or failure of an EMS provider.

Make no mistake about it, there's no easy money in this game. This is very, very hard work. The attention to detail and the internal coordination required just to break even at this business is very great. The reason these companies exist at all is that businesses in the industrialized economies need much higher value-add per employee than is derived from coordinating the enormous amount of materiel, manufacturing assets, and test equipment required to build on the scale that these companies do. Many tech companies much smaller than Flextronics will miss on earnings for a quarter or two and point to their internal manufacturing; Flextronics has held operating margins between 4 and 6 percent for forty-eight consecutive quarters and has never lost money. We think this is a safe bet, and with a multiple currently under 6, we think there's an opportunity for growth.

How's Business?

An encouraging development: Flextronics has found that service levels to India and Turkey now justify the opening of new facilities in each of those countries. These are two markets with growing middle classes who are very receptive to consumer electronics.

Upside
- Underpriced at $5.50
- Geographic expansion
- Good cash generation

Downside
- Inventory bloat
- Rising material costs
- Rising receivables

Just the Facts

SECTOR: Technology
BETA COEFFICIENT: 1.3
5-YEAR COMPOUND EARNINGS-PER-SHARE GROWTH: NA

	2007	2008	2009	2010	2011
Revenues (Mil)	27,558	30,949	24,111	28,680	31,500
Net Income (Mil)	694	543	378	633	685
Price: high	13.6	12.2	8.0	8.4	8.4
low	10.6	1.2	1.8	4.9	5.1

Flextronics International, Ltd.
One Marina Blvd., #28–00
Singapore, 018989
(408) 576-7000 (US)
Website: *www.flextronics.com*

INSTRUMENTS

Flow International Corp.

Ticker symbol: FLOW (NASDAQ) ❑ S&P rating: NA ❑ Value Line financial strength rating: C ❑
Current yield: Nil

Who Are They?

Ever find yourself staring at a 200-pound block of aluminum, wondering
how best to sculpt it into a flying pig for your sister's birthday? No? Well,
actually, neither have we, but if we had, we'd know the tool to use is a water
jet cutter. These clever machines are capable of accurately cutting almost
any material using nothing but a high-pressure stream of water. Flow International is the pioneer and market leader in the commercial use of high-
pressure water jet cutting tools and has delivered more than 10,000 systems
since 1974. The company also makes high-pressure surface cleaning systems,
but the bulk of its sales are from cutting tools.

Why Should I Care?

Both the company and the market have a number of attractive features. The
company is the technology leader in the field, having developed the initial
concept and then nearly all of the subsequent commercial refinements. Flow
has the broadest and deepest product line, with advanced robotics integration and 3D modeling software. And although all of the manufacturers took
a hit to the top line during the recession, Flow has the largest installed base,
the largest number of service contracts, and the largest recovery potential; it
is currently trading at less than half of its prerecession average.

The market itself, currently at about $500 million, is estimated to
be worth more than $1 billion with further upside when global markets
are more fully developed. The technology favors the new rapid prototyp-
ing production model and displaces several other alternative cutting/mill-
ing technologies. The high-end tools are expensive, but smaller systems are
affordable and almost as versatile. Some continuous-process manufacturers
(such as paper mills) use water jets exclusively for their cutting operations, as
they create no waste, run year-round with little downtime, and can be easily
reconfigured or repurposed, unlike most hard tooling. Textile and plastic
extrusion manufacturers would be large potential markets.

Although the company is relatively small, it maintains an advanced
systems business, which works with select accounts to develop custom,

integrated solutions for specific production problems. The company recently worked with Airbus to develop custom tooling for their wing production, for example. These quasi-partnerships are valuable to both companies, and Flow's maintenance of its advanced systems operation will pay benefits down the road.

How's Business?

Flow finished off FY2011 with a very strong quarter of revenue gains in its standard line, up 37 percent over the fourth quarter 2010. For the year, the standard segment system sales grew 44 percent over FY2010. The advanced segment sales were off 17 percent, as expected, primarily due to the timing of orders and the length of the product build cycle. Overall, consolidated sales were up 25 percent versus 2010, with while gross margin remained at 39 percent of sales and SG&A fell 4 percentage points, accounting for at least part of the improved profitability. There was encouraging news in the breakdown of the segments, as the standard line products (which ship quickly) were able to recognize most of their gains in the current year, while the advanced line products will not recognize revenue until 2012.

Upside

- Revitalized customer base
- Growing acceptance of technology
- New, impressive 3D functionality

Downside

- Nearly eighty competitors
- Cash flow is still lean
- High price still a problem on some capital budgets

Just the Facts

SECTOR: **Industrials**
BETA COEFFICIENT: **2.05**
5-YEAR COMPOUND EARNINGS-PER-SHARE GROWTH: **NA**

	2007	**2008**	**2009**	**2010**	**2011**
Revenues (Mil)	213	244	210	174	217
Net Income (Mil)	3.8	22.4	(23.8)	(8.5)	.76
Price: high	13.1	10.5	3.1	4.2	4.6
low	7.6	1.4	114	2.1	2.4

Flow International Corporation
23500 64th Avenue South
Kent, WA 98032
(253) 850-3500
Website: *www.flowwaterjet.com*

INTERNET

Google, Inc.

Ticker symbol: GOOG (NASDAQ) ❑ S&P rating: AA- ❑ Value Line financial strength rating: A++ ❑ Current yield: Nil

Who Are They?

Google owns and operates the world's leading Internet search engine. The vast majority of its income (97 percent in 2010) is derived from the delivery of targeted advertising through its Google AdWords and Google AdSense products. The licensing of its search technology (Google Search Appliance) to other companies generates the remainder of its revenue.

The revenue model is pretty simple. Google's AdWords scans the HTML code on an enrolled website, searching for keywords. When key-words are found, ads relevant to the keywords are displayed on the user's screen along with the page. Advertisers select their own target keywords and pay Google when a viewer clicks on their ads. Google and the advertiser are notified of every click, and other tracking information relevant to the click is transmitted as well.

Advertisers get targeted ads without a great deal of up-front cost, and the ads appear on pages from Google's large roster of partners, from AOL to the *Washington Post*. Partners in turn receive a share of the advertising revenue when ads on their pages are clicked.

Why Should I Care?

If you track Google's average annual price-to-earnings ratio you can get a sense of the market's expectations for this stock: in 2004, average P/E was 100; 2005, 53; 2007, 40; 2010, 20. Google's current P/E of 18 is typical for a mildly speculative tech stock and just above the median for the stocks in this book. Based on what the market seems to be saying with their money, then, Google is no longer the growth darling they once were. Or are they?

While it's true that Google's share price hasn't changed materially since the beginning of 2010, its earnings-per-share, revenue, margins, and cash position have all grown substantially over the same period. And while it's true the company's revenue model hasn't changed, Google's (free) browser and (free) smartphone OS have made significant advances in their respec-tive market shares. With $35 billion in the bank and a dominant position in search, the path forward with these assets seems pretty clear: Develop technologies to aid in the growth of mobile search, acquire promising companies working in those fields, and dominate those markets as well. While its core ad-placement business continues to spin off mountains of cash, Google knows the business it is in is the information business—knowing who its users are, where they are, and what they're interested in as *they* go about *their* business. Google's nonrevenue-generating businesses generate market intelligence, and the intelligence is what Google uses to monetize its core. New revenue-generating opportunities will arise; we look for Google, through acquisition in those markets, to position itself for significant growth.

We feel Google is simply undervalued in the current market. The shares are not inexpensive, but represent real value when compared to even a fine company such as Amazon. Amazon is currently trading at seventy times earnings, while Google is trading at a 20 multiple. That's an easy choice for us.

How's Business?

Google's offer for Groupon was rebuffed (in the long term, good for Google), but it has made forty other strategic acquisitions since March 2010, most of them targeted at the online retail and cloud computing spaces (including $400 million for AdMeld). The company's operating margins have settled into the 38–40 percent range, while annual revenues have grown $5 billion per year for the past five years.

Upside

- Undervalued
- Mobile search and ads just starting to take off
- One enormous wallet with which to defend AdSense

Downside

- The average investor may not commit to $600 shares
- China will be a tough nut
- Speculative push appears to have faded

Just the Facts

SECTOR: Technology
BETA COEFFICIENT: 1.1
5-YEAR COMPOUND EARNINGS-PER-SHARE GROWTH: 55%

	2007	2008	2009	2010	2011
Revenues (Bil)	16.6	21.8	23.7	29.3	35.0
Net Income (Bil)	4.20	5.30	6.52	8.50	9.81
Price: high	747.2	697.4	626.0	630.8	639.6
low	437.0	247.3	282.8	433.6	474.9

Google Inc.
1600 Amphitheatre Parkway
Mountain View, CA 94043
(650) 253-0000
Website: *www.google.com*

Greatbatch, Inc.

Ticker symbol: GB (NYSE) ❑ S&P rating: NA ❑ Value Line financial strength rating: B+ ❑ Current yield: Nil

Who Are They?

Greatbatch is a developer of technology-based products targeted at industrial and medical applications, and provides design and testing services groups for clients in similar markets. The company operates in two segments: Greatbatch medical and electrochem. A third operation, their QiG Group, is an advanced-development organization leveraging the company's technology into new products and processes.

Greatbatch medical designs and manufactures components for the medical device market with a focus on technical innovation. Many of the components are a legacy of the company's founding product—the first implantable pacemaker—and so include batteries, capacitors, etc., but it also produces precision metal products for orthopedic procedures and tools for vascular access and manipulation.

The company's electrochem segment produces batteries in a variety of form factors and chemistries, as well as wireless sensing devices. Its batteries are designed for unique, critical market applications such as oil drilling, undersea exploration, and military and aerospace. The wireless sensing devices are used for critical process-control applications, including machining, oil and gas, food and beverage, chemical, paper, and pulp, among others.

Why Should I Care?

Greatbatch is a company that started with one product—the implantable pacemaker. The development of that one product required the invention and/or refinement of a number of different technologies, all of which are evident in the company's current product line. For a pacemaker you need a long-lived battery in a custom form factor, and now Greatbatch has an entire business built around supplying exotic battery chemistries in custom form factors for unique applications. You also need the ability to work medical steel into unique shapes, and now Greatbatch has a business built around custom surgical tools. You need to be able to pass data and electrical signals through the human body, and now Greatbatch has an entire line of medical feedthroughs and remote sensing devices.

This is exactly the sort of company that motivates people to buy technology stocks. A company builds expertise in fundamental processes and technologies, then finds ways to adapt, apply, and exploit that expertise across a range of markets and applications. The newest area of focus for the company falls right along those lines: the $1.3 billion neuromodulation market. Neuromodulation is a technique that relies on the body's response to low-level electrical stimulation of the spinal cord and its therapeutic value as a treatment for chronic pain. The QiG group is leading this effort and expects to make regulatory submissions for the Algostim device in 2012. The QiG group also expects to commercialize three new cardiovascular devices later in 2011.

How's Business?

Greatbatch's 2011 got off to a great start in the first quarter, but business tapered off a bit in the second. Still, the first half came in well ahead of the prior year's results: sales up 4 percent, earnings up 9 percent, and $20 million in long-term debt paid down. Given the first half's revenue of $295.4 million our full-year estimate of $560 million may be on the low side, but the company is still cautious about the second half.

Upside

- Several new product introductions over the next six quarters
- Sales momentum growing
- Solid financials

Downside

- A submission is not a product
- Rising raw material costs
- Expect SG&A to increase regardless of new product performance

Just the Facts

SECTOR: **Technology**
BETA COEFFICIENT: **0.75**
5-YEAR COMPOUND EARNINGS-PER-SHARE GROWTH: **13%**

	2007	2008	2009	2010	2011
Revenues (Mil)	319	547	522	533	560
Net Income (Mil)	32.5	32.9	34.8	35.8	40.0
Price: high	35.0	27.1	27.5	25.1	29.0
low	18.5	15.5	17.3	19.0	20.5

Greatbatch Incorporated
10000 Wehrle Drive
Clarence, NY 14031
(716) 759-5600
Website: *www.greatbatch.com*

ENERGY

GT Advanced Technologies, Inc.

Ticker symbol: GTAT (NYSE) ❑ S&P rating: NA ❑ Value Line financial strength rating: B ❑ Current yield: Nil

Who Are They?

GT Advanced Technologies (formerly GT Solar) is one of the larger providers of polysilicon production technology for the solar industry. Its customers include several of the world's largest producers of solar cells and solar panels, as well as companies in the chemical industry. Its primary products are chemical vapor deposition (CVD) reactors, which are used to produce raw polysilicon; and directional solidification systems (DSS), which take polysilicon as an input and produce very large multicrystalline silicon ingots. These ingots are then cut into wafers, which are the platforms for individual solar cells.

The company typically sells multiple CVD and DSS units to larger customers. Unit sales figures are closely held, but it would not be unusual to find a single customer with hundreds of furnaces operating around the clock. It turns out that baking tasty silicon takes time; it takes three days in the oven for a 600kg loaf.

Why Should I Care?

GT Advanced Technologies occupies a unique position in the broader solar industry. Many of the more well-known players occupy niches built around either a single product or a single process. The big refiners make ingots, the huge panel assemblers build finished, installable product, and the integrated facilities do a lot of everything on their custom lines. GTAT produces nothing that goes into the end product but instead supplies the larger producers with the materials, tools, and support they need to do their jobs. If the solar energy boom is a gold rush, then GTAT is selling the picks and shovels.

The company has demonstrated some significant advances in the operating efficiency of polysilicon in solar cell applications. The crystalline silicon used in solar panels is typically either monocrystalline (each cell is one contiguous crystal lattice) or polycrystalline (each cell has more than one crystal) in form. Monocrystalline cells have higher efficiency, but their cost is substantially higher. GT Solar has built polycrystalline-based panels with efficiencies equivalent to some of the best production-quality monocrystalline devices. This combination of low production cost and high operating efficiency will be very attractive to equipment buyers.

The company's sapphire production technology (obtained in the August 2010 acquisition of Crystal Systems) is used to make large sections of pure sapphire for later processing. This type of sapphire has extremely high transmissibility across a broad spectrum of light and stands up to intense heat. It's been used in military and high-power laser applications for decades, and is now finding wide acceptance as a component of high brightness LEDs. The company has aggressive growth plans for this very complementary segment and looks for accretive earnings in mid-2012.

How's Business?

The company's name change reflects a broadening of its product line and its customer base. Prior to the recent acquisition of Crystal Systems, the company was strictly a play on the future of the solar industry. While that segment of the business is healthy (and getting healthier as the silicon production business desperately looks for more efficient processes), the future star for GTAT may just be its industrial sapphire line, acquired in the Crystal Systems deal. Sapphire is the overwhelming choice for substrates in LEDs, and GTAT's ability to provide volumes here will soon generate high-quality earnings for years to come. The original acquisition costs of Crystal Systems penciled out to around $75 million; since the acquisition, GTAT has received more than $700 million in orders for sapphire product and has tripled its original production capacity.

Upside

- Good representation in China
- Leading technology
- Pricing power from high demand

Downside

- Outside sourcing—production capacity a question
- One customer accounts for 19 percent of revenue
- Some open programs showing signs of weakening

Just the Facts

SECTOR: **Technology**

BETA COEFFICIENT: **1.65**

5-YEAR COMPOUND EARNINGS-PER-SHARE GROWTH: —

	2007	2008	2009	2010	2011
Revenues (Mil)	244	541	544	899	1065
Net Income (Mil)	36.1	88.0	87.3	178	212
Price: high	—	17.0	9.0	10.0	17.1
low	—	1.6	2.8	4.9	9.1

GT Advanced Technologies International, Inc.

243 Daniel Webster Highway

Merrimack, NH 03054

(603) 883-5200

Website: *www.gtat.com*

COMPUTERS

IBM Corp.

Ticker symbol: IBM (NYSE) ❑ **S&P rating: NA** ❑ **Value Line financial strength rating: A++** ❑
Current yield: Nil

Who Are They?

Big Blue is the world's leading provider of computer hardware and services. IBM still makes a broad range of computers, mainframes, and network servers, but the company has morphed over the past decade and now derives the majority of its earnings from software and services; it trails only Microsoft in software revenues. For all of the changes, though, IBM has not lost its focus on innovation and new product development—for the past nineteen years it has led the world in the number of U.S. patents issued.

Why Should I Care?

Improving margins have been the biggest part of IBM's past decade of financial success. Since 2001, revenues have increased 24 percent, while operating margin has increased 46 percent, and net margin has increased 63 percent. Part of this is certainly due to the company's operational excellence, but the move out of the low-margin commodity hardware businesses and the concentration on software and services has been (and will continue to be) the story here. It's worth re-iterating if only to stress the point that IBM has at least a six-year lead on many of its largest competitors with this business model.

For 2011, IBM will get 79 percent of its revenue from its software and service businesses. While hardware only accounts for 19 percent of sales, Big Blue is still committed to producing leading-edge hardware. Big Iron is healthy at Big Blue—the company continues to design and produce mainframes and has its label on five of the top ten supercomputers in the world. It also produces high-margin commercial servers and enterprise-level installations for cloud applications, but it has completely exited the lower-margin hardware businesses, such as consumer PCs, laptops, and hard drives.

IBM has offered long-term earnings projections that call for $20 per share by 2015. Not a lot of companies will offer this sort of prognostication and, were it from almost anyone other than IBM, you'd have to view it with a healthy skepticism. When IBM says, "This is going to happen," however, you have to pause, look over its recent history, and nod. Nearly everything it said it was going to do as part of its restructuring has been done, and often ahead of schedule. Yes, there are still companies like this that you can buy into.

Depending on your needs and investing profile, you can put together any number of different portfolios with the hundred stocks listed in this book. And yes, we know "no one ever got fired for recommending IBM," but we can't think of any reason you wouldn't want to build your new portfolio on a foundation of Big Blue.

How's Business?

The second quarter 2011 results should please investors. Per-share earnings were up 15 percent over the prior year on a currency-adjusted revenue increase of 5 percent. The company is very optimistic about the remainder of 2011 and has raised its earnings guidance from $12.75 to $13.25 per share. The company has also produced significant shareholder returns through buybacks. In the past ten years, the outstanding share count has been reduced by over one-third, and the company plans to continue this policy.

Upside
- Solid revenue streams from long-term services contracts
- Outstanding execution
- Revenue growth in emerging markets up 23 percent in 2010

Downside
- Lots of good competitors
- Geographic growth may be critical for sustainability
- Memo to IBM: Please cancel dividend and invest in IBM

Just the Facts

SECTOR: **Technology**
BETA COEFFICIENT: **0.85**
5-YEAR COMPOUND EARNINGS-PER-SHARE GROWTH: **NA**

	2007	2008	2009	2010	2011
Revenues (Bil)	98.8	103.6	95.8	99.9	106.4
Net Income (Bil)	10.4	12.3	13.4	14.8	15.7
Price: high	121.5	130.9	132.9	147.5	185.2
low	88.8	69.5	81.8	116	147.5

International Business Machines Corporation
New Orchard Road
Armonk, NY 10504
(914) 499-1900
Website: *www.ibm.com*

Insight Enterprises

Ticker symbol: NSIT (NASDAQ) ❑ S&P rating: NA ❑ Value Line financial strength rating: B+ ❑ Current yield: Nil

Who Are They?

Here at *100 Best*, we strive to provide insight, and so we present Insight Enterprises. Seriously, this retailer of computer hardware and software was an easy choice for our list. The world's largest software reseller, Insight focuses on the small business, education, and governmental customer base. It has operations in twenty-one countries and customers in 191 countries (fun fact: there are 195 countries in the world). It buys hardware and software directly from manufacturers such as HP, Apple, Cisco, Oracle, and IBM and resells it via catalog, phone, and online sales. It provides more than 250,000 products and services, from computer accessories up to planning services for an entire IT infrastructure.

Why Should I Care?

As a value-added reseller, Insight provides services over and above simply stocking and selling name-brand merchandise. After all, in many cases it is competing directly with the company that sold it the product in the first place. In order to be successful selling HP products against HP, the company has to offer the customer a compelling set of reasons to buy. Insight is able to compete with its suppliers by providing product bundling and pricing incentives that may simply be unavailable from the manufacturer. It also offers installation, financing terms, warranty options, service plans, integration, and support packages that may be a better fit for the customer than the (often) limited plans offered by the manufacturer. Finally, as a one-stop source, it can offer large buyers the opportunity to completely configure hundreds or even thousands of units with components from different suppliers and have all of them covered under a single purchasing and support plan.

Since we're talking about insight, this might be a good place to talk about PEG ratio. PEG is one of the ratios we at *100 Best* use as a filter when we're looking for potential stocks. The PEG ratio is a valuation measure that takes into account price, earnings, and predicted annual earnings-per-share growth rate (P/E/G or simply PEG). Since a stock's price is a bet on the company's future earnings, a price/earnings/growth ratio would yield a PEG of 1.0 for a company that is currently priced fairly. If a company's predicted earnings growth is greater than its P/E ratio, then the PEG would be less than 1.0 and the company's shares would be viewed as undervalued. As of August 2011, Insight's shares have a PEG of 0.50, which is considered very low for a company with its size and earnings predictability. PEG is certainly not the only measure we use to rate a stock for its growth potential, but it can be a handy place to start when you start your due diligence as a value investor.

How's Business?

A nice earnings surprise early in the year sent Insight's share price up over 20 percent in one day. Share price grew another 8 percent the following day, indicating there was even more good news once people started looking closely at the earnings report. In August, the company announced revised guidance for FY2011, bumping the per-share earnings up to a range of $1.90 to $1.98, up from analysts' consensus of $1.79 for the fiscal year. As the company continues to focus on cost controls, we expect more earnings surprises from this conservatively run, quality retailer as the year goes on and into 2012.

Upside

- Businesses are starting to update hardware again
- Stock is undervalued at its current price of 16
- Small share base

Downside

- Minimal pricing power
- Lackluster sales growth in EMEA
- Receivables at 90-plus days, worth keeping an eye on

Just the Facts

SECTOR: **Retail**

BETA COEFFICIENT: **1.30**

5-YEAR COMPOUND EARNINGS-PER-SHARE GROWTH: **1.5%**

	2007	2008	2009	2010	2011
Revenues (Mil)	4,800	4,826	4,137	4,810	5,300
Net Income (Mil)	72.0	48.2	30.8	75.5	80.0
Price: high	17.3	3.3	2.0	11.2	19.1
low	17.3	3.3	2.0	11.2	13.2

Insight Enterprises, Inc.
6820 South Harl Avenue
Tempe, AZ 85283
(480) 902-1001
Website: *www.insight.com*

SEMICONDUCTORS
Integrated Device Technology

Ticker symbol: IDTI (NASDAQ) ❑ S&P rating: NA ❑ Value Line financial strength rating: B ❑ Current yield: Nil

Who Are They?

IDT is a developer and manufacturer of digital, analog, and mixed signal semiconductors for the communications, consumer, and computing industries. Its current products are designed for the enterprise, data center, and wireless markets. End products include desktops, notebooks, storage and server applications, gaming consoles, set-top boxes, digital television, and smartphones for consumer-based clients. Its parts are sold primarily to OEMs based on design-in by its client firms. It also sells through distribution and direct channels.

In 2009, the company bought ICS, a semiconductor design company whose power management product line is now a mainstay in the IDT line and is the basis for further products.

Why Should I Care?

One of the few sure things in the technology space, even in a downturn, is the growth in consumer demand for cellular bandwidth. The next-generation 4G phones are shipping well and fueling the need for upgraded wireless infrastructure. One of IDT's strongest plays is in the 4G LTE base stations, where the company says it currently has $50 worth of silicon content in each station and a roadmap to get to $100 of content over the next three years. In these base stations, IDT is already selling digital infrastructure such as timing and switches, but customers have begun evaluations on IDT analog and hybrid parts for power management and variable gain amplifiers for the signal path.

The company is also confident it can triple its current $15 worth of silicon in every server sold to $45 each in three years. Again, its plan is to expand the number of seats in the end product by adding memory controllers, temperature sensors, and power management devices to its existing line of bus interfaces and timing components.

IDT has several nice niches in the PC and server architecture. As circuit geometries have shrunk and PCB layouts have become denser, the science of getting an electrical signal from point A to point B has really turned into an art. IDT's interface and communications components provide assurances of signal quality and data integrity without burdening the core logic with the cost of high-current output devices.

The company's confidence going into the new fiscal year and (with luck) an improved business cycle is encouraging, even refreshing. We agree that it is well positioned to take advantage of another recovery. We'll short-list it for a bargain play.

How's Business?

The company reports in two segments: communications, and computing and consumer. In the first quarter of FY2012, the company reported declines in revenue from both segments—a 1 percent decline from communications and a 7 percent decline from computing and consumer. All the declines were due to softness in demand, particularly from the consumer markets, partly offset by a larger increase in demand for DDR3-based devices for the server markets. Total revenue was off 5 percent from the year-ago period. Earnings were off almost 24 percent, most of which was accounted for in higher R & D expense. Net margin penciled out at 5 percent.

Don't be surprised to see IDT make one or two more small acquisitions to complement its existing line. It seems to do well with this strategy and its current financial situation is favorable.

Upside
- Interesting mix in the product line
- Great financials
- Considerable earnings potential

Downside
- Will carriers have money for 4G implementation?
- Wireless competition is stiff
- Actual earnings not that exciting

Just the Facts

SECTOR: **Technology**
BETA COEFFICIENT: **1.1**
5-YEAR COMPOUND EARNINGS-PER-SHARE GROWTH: **NA**

	2007	2008	2009	2010	2011
Revenues (Mil)	782	663	536	626	655
Net Income (Mil)	139	84.4	20.0	72.6	65.0
Price: high	17.2	12.7	7.4	7.4	8.6
low	11.1	4.2	4.0	4.8	5.2

Integrated Device Technology, Incorporated
6024 Silver Creek Valley Road
San Jose, CA 95138
(408) 284-8200
Website: *www.idt.com*

Intel Corp.

Ticker symbol: INTC (NASDAQ) ◻ S&P rating: A+ ◻ Value Line financial strength rating: A++ ◻ Current yield: 3.9%

Who Are They?

Intel is the world's largest chip manufacturer. It produces memory, large-scale logic, networking hardware, and motherboards (among other things), but is best known for its microprocessors, first introduced forty years ago. These processors, first given numerical designations like "8080" and "386" and now given names like Centrino, Pentium, and Core, are the heart (and mind!) of 90 percent of the personal computers sold today. Its share in the other markets in which it participates is not as dominant, but is still very significant. It is far and away the most important producer of processing units for the server and personal computer markets, both for Windows and OSX (Apple) operating environments.

In February 2011, the company acquired McAfee, a developer and marketer of security and utility software for the consumer markets.

Why Should I Care?

Intel's market share in servers had been dropping off prior to 2010, with an estimated market share in the low 70 percent range (what a shame!). Recently though, with the introduction of the Nehalem architecture to the Xeon server line, its full-year 2010 market share was close to 93 percent. One of the most important, if not *the* most important characteristic for server processors is their electrical efficiency. Operators of data centers pay rather large electricity bills, and so they want a processor that performs well in terms of work-done-per-watt and perhaps less so in terms of work-done-per-second. Speed is important, but at some point "fast enough" is fast enough. The recent Xeon parts are superior to AMD's offerings in both of those metrics, and the Xeon line has many more performance and price levels than AMD's Opterons.

The competitive landscape for Intel's desktop products has rarely looked better. Its major competitor, AMD, is still working through its acquisition of ATI and has fallen behind in its development of traditional processors. AMD's most recent CPUs are at least one generation behind Intel's in terms of raw performance and are far less efficient on a performance-per-watt basis.

Further, AMD's concentration on integrating CPU and GPU (graphics processing unit) technologies has not progressed as quickly as it had hoped. Its most recent Fusion processors will be competitive only at the low end of the desktop and laptop markets, where margins are already razor-thin.

The well-known cyclical nature of the semiconductor business is still with us, but you wouldn't know it by looking at Intel's share price. The company is in very good shape with bright prospects, but the share price has been essentially flat for the last eighteen months. We don't think this can last, and we would recommend getting in while the market still has the company valued in the low 20s.

How's Business?

Intel's current business and near-term outlook are both very good. Revenues for 2011 will be up 52 percent over a very-reasonable 2009 and 23 percent over a strong 2010. Second-quarter 2011 results showed double-digit revenue growth in the four main segments: consumer, server, mobile, and services. The company recently bumped its revenue forecast for Q3 from $13.5 billion to $14 billion. Its Atom processor continues to grow in volumes, but is losing market share rapidly to the less-expensive and more widely supported ARM processors shipped by a number of competitors.

Upside
- Significant technological lead
- Captive capacity fully utilized
- Dividend reasonable and rising

Downside
- Low-power Atom processor needs revamp
- Must grow with market
- Five and a half billion shares out there

Just the Facts

SECTOR: **Communications**
BETA COEFFICIENT: **1.0**
5-YEAR COMPOUND EARNINGS-PER-SHARE GROWTH: **2.0%**

	2007	2008	2009	2010	2011
Revenues (Mil)	38,334	37,586	35,127	43,623	53,270
Net Income (Mil)	6,976	5,292	4,369	11,692	12,765
Price: high	28.0	26.3	21.3	24.4	23.9
low	18.8	12.1	12.0	17.6	19.5

Intel Corporation
2200 Mission College Boulevard
Santa Clara, CA 95054
(408) 765-1549
Website: *www.intel.com*

International Rectifier

Ticker symbol: IRF (NYSE) ❑ S&P rating: BB- ❑ Value Line financial strength rating: B+ ❑ Current yield: Nil

Who Are They?

International Rectifier takes its name from the electrical function performed by its earliest products. Rectification of electrical current is the conversion of AC into DC, and this conversion takes place in nearly every electronic device in use today. Rectification still plays a big part in IR's product strategy, reflected in its broad product line of diodes and other power devices.

The company has been around from the beginning of the semiconductor industry and has some of the best patent portfolios and design talent around. It also has one of the best customer and developer support programs, with an extensive body of internally developed device models, application notes, design tools, training packages, white papers, and other technical content.

Why Should I Care?

Power management technology is one of IR's primary areas of focus, and IR's business differs from that of the mainstream semiconductor producer in the same way that Caterpillar's business differs from that of General Motors: Everything is built to a bigger scale. A complex logic device might be fabricated with 50,000 transistors on it, among other things. On a piece of silicon that same size, an IR product might be a single transistor. It'll operate at voltages and heat levels that would incinerate the logic device (literally) and instead of being mounted to the circuit board with solder, it'll be held in place with a fairly stout bolt.

Building devices meant to operate with very high current levels and high voltages require specialized design expertise. You won't find many semiconductor suppliers that live in both worlds (except through acquisition), as the fabrication processes for logic and power devices couldn't be much more different. What this means for the investor is that a company such as IR can carve out for itself a very comfortable niche in the world of semiconductors, and in fact that's just what it has done. There are several examples of this niche approach, but their power MOSFET line is a good story. Turning current on and off at levels higher than a few hundred milliamps turns out to be a complicated problem in the semiconductor world. In 1983, IR introduced a line of power MOSFETs that approximated, for practical purposes, an ideal switch. IR's technology and patents were so strong that most of the other semiconductor companies that wanted to get into this business found few alternatives to licensing IR's technology and processes. These devices are still in high-volume production and IR is still collecting license revenues on every part sold.

How's Business?

For FY2011 (ended June 26), the company posted revenue of $317.2 million and earnings of $.55 per share. This bested the consensus $315.4 million and $.51, but the company's downbeat message for the upcoming quarter (which had almost nothing to do with the company itself but rather the state of the economy) sent many for the exits. Gross margin declined from the previous quarter but was up a full percentage point from a year ago. Further growth in operating margin is predicted for the first quarter of 2012, though revenues will be under forecast by 3–5 percent.

Upside

- Well positioned with valued products
- Good balance sheet
- Quick design turnaround

Downside

- No product heroes for a down economy
- Distribution channel appears to be full
- Lowered guidance will keep buyers away

Just the Facts

SECTOR: **Technology**
BETA COEFFICIENT: **1.00**
5-YEAR COMPOUND EARNINGS-PER-SHARE GROWTH: **NA**

	2007	2008	2009	2010	2011
Revenues (Mil)	1,203	985	740	895	1,175
Net Income (Mil)	73.5	(6.2)	(247)	73.1	145
Price: high	44.4	34.2	2.4	30.7	34.6
low	30.5	9.3	11.5	17.5	19.3

International Rectifier Corporation
101 North Sepulveda Boulevard
El Segundo, CA 90245
(310) 726-8000
Website: *www.irf.com*

SOFTWARE/SERVICES

Intuit, Inc.

Ticker symbol: INTU (NASDAQ) ❑ S&P rating: BBB ❑ Value Line financial strength rating: A ❑ Current yield: Nil

Who Are They?

Most of us know Intuit primarily as the producer of TurboTax, a software package that helps us get through April without doing violence to innocent state and federal forms. The company is also well known for its Quicken family of personal finance products, but the majority of its revenues are derived from the sales of software for professional and institutional financial management and institutional personnel management.

Intuit serves the small business community with a family of software products known as the QuickBooks series. The functionality (and price) of QuickBooks grows with the level of features and requirements, but all are targeted at users needing an integrated package that handles billing, inventory, payroll, banking, payments, and other tasks normally handled by a dedicated finance staff. The company also produces training and support software for professional accountants, point-of-sale software, and supplies such as checks, forms, and other documents used in the day-to-day of accountancy.

Why Should I Care?

People like to talk about "killer apps"; software that's so indispensable you don't think twice about buying it and maybe the underlying hardware as well just so you can run the software. For us, those earliest killer apps were a word processor (because editing is fun), a spreadsheet (because math is tedious), and TurboTax. Those three programs embodied what computers did best: freeing up the mind by taking the drudgery out of the task, saving time, and eliminating errors.

This, it seems to us, is what has driven Intuit's product development ever since—providing the average person with tools that offer real value by doing the nasty, boring, humdrum work quickly and reliably. We also think this is why Intuit has posted record revenues for each of the past twelve years, even through two recessions. The relative revenue contribution from each of its top five business segments hasn't varied more than 1 percent over the past four years, even though overall revenue is up 30 percent. The products it sells are the staples of most people's financial world; you don't buy more of it when times are good, but you don't dare do without it when times are bad.

Intuit is not content to produce some of the most widely used software in the world, however. Leveraging its broad appeal among small businesses, Intuit has released a set of website development and hosting tools with which businesses can quickly and easily establish a presence on the Internet. Included in this platform are purchasing and payment methods that link to Intuit's accounting software. The company is also in the process of developing a full suite of complementary mobile apps designed to allow users to make queries while on the go. Being able to check inventories and shipments remotely used to be the domain of large CRS systems, but now Intuit plans to offer that functionality to small businesses as well.

In 2010 Intuit Health acquired Medfusion, Inc., which provides online patient-to-provider communication solutions. Services are delivered through a standard Web browser on a subscription basis and include features such as appointment scheduling, patient preregistration, prescription renewal, and electronic bill payment.

Intuit is not waiting for someone else to find the next killer app.

How's Business?

Steady as she goes. The company's net margin has been between 17 and 20 percent for each of the past ten years, reflecting its steady, nearly predictable growth in sales over the same period. The 2011 earnings should come in at 16 percent over prior year's results, and the early predictions for 2012 show similar growth. What's not baked into most assumptions, though, are any game-changing moves, such as a shift to cloud services, where we feel Intuit could shine.

Upside
- Reliable earnings
- Some interesting new initiatives
- Good execution

Downside
- Large share base (310 million)
- H&R Block looks strong in the segment
- Aggressive enough?

Just the Facts

SECTOR: **Technology**

BETA COEFFICIENT: **0.85**

5-YEAR COMPOUND EARNINGS-PER-SHARE GROWTH: **17%**

	2007	2008	2009	2010	2011
Revenues (Mil)	2,673	3,071	3,183	3,455	3,825
Net Income (Mil)	507	542	601	685	735
Price: high	33.1	32.0	31.3	50.3	55.9
low	26.1	20.2	21.1	29.0	40.9

Intuit, Inc.

2700 Coast Avenue

Mountain View, CA 94043

(650) 944-6000

Website: *www.intuit.com*

COMMUNICATIONS

Itron, Inc.

Ticker symbol: ITRI (NASDAQ) ❑ S&P rating: BB- ❑ Value Line financial strength rating: B+ ❑ Current yield: Nil

Who Are They?

Itron is the world's largest provider of "intelligent" metering systems for residential and commercial gas, electric, and water usage. Intelligent meters, in addition to tracking raw usage over a period of time, also measure point-of-use operating parameters such as pressure, temperature, voltage, phase, etc. This information can be extremely valuable to the supplying utility, but in the past has been difficult and expensive to obtain. Itron supplies a range of products from basic manual-read meters to meters that act as network devices and transmit their data in real time to the managing utility. Itron also sells a range of software platforms for the management of the installed base and the analysis and optimization of usage.

The company was founded in 1977 and in 2004 acquired the electric meter operations of Schlumberger, which at the time was the largest global supplier of this equipment.

Why Should I Care?

The push for a more intelligent infrastructure has been a getting a lot of press recently, but Itron has been in the business of supplying products and services to utilities for more than thirty years. Itron is the biggest player in the business, with an enormous installed base and a Rolodex of more than 8,000 utility customers in 130 countries.

The case for the implementation of these systems can be very strong. In a typical scenario, a utility might require 100,000 meter reads for water, gas, and electric usage. Only half of these will be done per month, as the cost of reading all would be prohibitive. Of the meters that are read, only 80 percent are actually correct, while the other 20 percent require adjustments on the next billing cycle. In any given month, then, 60 percent of the billings are actually estimates. Doubling the number of meter readers would only reduce the number of inaccurate billings to 20 percent.

In the case of a utility in Ohio, the implementation of an AMR system improved the accuracy of the meter readings to over 99.85 percent, with every reading taken monthly. Customer billings now line up with actual usage, and all of the customers receive accurate data on which to base their own usage decisions. Meter tampering and theft of service have been reduced, and the number of readers has been reduced from nine to one, with many associated costs cut out.

Due to sharply reduced tax revenues and the virtual evaporation of state and federal program matching grants, municipalities across the country are scrambling to come up with ways to save money and reduce pension exposure. And though the up-front costs of a system-wide AMR implementation is a big budget item, these systems are typically rolled out incrementally over the course of a few years, softening the fiscal impact to any single year's budget. Any municipality with a long-term view is going to look hard at this sort of system; the opportunities at the municipality level to provide a higher level of service at a lower cost are few and far between.

How's Business?

The company reported record sales and earnings in 2010 and should do so again in 2011. Note that this company is evaluated very conservatively— Itron has outperformed analysts' estimates five out of the six previous quarters. The results from second quarter 2011 were no exception, as EPS came in at $1.20, $.15 higher than the consensus estimate of $1.05. Fewer than 10 percent of utilities in the United States are currently using smart metering, so the potential for growth is encouraging, particularly given the success stories from early adopters in the European market.

Upside

- Compelling product benefits
- Low-cost sourcing
- Solid financing

Downside

- Rollout may lag, given municipal budgets
- Management tempered guidance for 2011
- Share base has doubled in seven years

Just the Facts

SECTOR: **Technology**

BETA COEFFICIENT: **1.10**

5-YEAR COMPOUND EARNINGS-PER-SHARE GROWTH: **20%**

	2007	2008	2009	2010	2011
Revenues (Mil)	1,464	1,910	1,687	2,259	2,300
Net Income (Mil)	87.3	117	44.3	130	170
Price: high	112.9	106.3	69.5	81.9	64.1
low	51.2	34.3	40.1	52.0	36.6

Itron, Inc.

2111 North Molter Road

Liberty Lake, WA 99019

(509) 924-9900

Website: *www.itron.com*

Jabil Circuit, Inc.

Ticker symbol: JBL (NYSE) ❑ S&P rating: BB+ ❑ Value Line financial strength rating: B+ ❑ Current yield: 1.4%

Who Are They?

Jabil Circuit, based in Florida, is a leading global provider of electronics manufacturing services and products. It offers design, engineering, and manufacturing solutions for Original Equipment Manufacturers (OEMs), as well as programs for aftermarket services and repairs. Founded in 1966 in Michigan, Jabil emerged as a leading EMS provider in 1976 when it signed a manufacturing and engineering contract with GM. Its current customer list includes large technology firms such as Apple, Hewlett-Packard, IBM, Cisco, Agilent, Research in Motion, Philips, and Nokia.

The company operates three segments: diversified manufacturing systems (DMS), enterprise and infrastructure (E&I), and high velocity systems (HVS), each generating about one third of 2010's revenue.

- The E&I segment is focused primarily in the computing, storage, networking, and telecommunications sectors.
- The HVS segment provides global supply chain and manufacturing services in quick-turn and short life-cycle products primarily in the automotive, mobile, set-top, and peripheral (printers, displays) markets.
- The DMS segment manages higher complexity products (often) in regulated industries such as defense, aerospace, life sciences, and materials.

Why Should I Care?

The global EMS industry lives on very low margins, but someone has to be doing better than all the others in this regard, and in this case it's Jabil Circuit. Its DMS segment generates higher margins than its other segments and has been growing at a much higher rate. The company has targeted growth rates for HVS and E&I in the 5–10 percent range but expects DMS to grow long-term at a rate closer to 20–30 percent. With the results thus far in 2011 far exceeding these targets, Jabil now expects to post revenues of $20 billion by 2013.

In April 2011, Jabil entered into a two-year partnership with JA Solar to manufacture up to 200 megawatts per year of solar modules using JA Solar Cells. Jabil should also benefit from a new agreement with AuthenTec to deliver a next-generation mobile phone with Jabil-owned technology in the keypad. Jabil will be utilizing its acquired operations of Green Point Enterprises to design and produce the advanced plastics and metals used for the mobile products market. The product will enhance Jabil's position in the mobile products market and show an end-to-end capability, attracting new customers. Finally, the ramp up of Apple's iPhone should provide meaningful growth through the remainder of 2011 and beyond.

How's Business?

Jabil's third quarter (ended June 21) put them well ahead of their schedule and prompted the CEO to guide for record revenue and earnings for the year. Third-quarter revenues and earnings were up 20 percent and 101 percent over the prior year. The fourth quarter is expected to come in with flat growth quarter over quarter. The mood in the market for EMS firms could not be worse at the moment, so there's a very good chance that despite the record results, you will be able to pick up Jabil on the cheap (a P/E of 9 or less).

Jabil continues to develop new, low-cost, localized manufacturing in locations such as India, China, and Russia. This should provide continued momentum to operating margin for the company.

Upside
- Good track record of revenue growth
- Steady organic growth
- Shortest cash cycle in the industry

Downside
- HP, RIM, Cisco may underperform
- Still very little pricing power
- Green Point acquisition dropped debt rating

Just the Facts

SECTOR: Technology
BETA COEFFICIENT: 1.35
5-YEAR COMPOUND EARNINGS-PER-SHARE GROWTH: -4.5%

	2007	2008	2009	2010	2011
Revenues (Mil)	12,291	12,780	11,685	13,409	16,400
Net Income (Mil)	168	193	89.2	227	415
Price: high	27.9	18.8	17.9	20.4	23.0
low	14.3	4.8	3.1	10.2	14.1

Jabil Circuit, Inc.
10560 Dr. Martin Luther King, Jr. Street North
St. Petersburg, FL 33716
(727) 577-9749
Website: *www.jabil.com*

COMMUNICATIONS

JDS Uniphase Corporation

Ticker symbol: JDSU (NASDAQ) ❑ S&P rating: NA ❑ Value Line financial strength rating: B ❑ Current yield: Nil

Who Are They?

JDS Uniphase is an optoelectronics company. It uses its expertise in the manipulation and conversion of light to electricity (and vice versa) to produce some of the most sophisticated fiber-optic telecommunications equipment in the industry. It designs, manufactures, and markets its products for customers in the telecom and cable television industries. Its products are also used anywhere long-haul data connections require the highest possible bandwidth and lowest possible latency.

Formed in 1999 by the merger of JDS Fitel and Uniphase Corporation, the company became JDS Uniphase (still its legal name, though it refers to itself now as just JDSU). JDSU was one of the most overvalued stocks in the tech bubble of 2000—its shares fell from more than $150 to less than $2 in weeks. The company took a $45 billion write-down to goodwill as the smoke cleared and 80 percent of its employees were let go. The company today bears little resemblance to that of 2000, but we thought you should know about it.

Why Should I Care?

Okay kids—who's ready for Mr. Frog's Wild Ride? Don't get us wrong, we like this company. We like its products, we like its position in the marketplace, we like its steady progress over the last five years. But wow, the volatility here is really something. It's not all JDSU's fault, though. It happens to be a small-ish company in the middle of the speculation surrounding the on-again, off-again battles over the rollout of fiber optics in the United States telecommunications infrastructure. That's all. No big deal. Just the mother of all infrastructure projects, the one that refuses to make sense or the only one that makes sense, depending on where you live, whom you talk to, and who your local cable provider is. JDSU makes many of the most commonly used fiber diagnostic and test tools that are used when installing and maintaining fiber networks, which sort of makes it the flea on the tail of the dog that is a wide-area fiber rollout. Any major new rollouts of fiber networks will be very good for its business. Thus the volatility.

JDSU also has exposure to the 4G upgrades that wireless providers are installing now. The backhaul (the part of the network from the tower to the local exchange) for many of these networks will require a very high bandwidth connection in order to support the greatly increased data rates of 4G technology. Verizon uses JDSU equipment to get this done, and AT&T and others will need to choose between JDSU and a Finnish competitor as they upgrade over time.

How's Business?

Earlier this year, JDSU was trading at just over $29 and is now going for less than a sawbuck (that's $10 for you nonhipsters). We like this as a very reasonable buy-in point for a share that, frankly, needed some of the speculative juices wrung out of it. Again, the presence of speculation does not mean that it's not a potential value buy; you just have to find the right price. We think JDSU at less than $10 is a very good value and have no qualms about recommending it there. If it should float back up to the $25–$30 range, we'd take a pass.

Upside

- Mainstay products are the standard of the industry
- Diverse and intriguing product line
- Solid financials

Downside

- Still attracts a lot of speculative play
- Comm stocks may have to follow lead of overall market
- Finisar has market share lead on most components

Just the Facts

SECTOR: **Technology**
BETA COEFFICIENT: **2.35**
5-YEAR COMPOUND EARNINGS-PER-SHARE GROWTH: **NA**

	2007	2008	2009	2010	2011
Revenues (Mil)	1,397	1,530	1,294	1,364	1,800
Net Income (Mil)	63.6	115	39	91.9	220
Price: high	18.0	15.3	8.8	14.7	29.1
low	12.4	2.0	2.2	7.7	9.9

JDS Uniphase Corporation
430 North McCarthy Boulevard
Milpitas, CA 95131
(408) 546-5000
Website: *www.jdsu.com*

KLA-Tencor

Ticker symbol: KLAC (NASDAQ) ❑ S&P rating: BBB ❑ Value Line financial strength rating: B++ ❑ Current yield: 3.9%

Who Are They?

With more than 50 percent market share, KLA-Tencor is the world's lead-ing supplier of process control and yield management systems for the semi-conductor and related industries. Its systems combine advanced optics with custom digital electronics and software to replace human inspection and interpretation methods. KLA's tools are used by nearly every major wafer and semiconductor manufacturer.

Its quality assurance tools are designed to minimize process defects and thus improve the all-important yield of a semiconductor process. As chip geometries continue to shrink, the use of automated tools becomes more and more important. The implementation of new process technologies such as SOI and high-k dielectrics requires a new level and type of vigilance dur-ing process characterization and the early stages of production. And with the cost of a state-of-the-art fab now running well north of $5 billion, process downtime is much more expensive than in the past, making the cost of KLA's tools easier and easier to justify.

Why Should I Care?

KLA-Tencor had a terrific FY2011. Revenues were up 73 percent and per-share earnings were up 218 percent. It was just a blockbuster of a recovery year with a perfect storm of steady orders and available capacity. FY2012 won't duplicate those numbers, but the decline on the top end will be mini-mal and the company will maintain solid profitability. FY2012 will be, in fact, KLAC's second-best year in the company's history—it just happens to be coming on the heels of the best year in the company's history.

Even though 2012 will be somewhat off, KLAC is still a buy. This is one of the quality issues in the semiconductor equipment market, and to find it trading at a multiple under 7 in the middle of a growth cycle points to opportunity. The median P/E ratio for the sector is currently at 24. The shares have taken a step back lately and are now trading in the low 30s, while the analysts' range for the stock is $48–$59. Two-year target prices range from $64–$96, and the stock will be paying you a 4 percent dividend while you wait.

None of these predictions are guaranteed, obviously, but the numbers are not misleading: KLAC's per-share levels of cash, cash flow, earnings, dividends, and sales are all at record highs, while the share price relative to earnings is less than half of the previous record low. Its gross margin and net margin (over 60 percent and 25 percent, respectively) are among the best in the industry. When this current fog of uncertainty lifts, we have to believe that KLAC is going to be one of the first stocks to be bid up.

How's Business?

KLA's big 2010 was all about broad-based growth in all of the major semi-conductor markets (memory, foundry, and logic) and all of its product lines. Customers continue to grow capacity, particularly in Korea, China, and Taiwan. Revenue has increased every quarter for the past two years, and acceptance of the company's new higher-end tools has been good. We would expect to see continued growth in two of the hot markets—solar wafer production and high-brightness LEDs—but KLA does not disclose PL data.

Upside

■ Broad geographic coverage—only 20 percent of sales are U.S.
■ New lines doing well
■ Healthy customer base

Downside

■ Revenue growth tapering
■ Some Japanese exposure
■ Patent-infringement suit from competitor

Just the Facts

SECTOR: **Semiconductor**
BETA COEFFICIENT: **1.20**
5-YEAR COMPOUND EARNINGS-PER-SHARE GROWTH: **NA**

	2007	2008	2009	2010	2011
Revenues (Mil)	2,731	2,522	1,520	1,821	3,175
Net Income (Mil)	633	512	(37.5)	267	820
Price: high	62.7	48.3	37.7	40.4	51.2
low	46.6	14.8	15.3	26.7	33.7

KLA-Tencor Corporation
One Technology Drive
Milpitas, CA 95035
(408) 875-3000
Website: *www.kla-tencor.com*

SEMICONDUCTOR EQUIPMENT

Kulicke & Soffa

Ticker symbol: KLIC (NASDAQ) ▫ S&P rating: NA ▫ Value Line financial strength rating: C+ ▫ Current yield: Nil

Who Are They?

Kulicke & Soffa produce assembly and test equipment for semiconductor manufacturers. It is one of the leaders in the bonding process and has some special capabilities in copper bonding technology. It produces die, ball, and wedge bonders for gold, aluminum, and copper processes. Bonding equipment accounts for 90 percent of the company's sales, with sales of IC packaging material making up the balance.

The company is not the largest player in the semiconductor equipment game, but its list of customers includes names like Samsung, TI, STMicroelectronics, Amkor, and Renesas.

Why Should I Care?

First, let's do a quick review on bonding for those of you who may have missed it the first time around. Step 214 in building an integrated circuit (after you've created the working silicon with all the circuitry on it) consists of connecting the die to something that can be soldered to a circuit board. This something is called a leadframe, an aluminum structure with lots of "legs" around its periphery and a hole in the middle for the die. The die and leadframe have to be connected by tiny wires—sometimes hundreds of them—that carry the electrical signals into and out of the circuit. The process of making those wired connections is called bonding, and the majority of the integrated circuits on the planet go through this step. That means there's a lot of bonding going on and a need for lots of bonders.

Classic bonding technology uses high-purity gold/beryllium alloy wire for these connections. Gold is easy to work with and creates clean, nonoxidizing connections, but as you may have noticed lately, it's kind of expensive and getting more expensive. This is where Kulicke & Soffa come in. It turns out that with the right metal chemistry and the right process parameters, you can bond out most ICs nearly as quickly and just as reliably with a copper alloy wire. The machine that does this is built almost exactly like a gold bonder but works with the far less expensive copper wire. Copper also provides higher electrical and thermal conductivity than either gold or aluminum (aluminum being another potential bonding material, but with greatly restricted applications).

To put the costs in perspective, the gold content of all the bond wire used in 2008 worldwide came to just over $67 million. If copper had been used instead, that cost would have been $8,815.79 (plus applicable sales tax, unless you ordered it from Amazon).

Kulicke & Soffa's copper bonders and wire are considered the gold standard (sorry) in the industry. With the price of gold continuing to sky-rocket and the price of copper bonders essentially identical to that of their gold counterparts, many IC manufacturers will be qualifying and specifying copper-bonding processes for their new parts. This is a nice demand multiplier for K&S on both incremental sales and displacement installations because, as we said, there are a lot of bonders out there.

How's Business?

Third-quarter FY2011 revenues were up 33 percent and earnings were up 42 percent over a pretty good quarter in the prior year. Costs and inventory appear to be well in control, receivables are down, and the company has socked away more than $100 million in cash so far in 2011. The company is bringing on-line some lower-cost suppliers, so we see several good quarters to come.

Upside

- Riding an industry-wide wave
- Market-share leader in their top lines
- Great financials

Downside

- May not be able to meet full demand
- The V-word applies (volatility)
- Cheap now, but may get bid up quickly

Just the Facts

SECTOR: **Technology**

BETA COEFFICIENT: **1.7**

5-YEAR COMPOUND EARNINGS-PER-SHARE GROWTH: **NA**

	2007	2008	2009	2010	2011
Revenues (Mil)	700	328	225	763	840
Net Income (Mil)	37.7	3.8	(58.0)	142	150
Price: high	12.5	7.9	6.7	9.6	12.5
low	6.5	1.1	1.2	4.6	7.9

Kulicke & Soffa Industries, Inc.

1005 Virginia Drive

Fort Washington, PA 19035

(215) 784-6000

Website: *www.kns.com*

L-3 Communications

Ticker symbol: LLL (NYSE) ❑ S&P rating: BBB- ❑ Value Line financial strength rating: B++ ❑ Current yield: 2.3%

Who Are They?

L-3 is a prime contractor in materiel and service contracts for the U.S. Department of Defense and the General Services Administration. The company is organized into four business segments with fairly descriptive names: command, control communications, surveillance and reconnaissance; aircraft modernization and maintenance; electronic systems; and government services. The company's customers include the Department of Defense and its contractors, U.S. government intelligence agencies; various U.S. Departments, including Homeland Security, State, and Justice; allied foreign governments; domestic and foreign commercial customers; and other federal, state, and local government agencies. In other words, people who pay their bills.

The company has operations in eight countries, with many separate operating entities. L-3 has grown tremendously through acquisition. We count no fewer than ninety-five individual profit centers, plus a dozen or so corporate and organizational offices. We were surprised to find out that one of us actually worked for a company that's now part of L-3. We can't say which one . . . they might be listening.

Be aware, an activist investor is pushing for L-3 to sell off its Government Services and Aircraft Modernization & Maintenance segments and concentrate on its more profitable communication and electronic systems segments. The company has said that it is looking into possible divestiture of perhaps 25 percent of its GS segment (nonstrategic assets representing $1 billion in sales) but has not committed to a plan as yet.

Why Should I Care?

Early in the second half of 2011, it's pretty clear that defense contracts will not be as plentiful as they have been in the past ten years. Congress has agreed to (and the president has signed off on) budget changes that will reduce planned defense spending by $400 billion over the next ten years. Major platform programs are bound to be affected, but L-3's areas of focus (communications and surveillance) will have less exposure than will the large platform programs. The military has always found it to be more cost-effective, whenever possible, to upgrade the electronics packages in existing platforms than to build entirely new ships, tanks, and planes, and this is the sort of business environment where L-3 can excel. L-3 does have some exposure in its current marine propulsion operations, but we feel there will be accelerated business in the remote sensing and unmanned vehicle areas, which should ameliorate those declines.

L-3 has a record of successful development programs with a number of agencies, not just defense. Approximately 25 percent of its business is non-defense related, and the current growth in the commercial aviation markets is going to help the top line.

The board has authorized the repurchase of up to $1.5 billion worth of stock, which, at current prices, represents about 20 percent of the outstanding shares. This should make for a nice bump to the comps at the end of 2012.

How's Business?

Coming into FY2011, L-3's funded backlog stood at $11.1 billion. It held sole-source position on 53 percent of its total sales, with the other 47 percent coming from wins on competitive bids. The large majority of the company's businesses enjoy a number-one or number-two position in their respective niches. The company's strong cash flow and cash position have provided for healthy increases in R & D funding, including a 5 percent increase just last year.

Upside

- Very large customer base
- Diverse, in-demand capabilities
- Solid financials

Downside

- Significant percentage of fixed-price contracts
- GSA service contracts bidding downward
- Incoming budget missiles, L-3 targeted?

Just the Facts

SECTOR: Defense
BETA COEFFICIENT: 0.90
5-YEAR COMPOUND EARNINGS-PER-SHARE GROWTH: 16.5%

	2007	2008	2009	2010	2011
Revenues (Mil)	13,961	14,901	15,615	15,680	15,520
Net Income (Mil)	756	858	867	950	910
Price: high	111.7	115.3	89.2	97.8	88.3
low	79.3	58.5	57.1	66.1	63.0

L-3 Communications
600 Third Avenue
New York, NY 10016
(212) 697-1111
Website: *www.l-3com.com*

SEMICONDUCTOR EQUIPMENT

Lam Research, Inc.

Ticker symbol: LRCX (NASDAQ) ◻ S&P rating: BB+ ◻ Value Line financial strength rating: A ◻ Current yield: Nil

Who Are They?

Lam Research has been one of the major suppliers of wafer fabrication equipment to the worldwide semiconductor industry for more than thirty years. It produces two lines of equipment: etchers and single-wafer cleaners. The etching line consists of four different classes of machine: dielectric etch, conductor etch, three-dimensional circuit etch, and MEMS and deep silicon etch. These machines are all used in different steps of the fabrication process, with their use dictated by the circuit and process design. Customers will choose the number and type of machine based on their targeted volumes and process requirements. Lam's etching equipment is considered some of the very best available, and Lam has the largest installed base and the leading market share in etching equipment (48 percent, based on 2009 sales).

Its other product line, single-wafer cleaners, consists of three classes of equipment: spin clean, linear clean, and plasma-based bevel clean.

Although Lam is a market leader in etch technology and market share, it is many times smaller than Applied Materials or Tokyo Electron, which have much larger product lines in other processes.

Why Should I Care?

Etching and wafer-cleaning processes are critical steps in semiconductor device manufacturing and are used numerous times throughout chip fabrication. Etch processes are used to create the finely delineated features in conductive and dielectric layers. Wafer cleaning removes residues and particles after etching or photoresist strip, or simply prepares a wafer surface for subsequent processing steps. IC geometries shrink for every eighteen to twenty-four months, on average, and at each new level of process geometry the number and complexity of etch and clean steps increase significantly, providing an ongoing need for new designs and equipment capabilities. Lam has always been at the forefront of new processing nodes and so captures the larger share of high-demand, high-margin shipments.

Not every semiconductor fabrication process requires the very latest, cutting-edge, state-of-the-art equipment in order to produce reliable parts at a good yield. For those processes that do require the most advanced equipment available, though, Lam is one of the few players in consideration. Lam produces the equipment used to fabricate the most complex, smallest featured, most difficult-to-produce chips available.

How's Business?

As expected, Lam reported very strong increases in both revenues and earnings for FY2010. It also cautioned for lower shipment levels for the remainder of calendar 2011, with word that customers are delaying orders for additional equipment in the 32 and 28 nanometer nodes until they can fully address the yield issues. These issues routinely occur with each new process node, and Lam is expecting steady growth beginning in 2012. IC unit volume is expected to increase 10–11 percent annually for the next three years, leading to an estimated $30–$33 billion per year spend on wafer front-end equipment, compared to an annualized $32 billion in the first half of calendar 2011.

Upside
- Significant cash generation
- Negligible debt
- Good opportunity to buy in before calendar 2012

Downside
- Flat growth out to 2013 looks more likely
- PC volumes could hold downside surprise
- Consumer confidence far from robust

Just the Facts

SECTOR: **Technology**

BETA COEFFICIENT: **1.20**

5-YEAR COMPOUND EARNINGS-PER-SHARE GROWTH: **13.5%**

	2007	2008	2009	2010	2011
Revenues (Mil)	2,567	2,475	1,116	2,134	3,230
Net Income (Mil)	686	450	(126)	347	730
Price: high	60.8	44.7	39.8	52.9	58.4
low	42.7	14.7	18.2	32.1	35.8

Lam Research Corporation

4650 Cushing Parkway

Fremont, CA 94538

(510) 572-0200

Website: *www.lamresearch.com*

SEMICONDUCTORS

Linear Technology Corp.

Ticker symbol: LLTC (NASDAQ) ❑ S&P rating: NA ❑ Value Line financial strength rating: B++ ❑
Current yield: 3.0%

Who Are They?

Linear Technology designs, manufactures, and markets high-performance
linear integrated circuits for end-market applications such as communications, power, multimedia, medical, instrumentation, and automotive.
Its products are used in consumer, industrial, commercial, and aerospace
equipment produced by customers around the world. It markets more than
7,700 products to over 15,000 OEMs, with manufacturing in California,
Washington, Singapore, and Malaysia. This is a company run by engineers for engineers (easily witnessed on their website: fast, functional, and
marketing-lite).

Why Should I Care?

With its broad catalog and outstanding technical support, Linear has earned
the reputation as one of the go-to companies in the electronics business. If
you need it, chances are very good they sell it. And because it has such a specialized product line, there's also a pretty good chance that it is the only one
that does sell it, which is a great position to be in if you happen to be Linear
Technology (or an investor). Linear makes excellent products and supports
them very well . . . and it makes money doing so.

We do love our analog chip companies here at *100 Best*. We're not dis-
missing the enormous output of CPUs, graphics processors, memory devices,
or the people who produce them. We just think that right now, analog and
interface chips are where the action is. Consider the products that require
specialized analog parts: smartphones, tablets, music devices, digital cameras. Consider the hot initiatives in the industry: wireless, energy efficiency,
touch interface, mobile. Consider the industries starting to build increasing
levels of functionality into their products: automotive, appliances, consumer
electronics. There's some real synergy here, and linear/analog parts are at the
core of most user-centric designs. Things are getting interesting.

When people think of the semiconductor industry they typically think
of Intel and all of the chips that go into a personal computer. No question
about it, the PC was (and still is) a big revenue generator for the bus-oriented

data-processing silicon that created so many fortunes in Silicon Valley. The fact is, though, that right now the PC and server markets are basically flat with regard to the development of new "big" silicon. Yes, generational changes in CPUs will continue to produce higher data throughput, but the truth is that for the past three years the really exciting, interesting, and useful developments in the semiconductor market have been in the mixed-signal and analog areas.

How's Business?

Linear's fourth-quarter earnings grew 27 percent on lower revenue, in part due to a reduced tax rate and a prior-year charge. The company said bookings declined toward the end of the quarter. For the year, the company saw revenue growth of 27 percent and earnings growth of a rather impressive 61 percent. During the year, the company retired $400 million in debt, repurchased over 38 million shares of stock, and paid out $217 million in dividends. All in all, a pretty good year. Looking ahead, the company remains downbeat on 1Q2012, although analysts are expecting a modest increase over the fourth-quarter results. Linear's guidance is for a 6–8 percent sequential decline as the effects of the Japanese downturn continue to ripple through Linear's automotive customers.

Upside

- Terrific recovery
- Google-like margins
- Trading at half of its historical multiple

Downside

- Automotive sector still in recovery
- Full-value horizon may be out in 2014
- Inventory—a necessary evil, given the catalog

Just the Facts

SECTOR: **Technology**

BETA COEFFICIENT: **0.95**

5-YEAR COMPOUND EARNINGS-PER-SHARE GROWTH: **8.5%**

	2007	**2008**	**2009**	**2010**	**2011**
Revenues (Mil)	1,083	1,175	969	1,170	1,484
Net Income (Mil)	412	388	297	372	581
Price: high	38.8	37.8	31.1	35.1	36.1
low	26.1	30.2	15.3	17.8	26.1

Linear Technology Corporation

1630 McCarthy Boulevard

Milpitas, CA 95035

(408) 432-1900

Website: *www.linear.com*

Manhattan Associates

Ticker symbol: MANH (NASDAQ) ❑ S&P rating: NA ❑ Value Line financial strength rating: B++ ❑ Current yield: Nil

Who Are They?

Manhattan Associates develops and markets supply-chain software and services for manufacturers, distributors, retailers, suppliers, transportation providers, and consumers. Its solutions are designed to optimize inventory distribution, equipment and personnel management, and distributor communications. The company gets the bulk of its revenue from configuration and implementation services, with the actual operating licenses accounting for less than 20 percent.

The company has three main product lines: SCOPE, SCALE, and Carrier. SCOPE is its supply-chain technology implemented on an open-source (Linux) platform. SCOPE is targeted at complex supply-chain environments, with the goal of a unified, integrated, and highly scalable global supply-chain operation. The product covers core processes such as planning and forecasting, inventory optimization, and transportation management. The SCALE product, written for the Microsoft.NET platform, is designed for quick deployment as a low-risk supply-chain system for companies that need core logistics execution capabilities. Its main advantages are simple rollout and low IT support costs. The Carrier platform is used by nearly half of the top 100 motor carriers in North America to manage and optimize their fleet operations. It performs load assignments, route swapping, profitability, and fuel optimizations for a wide range of carrier classes and operations.

The company's current active client base includes more than 1,200 individual customers worldwide.

Why Should I Care?

Logistics management is an application that has benefited perhaps more than any other from the proliferation of modern data processing. Moving material, for instance, means tracking the material, tracking the data associated with the material (lot numbers, serial numbers, etc.), accounting for the value of the material, accounting for the costs of moving the material, accounting for the warehouse space at the source and at the destination, accounting for any tax implications . . . the list goes on and on. And while the movement of material is a fundamental part of most businesses in this country, for the distribution business it *is* the business. Consequently, any distributor, wholesaler, or retailer that is not using the best and most applicable logistics tools available is leaving money on the table.

Manhattan Associates claims to have one of the better approaches to logistics software in that its platform integrates the organization's entire process. Many applications have come to market over the years that will focus on some segment of the supply chain (warehousing, for example) without providing a solution that comprehends the process beyond the warehouse's walls. Manhattan's platform approach is very scalable and allows the customer not only to optimize internal warehouse operations, but also to optimize the warehouse so that it benefits both the distribution and retailing processes at either end.

Customers have taken a liking to Manhattan's approach; new orders have driven revenue increases of 20 percent in 2010 and 10 percent in 2011, with another 10 percent estimated for 2012. License revenue from these new seats will drive profitability growth down the road.

In the past five years, the company has put more than $200 million into R & D, focused almost entirely on the supply chain. These efforts are showing up in customer satisfaction, with reports from the customer base of improved labor costs, lower inventory costs, and better asset utilization.

How's Business?

This is another company whose business level reflects the health of the economy at large, although its earnings reliability have been better than average. Those earnings have very good leverage, with only 21 million shares outstanding and the company having announced plans for further reductions via buyback.

Upside
- Stable core business
- Large, geographically diverse customer base
- Great balance sheet

Downside
- Many competitors in this space
- Long term looks better than short term
- Customers may be rolling back on spend

Just the Facts

SECTOR: Software

BETA COEFFICIENT: 0.85

5-YEAR COMPOUND EARNINGS-PER-SHARE GROWTH: NA

	2007	2008	2009	2010	2011
Revenues (Mil)	337	337	247	297	330
Net Income (Mil)	30.8	28.4	16.6	28.1	43.0
Price: high	31.6	27.7	25.0	32.1	40.0
low	23.5	13.7	13.9	20.9	29.2

Manhattan Associates, Inc.

2300 Windy Ridge Parkway, Suite 1000

Atlanta, GA 30339

(770) 955-7070

Website: *www.manh.com*

SOFTWARE/SERVICE

ManTech International

Ticker symbol: MANT (NASDAQ) ❑ S&P rating: NA ❑ Value Line financial strength rating: B+ ❑ Current yield: 2.4%

Who Are They?

ManTech International is a provider of information technology services to the U.S. government. Founded in 1968 and with a current employment base of 10,000 (half of whom are former military personnel), the company has over a thousand active contracts with more than forty different government agencies. Given the nature of its expertise, which is in data and communications security, it is a prime contractor for the Department of Defense and "the intelligence community" (nudge/wink).

It provides systems, systems support, logistical management, supply-chain management, and infrastructure support for a broad range of programs in the intelligence, surveillance, and reconnaissance areas. Its value-add on contracted work emphasizes systems engineering and integration, hardware and software development, enterprise security, intelligence operations, and computer forensics.

Why Should I Care?

When people hear the phrase *government contracts*, what comes to mind are often the old stories about thousand-dollar hammers, million-dollar toilets, etc. Although these stories are sometimes true, they tend to obscure the larger truth about working with the government, which is this: When the government finds a problem (another process altogether), it doesn't buy a product, it buys a solution. When that solution ends up costing $1,000 and looks a lot like a hammer, people naturally complain. But when the problem is what to do about the millions of cyber attacks on U.S. government systems that occur daily, the solution is not something you can buy off the shelf. The solution the government pays for, like that mythical $1,000 hammer, is specifically suited to its needs (both current and future), its performance requirements, and the price is determined not by the government but by the most competitive bidder. Companies such as ManTech have to provide the best solution to the problem at hand not only because the work is closely specified but also because they have to compete with half a dozen other companies all looking to do the same work.

Some investors shy away from companies such as ManTech in times of budget cutbacks, but it's when money is tight that the suppliers of mission-critical systems like ManTech do well. The Department of Defense may be buying fewer offensive platforms, but the government will not be turning off its intelligence, security, and early-warning programs.

Mantech's EPS growth over the past five years has averaged over 20 percent. Most analysts have pegged the forward growth in the 7 percent range, but we can't support such a sharp reduction. The company is trading at a record-low multiple (versus trailing earnings) at the moment and is a solid choice, given its low volatility, strong balance sheet, and history of steady earnings.

The company recently instituted a dividend, and not a small one. Companies will often institute dividends when they sense flagging interest in their shares or they find themselves in a particularly strong cash position. The company is flush with cash at the moment, but there's no loss of interest in the shares here at *100 Best*. Take the 2.5 percent bonus and do something nice for yourself.

How's Business?

At a time when many contractors are looking ahead with some trepidation, Mantech exited the second quarter with a funded backlog up 14 percent, to $1.5 billion. The company reaffirmed its full-year forecasts for 2011 revenues of $3.0 billion (up 15 percent) and earnings of $138 million (up 10 percent).

Upside
- Little exposure to at-risk programs
- Very good win ratio on bids
- Defies market volatility

Downside
- Not low growth, but slow growth
- Very low commercial sector exposure
- Exposure to political budgetary shenanigans

Just the Facts

SECTOR: **Technology**

BETA COEFFICIENT: **0.75**

5-YEAR COMPOUND EARNINGS-PER-SHARE GROWTH: **21.5%**

	2007	**2008**	**2009**	**2010**	**2011**
Revenues (Mil)	1,448	1,871	2,020	2,604	3,000
Net Income (Mil)	67.3	90.3	112	125	138
Price: high	48.4	62.1	60.6	51.8	45.8
low	29.7	36.6	32.9	34.7	33.3

ManTech International

12015 Lee Jackson Highway

Fairfax, VA 22033

(703) 218-6000

Website: *www.mantech.com*

Marvell Technology

Ticker symbol: MRVL (NASDAQ) ❑ S&P rating: NA ❑ Value Line financial strength rating: B++ ❑ Current yield: Nil

Who Are They?

Marvell Technology, founded in 1995, is a fabless semiconductor company. It provides application-specific standard process semiconductors in analog, digital, and mixed-signal technologies for the storage, mobile and wireless, and networking markets.

Its storage segment products (46 percent of FY2011 sales) are targeted for the hard drive, optical drive, and SSD markets. The mobile/wireless segment includes communications devices and processors made largely for handsets and tablets. The line provides parts for wireless connectivity, including Wi-Fi, Bluetooth, and FM radio for a wide range of devices such as handsets, tablets, TVs, Blu-Ray players, and gaming consoles, among other consumer electronic devices. The networking segment includes the wired and wireless solutions for Ethernet and Wi-Fi connectivity. Its parts are sold into many markets, including PCs, servers, switches, and routers, with a diverse customer base that includes Brocade, Cisco, Dell, HP, Huawei, Intel, and Juniper Networks.

Why Should I Care?

Marvell's processor line is getting some traction with smartphone makers. Earlier this year, ASUS announced it would be using Marvell's PXA920 platform for its T10 and T20 series smartphones. These are the first available phones with a single-chip solution for the Chinese market. In order to get around western licensing fees, China has developed its own cell access method, known as TD-SCDMA. Service providers in China are free to implement other protocols, but since TD-SCDMA is the "official" system, the expectation in China (and most of southeast Asia) is that TD-SCDMA is the way forward. Marvell's implementation has support for both TD-SCDMA and GSM/EDGE (used almost everywhere else in the world) in one device, which also includes video processing and ARM-based core. With little competition in the nascent Chinese mobile market, Marvell is making a strong bet on the build-out of the Chinese smartphone market, and it's a bet we like. Marvell's mobile sales in Q2 were up 18 percent over the previous quarter. Keep an eye on this.

Marvell has developed one of the better solid-state-disk (SSD) controllers for enterprise applications. While the SSD market is still more or less in its infancy, the margins there are very good, and we expect strong growth in their use over the next year as flash NAND prices continue to fall. Fabs have moved capacity out of DRAM and into NAND and prices have not yet leveled out.

How's Business?

Marvell is significantly undervalued compared to the rest of the semiconductor market and the stock market as a whole. The overall market's price/earnings/growth ratio is currently at 1.3, which indicates a somewhat overbought condition, but forward earnings estimates right now are quite low, driving this figure higher. Interestingly, the semiconductor market, which has traditionally commanded more money for a unit of growth, is at a 0.9 PEG. This indicates it is slightly undersold compared to the nominal 1.0 value for a balanced market, and well undersold compared to the market at large. Marvell is even further down the scale with a PEG of 0.7, which means that the price you would pay for the stock is very low, relative to its future earnings and growth estimates.

Upside
- Innovative products
- $2.2 billion in the bank
- No debt

Downside
- China predictably unpredictable
- Blackberry volumes in some doubt going forward
- Significant volumes in the low-margin PC business

Just the Facts

SECTOR: **Technology**
BETA COEFFICIENT: **1.20**
5-YEAR COMPOUND EARNINGS-PER-SHARE GROWTH: **16%**

	2007	2008	2009	2010	2011
Revenues (Mil)	2,895	2,951	2,808	3,612	3,700
Net Income (Mil)	114	147	354	904	790
Price: high	21.2	18.3	21.1	22.9	22.0
low	13.5	4.5	5.7	13.9	11.9

Marvell Technology Group Ltd
Canins Court, 22 Victoria Street
Hamilton HM12 Bermuda
(408) 222-2500
Website: *www.marvell.com*

Mentor Graphics

Ticker symbol: MENT (NASDAQ) ❑ S&P rating: NA ❑ Value Line financial strength rating: B ❑ Current yield: Nil

Who Are They?

Mentor Graphics is one of the leading electronic design automation (EDA) suppliers.

The company is one of the originators of the EDA market, and its products are some of the most respected and trusted anywhere. Mentor's products are tools that many companies have come to rely on heavily. Converting to another tool base (from one of Mentor's competitors, for instance) is a tricky and lengthy process, and companies don't often do it. Once an EDA firm is ingrained and established in another company's design process, the account is guarded and protected and the relationship becomes very much akin to a partnership. Software license contracts have typical durations of three to four years, with large enterprise-scale customers accounting for over half of Mentor's total revenue.

Why Should I Care?

Designing and manufacturing a complex integrated circuit is an expensive and risky process. It's a bit like building a mid-sized American city—buildings, roads, subways, sewers, power distribution, everything—in a few months or more, and having it work perfectly right away. Well, that's the goal, anyway. What usually happens is the first parts come out of the Easy-Bake and go straight to a test environment where each part is poked and probed to determine how much of it actually works as intended. Once these first parts are characterized, it's back to the drawing board for a second pass, fixing the errors and adding in some features that may not have made it into the first parts. This iterative process continues for as long as it takes, and it can take a long time and a lot of money. Companies (some of them named Transmeta) have gone out of business trying to perfect their implementations in silicon.

Mentor's EDA software attempts to minimize the number of iterations required to produce working silicon. It does this by modeling the physics of the underlying structures in the circuit and applying a set of rules that virtually guarantees a highly functional first part, as long as it has passed Mentor's simulations of its behavior.

As a client gains expertise with their own technology and becomes more proficient with the Mentor toolset, they're able to design more complex parts with higher levels of functionality, which often leads in turn to more software sales for Mentor. This is the win-win scenario that tool companies like to sell and that has worked well for Mentor in the IC and PCB design markets. Mentor has branched out and is supplying design tools for many other high-demand applications, such as mechanical analysis, wire harness design, EMI simulations, and, most recently, software simulation.

How's Business?

After two years of losing money, Mentor is back in the black with greatly improved prospects for the rest of 2011 and well into 2012. Pent-up demand in the automotive and consumer electronics industries should lead to healthy improvements in earnings and cash flow. The service and support contracts that follow the new licenses will provide further momentum to the financials in 2012. In February 2011, Carl Icahn offered to buy the company for $17 per share. Icahn is the largest individual shareholder in Mentor, and his offer wasn't so much a real offer but an attempt to stir up interest in other potential buyers. There were no nibbles, however, in large part due to concerns over the consolidation of this market and the likelihood of such a deal being approved by regulators.

Upside
- Fairly stable revenue
- Good international growth
- Robust return to profitability

Downside
- Margin/cash flow volatility
- Increasing share base
- Likely to be a relatively high buy-in

Just the Facts

SECTOR: **Technology**

BETA COEFFICIENT: **1.05**

5-YEAR COMPOUND EARNINGS-PER-SHARE GROWTH: **-9.5%**

	2007	2008	2009	2010	2011
Revenues (Mil)	880	789	802	915	1000
Net Income (Mil)	28.8	(88.8)	(21.9)	28.6	110
Price: high	19.4	16.0	9.7	12.4	16.0
low	10.3	3.4	3.3	7.6	8.75

Mentor Graphics Corporation
8005 S.W. Boeckman Road
Wilsonville, OR 97070–7777
(503) 685-7000
Website: *www.mentor.com*

MICROS Systems

Ticker symbol: MCRS (NASDAQ) ❑ S&P rating: NA ❑ Value Line financial strength rating: B+ ❑ Current yield: Nil

Who Are They?

MICROS Systems, founded in 1977, designs, manufactures, markets, and services enterprise information solutions for the hospitality and specialty retail industries. The scope of the industries served is impressive—it includes hotels, restaurants, hardware stores, fast-food stores, casinos, shoe stores, theaters, airports, jewelry stores, stadiums, theme parks, cruise lines, sports venues, major chains, local independent operations, and government facilities. The company began by selling just the point-of-sale terminal, but grew its service base to include items such as inventory planning and control, ordering, employee scheduling, guest management, reservations, and many others.

MICROS continues to sell OEM hardware but now offers complete information management solutions including software, hardware, enterprise systems integration, consulting and support. MICROS distributes its products through subsidiaries, independent dealers/distributors, and company-owned sales and service offices, including more than forty-five wholly or majority-owned subsidiaries and branch offices in major markets, and ninety distributors in fifty countries. Its hotel and retail client lists include some of the biggest names in the industry: InterContinental Hotels, the Four Seasons, Best Western, Shangri-La Hotels, IKEA, Starbucks, NIKE, and Staples.

MICROS is the market share leader in the restaurant industry with more than 330,000 installations worldwide.

Why Should I Care?

MICROS closed out fiscal 2011 on a high note, with two good quarters of growth. The fourth quarter produced revenue and earnings growth of 10.4 and 22.6 percent, respectively. It announced several new wins in the quarter for its Opera and Simphony products and was rewarded for bucking the downward trend in the industry with a 5 percent bump in its share price on the earnings announcement.

MICROS began to realign its professional services business model during the second half of 2009, resulting in the disposal of certain low-margin businesses. The company also streamlined its cost structure to combat the difficult economic downturn. The company's operating expense ratio was cut to 35.4 percent in the first three quarters of FY2011 from 37.4 percent in the prior year, resulting in an improved operating margin of 19.8 percent, up 230 basis points. Additionally, MICROS continues to work on cost-reduction measures, including headcount and other discretionary costs.

The company recently integrated a service called Tabbedout, which lets patrons open, review, and pay restaurant or bar tabs with a smartphone. This may be the best idea we've heard of in quite a while. Just be careful who you loan your phone to when dining out.

While the hospitality industry recovers, MICROS management is taking steps to increase shareholder value (and support the share price). The company's board approved a stock buyback of up to 2.2 million shares over the next three years. And as has been its practice, the company is also looking for complementary acquisitions in its core markets, and the cash flow to support the strategy is in place.

How's Business?
As bad as the hospitality and leisure markets have been, MICROS has pulled through with steadily improving sales and earnings, with just a minor setback in 2009. The service revenue model has helped a great deal here, as has the acquisition strategy.

Upside
- Strong market presence
- Creative M&A
- Still making money in a weak environment

Downside
- On everyone's radar now
- Buying growth can be habit-forming
- Europe still weak, and may be getting weaker

Just the Facts

SECTOR: **Software**

BETA COEFFICIENT: **1.0**

5-YEAR COMPOUND EARNINGS-PER-SHARE GROWTH: **22.0%**

	2007	2008	2009	2010	2011
Revenues (Mil)	786	954	912	914	1,008
Net Income (Mil)	80	101	99.3	114	158
Price: high	37.5	37.3	32.4	46.8	52.9
low	25.1	13.3	13.5	26.2	38.7

MICROS Systems, Inc.

7031 Columbia Gateway Drive

Columbia, MD 21046–2289

(443) 285-6000

Website: *www.micros.com*

SOFTWARE

Microsoft

Ticker symbol: MSFT (NASDAQ) ❑ S&P rating: AAA ❑ Value Line financial strength rating: A++ ❑ Current yield: 2.5%

Who Are They?

Seriously? You have to ask who Microsoft is? Oh wait, that was us asking the question. In that case, Microsoft is the largest independent maker of software on the planet. It belongs in a book about tech stocks the way Pete Rose belongs in a book about people who should be in the Baseball Hall of Fame but aren't. Both are at the top of the list. And though Pete is probably not founding a tech start-up anytime soon, wouldn't we all love to see Bill Gates take out Larry Ellison with a headfirst slide at home?

Microsoft is, of course, the developer of the Windows line of operating systems, the Microsoft Office suite of applications (Word, Excel, etc.), Windows Live, the Xbox/Kinect entertainment systems, and countless other products and services that have become as ubiquitous as aspirin. The company operates in five reporting segments, the two largest being Windows and the Microsoft Business Division (makers of the Office suite). The three other segments (server and tools, entertainment and devices, and online services) have smaller revenues and margins. Online services, in fact, operates in the red at this time.

Why Should I Care?

Windows has a dominant market share in the PC market, and Windows 7 attach rates appear to be holding steady. Upgrades in the business market are far from complete, and new PC sales, while softening somewhat in 2011, are expected to accelerate in 2012.

In 2010 the company signed an architectural license agreement with ARM Holdings, which will give Microsoft access to the ARM processor architecture and the freedom to design its own ARM chips. This is a path already taken by the likes of Qualcomm and Marvell in designing CPUs for mobile devices. Significantly, this is also the path taken by Apple when it needed a mobile CPU—the Apple A4 is an ARM-based design used in the iPad, the iPhone 4, the iPod Touch, and Apple TV. A licensee of the ARM core is permitted to make customizations and extensions to the basic architecture for their own needs, and we'd be shocked to learn that there weren't already very good resources already in place at Microsoft doing just that. The x86 architecture does not scale well into these very low-power regimes, so Microsoft's announced move to support ARM on Windows 8 is seen as the precursor to a full-on custom CPU for mobile devices running an optimized Microsoft OS. The company certainly has the resources, and the market is there—if and when it happens it will be an earthshaker in the mobile space.

Microsoft's Windows server products seem to have surprised a lot of watchers (okay, including us) with how well they've been received. Revenues have continued to beat predictions, and the product's performance in 2010 pushed the entire segment into record territory. Unit volumes are still outstripping the server sales market, indicating further market share gains.

How's Business?

It's Microsoft—business is great. Revenue is on a tear, operating margins are in the low 40s, there's cash everywhere, and last year they had a lower tax rate than we here at *100 Best*. The problem is that all those earnings were spread out over *8.4 billion* shares of stock. And that was after buying back *2 billion* shares over the past five years. It almost doesn't matter how much money is in the bank—if you rob it with 8 billion accomplices, your cut is pretty thin.

Upside
- Godzilla-like business core
- Bing is catching on
- Xbox is actually profitable

Downside
- Nearly two shares for every human on the planet
- Mobile turnaround will require patience
- Competition? Just Google and Apple

Just the Facts

SECTOR: **Software**

BETA COEFFICIENT: **0.80**

5-YEAR COMPOUND EARNINGS-PER-SHARE GROWTH: **12%**

	2007	**2008**	**2009**	**2010**	**2011**
Revenues (Mil)	51,112	60,420	58,437	62,484	69,943
Net Income (Mil)	14,065	17,681	14,569	18,760	23,150
Price: high	37.5	36.0	31.5	31.6	28.9
low	26.6	17.5	14.9	22.7	23.9

Microsoft Corporation

One Microsoft Way

Redmond, WA 98052–6399

(425) 882-8080

Website: *www.microsoft.com*

Molex, Inc.

Ticker symbol: MOLX (NASDAQ) ❑ S&P rating: NA ❑ Value Line financial strength rating: A ❑ Current yield: 3.2%

Who Are They?

Molex, Inc., could probably be viewed as the lowest-tech company in this book of high-tech stocks. Don't be put off, however, as this company absolutely belongs in any discussion of technology companies and quality stocks. Founded in 1938 in Illinois, Molex manufactures more than 100,000 electrical and fiber-optic connections, switches, and integrated products (connectors with embedded active circuit elements). Its actual output is more than 60 billion connectors per year. Its shipments are split roughly evenly among consumer electronics, telecom, and data applications at about 25 percent each, with automotive, industrial, and medical applications making up the balance.

The connector market is more than $40 billion per year, giving Molex (the market leader) a 9 percent share. The company has thirty-nine manufacturing facilities in sixteen countries, and more than 35,000 employees.

Why Should I Care?

You could make the argument that the connector industry has been as innovative and as important to the growth of electronics in modern life as has been the semiconductor industry. Okay, that might be a bit of a stretch, but for illustrative purposes it's a worthwhile exaggeration. Consider: One of the great feats of the semiconductor has been its incredible shrinking act. At the dawn of the commercial transistor the most commonly used device was perhaps a tenth of an inch across, and now we fit billions of them on a single chip. Now consider wire: A modern CPU from Intel has 1,156 individual connections on it. Without a high-density connector to support it there would be no point in miniaturizing the CPU, as the structures required to connect 1960s-era wire to it would be enormous. This is just one example of how the miniaturization of the connector has enabled much of what we take for granted in the industry. In the Molex catalog you can find tens of thousands more.

Higher-density connections are where the higher margins are, and smartphones and tablets have some of the highest-density connections of any device. Given projected 50 percent unit growth in those markets we should see about 500 million additional connectors sold into those two markets, where Molex has roughly a 15 percent share. This means an incremental 75 million units in 2012 from those two markets alone. The automotive market is also growing its use of higher-density connectors, and Molex has a 17 percent share there.

Molex ran into some problems in the timing of its move of some production capacity to Asia. The move occurred just as the recession hit and Molex's margins took a disproportionately large hit. We feel its margins will settle in well above the prerecession levels, making its current valuations quite low. We like the company for a good early buy before the numbers catch up.

How's Business?
Molex closed out its FY2011 on June 30 with good numbers in both the quarter and for the full year. Revenue of $3.6 billion was up over 19 percent from the prior year, while per-share earnings of $1.70 were up 55 percent. The company's gross margin increased for the second consecutive year, even in the face of rising commodity costs (gold was up 25 percent during the year, and will continue to present challenges in 2012).

Upside
- Record revenue and earnings despite events in Japan
- Good projections for 2012
- Two dividend increases in one year

Downside
- Gold price only 60 percent hedged
- SG&A to rise in advance of anticipated growth
- New FY2012 will start slowly with reduced sequential revenue

Just the Facts

SECTOR: Industrial

BETA COEFFICIENT: 1.56

5-YEAR COMPOUND EARNINGS-PER-SHARE GROWTH: 2.0%

	2007	2008	2009	2010	2011
Revenues (Mil)	3,266	3,328	2,582	3,007	3,587
Net Income (Mil)	263	254	52.4	192	299
Price: high	32.3	30.6	22.4	23.7	28.2
low	23.5	10.3	9.7	17.5	18.6

Molex, Inc.

2222 Wellington Court

Lisle, IL 60532

(630) 969-4550

Website: *www.molex.com*

COMMUNICATIONS

Motorola Mobility

Ticker symbol: MMI (NYSE) ❑ S&P rating: NA ❑ Value Line financial strength rating: B++ ❑ Current yield: Nil

Who Are They?

Motorola Mobility is the mobile services business of the former Motorola, Inc., which in January 2011 divested its mobile business and split into MMI and Motorola Solutions (MSI). MMI's revenues in 2010 (retroactive) were about $11.5 billion and should reach $15.5 billion in 2012, while MSI's revenues should grow from $7.9 billion to $8.7 billion over the same period (MMI licenses the Motorola brand name to MSI). MMI's post-split charter is to focus on the consumer with mobile products such as cell phones, accessories, tablet products, navigation systems, and two-way radios. It also designs and manufactures products for the home market, including cable set-top boxes, cable and DSL gateways, wireless networking gear, POTS phones, and IP video interfaces. Many of both the home and mobile products are produced for and branded by the service provider. MMI also produces and markets the back-end hardware for large-scale video distribution systems.

The split was motivated in no small part by a long series of legal pressures applied by a very fussy Carl Icahn. Mr. Icahn believed strongly that the company should have been split in 2008, but Motorola's board (which offered Icahn two seats—he declined) held out for several years until agreeing to the change.

Why Should I Care?

MMI is one of the leading innovators in the marketplace, with very few low-margin, me-too offerings. Its new Atrix 4G smartphone, for example, employs a dual-core, 1GHz processor; 1GB of RAM; 16GB of storage; and a very high resolution/high-contrast display. In terms of raw performance, it's the most capable phone on the market, and it includes many other high-end features, including the ability to dock to a large display and function as a desktop. Motorola holds nothing back on this product, and its recent Xoom tablet product is also aggressively featured. Given the apparent bifurcation of the smartphone market (Apple and everybody else), the innovators in the non-Apple camp are the players to watch. Motorola is pretty clearly at the top of this pile, with perhaps only HP (with Web OS) being in a position to upset the non-Apple cart.

The company would probably benefit from further attrition. The networking business has been up against very stiff pricing pressure for years, and the set-top market has been basically flat since 2008. Motorola was looking for buyers for these units prior to the split, but interest was low. MMI may test the waters again in the next few years, unless they can develop a particularly compelling convergence message around the phone/set-top link.

How's Business?

MMI is doing well in developing markets. It is the share leader in Brazil and has a 7.5 percent share in China, compared with 4 percent of the global market. The second quarter 2011 revenues topped $3.3 billion with earnings of $.09 per share. The earnings were 50 percent higher than estimates and should lead to MMI beating guidance for the year. During the period, the company shipped 11 million devices, including 4.4 million smartphones and 440,000 Xoom tablets. Motorola's Mobility business had been losing money since its inception ($1.2 billion in 2007 alone). It seems ironic then that just as the split takes place, MMI turns its first-ever quarterly profit, good for $3 million in the third quarter of 2010. Earnings will continue to be based on narrow margins through 2012, but the revenue and operating margin acceleration is promising.

Upside
- Strong recent product introductions
- Android application base continues to grow
- Debt-free and healthy cash flow

Downside
- Lackluster network business
- Service provider consolidation could impact ASPs
- Competition? Just Apple and HP . . .

Just the Facts

SECTOR: Communications
BETA COEFFICIENT: NA
5-YEAR COMPOUND EARNINGS-PER-SHARE GROWTH: NA

	2007	2008	2009	2010	2011
Revenues (Mil)	—	—	11,050	11,460	13,650
Net Income (Mil)	—	—	(1,342)	(86.0)	75.0
Price: high	—	—	—	36.5	36.3
low	—	—	—	23.0	21.0

Motorola Mobility
600 North U.S. Highway 45
Libertyville, IL 60048
(847) 523-5000
Website: *www.motorola.com*

NetApp, Inc.

Ticker symbol: NTAP (NASDAQ) ❑ S&P rating: NA ❑ Value Line financial strength rating: A ❑ Current yield: Nil

Who Are They?

NetApp provides storage and data-management solutions designed to reduce the cost of provisioning and protecting data while at the same time increasing its availability. The company develops systems, software, and services that implement secure backup, archival, and online storage/retrieval of business-critical data across a number of operating system and networking platforms. NetApp's products are designed for large, network-leveraged installations. As such, the company works with key partners such as Cisco, IBM, Microsoft, SAP, and VMware to develop integrated solutions that optimize final system performance for their applications and infrastructure.

The company operates in three segments defined by sales: product, which generally means preconfigured hardware and software sold as a bundle; software entitlements and maintenance, which consists of the initial sale of a software license and the cost of updates, patches, etc.; and service, which consists of hardware maintenance, professional services, and training. Over the past three years, growth in service revenues has exceeded that of both product and software revenues. Indirect sales channels (VARs, etc.) accounted for approximately 70 percent of the company's sales in 2010.

Why Should I Care?

You can never be too rich, too thin, or have too much fast, deep, hard drive space. Massive amounts of space solve a lot of problems in the IT universe, from safety to security to performance. Companies have found that throwing hard drives at a problem is often the fastest and cheapest way to make it go away. Storage is also a massive enabler for many of the new business models that leverage a company's internal data. Drive space can turn out to be very inexpensive when it provides instant access to any and every piece of data in a company's arsenal.

NetApp's revenue stream had been trending away from hardware prior to the most recent product launch. The new systems have been well received in the marketplace, and hardware sales numbers should rise significantly over the next year. This will have the effect of reducing margins somewhat, but the systems will act as platforms for future system and service revenue generation.

NetApp's business is in large part a play on the growth of cloud and mobile computing in general and social media in particular. People want access to their music, photos, videos, and documents from anywhere and everywhere, and storage on mobile devices can be expensive. The popularity of all-you-can-eat data plans reveals this shocking truth about human nature: People are lazy. Rather than store and organize documents on their own devices, folks will pay to connect to the giant thumb drive in the sky that is cloud storage in order to access data they already have. NetApp, EMC, and others will do well in this sort of environment, regardless of who wins in the social media space.

How's Business?

NetApp's FY2011 results beat both the market and its own expectations with a 33 percent increase in revenues and a 79 percent increase in earnings. There were a few who cried, "Sandbag!", but not many expected the company to beat its guidance by such a margin, if at all. Excellent execution in the fourth quarter, in spite of some material shortages, led to numbers that surprised everyone involved.

The company recently took over second place in external storage systems market share, moving ahead of IBM to 13.5 percent. EMC is still the market leader with 27 percent share, but NetApp is beginning to put some distance between it and the rest of the field, including generalists IBM, HP, and Dell.

Upside

- Leading technology
- Nice ongoing service revenues
- Application base continues to expand

Downside

- Two customers account for one-third of revenue
- Somewhat cyclical business
- May not be cheap (low 40s) for long

Just the Facts

SECTOR: **Technology**

BETA COEFFICIENT: **1.10**

5-YEAR COMPOUND EARNINGS-PER-SHARE GROWTH: **19.9%**

	2007	2008	2009	2010	2011
Revenues (Mil)	2,804	3,303	3,406	3,850	5,123
Net Income (Mil)	298	310	87	375	673
Price: high	40.9	27.5	35.0	58.0	61.0
low	22.5	10.4	12.4	28.9	44.5

NetApp, Inc.

495 E. Java Drive

Sunnyvale, CA 94089

(408) 822-6000

Website: *www.netapp.com*

Newport Corp.

Ticker symbol: NEWP (NASDAQ) ❑ S&P rating: NA ❑ Value Line financial strength rating: B ❑ Current yield: Nil

Who Are They?

Newport is a global supplier of advanced technology products such as lasers, optical instrumentation, robotics, ultra-precise positioning systems, and specialized laboratory equipment. Its customers are in a broad set of markets, including microelectronics, health sciences, precision industrial manufacturing, aerospace and defense, and general research. The company's products are used to advance the state of the art in engineering, manufacturing, and research applications.

Founded in 1969, the company started out as a provider of vibration-controlled tables used in the precision optics field. As lasers became more widely used in research and manufacturing and as the price of lasers dropped, the need for more optical tools increased, and Newport grew with the technology. It is now one of the world's largest manufacturers and suppliers of custom and off-the-shelf precision equipment. The company sells to the end-user through its own direct sales force (no distribution) and so is able to establish close relationships with its customers.

Why Should I Care?

This is clearly a company that likes to work closely with its customers. There are no distributors—sales are through Newport's direct staff. Most of its products can be ordered off the company's corporate website, and prices are on display for all to see. The number and variety of products available is very impressive (a confession: we love technical catalogs). We get the strong impression that Newport's customers:

- Are smart enough to know exactly what they want
- Are smart enough to know where to find it
- Have probably shopped here before
- Don't do a great deal of comparison shopping before making a decision to purchase

In fact, calling it "shopping" is a bit of a misnomer. What's for sale at Newport is, by and large, advanced laboratory-grade equipment targeted to sane and sober people who need the right tool for the job and who are willing to pay the price to get it. The "impulse" buys here are pulsed lasers. The company's products carry good margins and in many cases are available only from Newport. From 2010 to 2012, the company's operating margin should average about 17 percent, which is very good for what is essentially a direct seller/reseller with a high level of technical service. As long as demand holds, its current P/E of 7 looks pretty cheap.

How's Business?

The first half of FY2011 has been very good for Newport. Sales are up 17 percent over the first half of 2010. All four end-market reporting segments showed gains, with particular strength in microelectronics and industrial/manufacturing. Orders for the first half were up just over 9 percent with 30 percent growth in the second quarter in microelectronics. Earnings for the first half were up 160 percent to $34.7 million. Receivables are up only slightly, far less than the $18 million the company added to its cash assets through the period.

Upside

- Loyal customers
- Miniscule SG&A
- Flying under a lot of radar

Downside

- Watch orders closely
- A bit more in the bank wouldn't hurt
- Institutions own 83 percent of shares

Just the Facts

SECTOR: **Technology**
BETA COEFFICIENT: **1.35**
5-YEAR COMPOUND EARNINGS-PER-SHARE GROWTH: **NA**

	2007	2008	2009	2010	2011
Revenues (Mil)	445	445	367	480	530
Net Income (Mil)	43.9	(147)	(17.4)	41.1	64.0
Price: high	21.3	13.9	9.7	18.2	19.2
low	11.9	4.8	2.9	7.7	11.3

Newport Corporation
1791 Deere Avenue
Irvine, CA 92606
(949) 863-3144
Website: *www.newport.com*

Novellus Systems, Inc.

Ticker symbol: NVLS (NYSE) ❑ S&P rating: NA ❑ Value Line financial strength rating: B ❑ Current yield: Nil

Who Are They?

Headquartered in San Jose, California, Novellus Systems is a manufacturer of new and refurbished front-end semiconductor manufacturing process equipment, wafer manufacturing equipment, and various other types of industrial equipment. However, the majority of its revenue comes from new semiconductor equipment sales.

Front-end semiconductor manufacturing processes are those that create the silicon die prior to packaging and testing. Novellus's particular expertise is in interconnect formation gear, with most of its equipment focused on various deposition technologies, such as chemical vapor deposition, physical vapor deposition, and electrochemical deposition. It also offers equipment for etching and polishing, processes that take place between deposition steps. The industrial applications group, formed through acquisitions, produces precision equipment for surface treatments such as grinding, de-burring, lapping, honing, and polishing of various industrial materials.

The company builds product in-house from completed subassemblies and sells systems through its direct sales force worldwide. The company's top three customers account for more than 40 percent of sales. Its largest competitor in the semiconductor equipment segment is Applied Materials.

Why Should I Care?

Prior to the current broad retreat in the economy, projections for spending on semiconductor capital equipment through 2011 were quite positive, with both Gartner and SEMI expecting low double-digit growth. Novellus, with its innovative products, would stand to increase market share in such an environment. In addition, the top Novellus customers Samsung, Intel, and TSMC are expected to be some of the biggest spenders this year ($9.2 billion, $9 billion, and $5.7 billion, respectively). Driving the spending is the increasing demand for tablets and smartphones, which are expected to see strong growth through 2012. In 2010, Novellus's semiconductor business grew 125 percent, and we think it likely that they picked up some market share in the process.

About 65 percent of Novellus's revenue currently comes from Asia, where most semiconductor manufacturing takes place. Business there grew 140 percent in 2010, and although growth will probably slow this year, Novellus's strong market position will ensure it a piece of the growth to which both TSMC and Samsung have committed.

We like the company's used equipment business. Recognizing the cyclical nature of the semiconductor business, it's not a bad move to keep ready-to-ship hardware on hand at a reduced valuation. Sell it when it's hot, and buy it back when it's not. We also like the industrial equipment and wafer processing business, as it helps to buffer the revenue during down cycles in the IC business.

Finally, we like the outsourcing model, as it helps to keep the company's debt low (just 8 percent of capitalization) and frees up cash for other purposes. Cash growth has been moderate but steady, and the recent surge in sales has given the bank account a nice bump.

How's Business?

The recent uptick in business has shown the company in a favorable light. The leaner business model has produced record operating margins. The company's strong cash position allowed it to repurchase approximately 15 percent of outstanding shares (although a recent convertible bond offering will dilute shares somewhat). There are concerns about the recent pullback lasting into early 2012, but Novellus's longer-term growth prospects seem secure.

Upside
- Improved cost model
- Some product diversification
- Good presence in Asia

Downside
- Phone/tablet demand softening?
- Sales concentration in top five customers
- Revenue closely tied to memory market

Just the Facts

SECTOR: **Technology**
BETA COEFFICIENT: **1.05**
5-YEAR COMPOUND EARNINGS-PER-SHARE GROWTH: **NA**

	2007	2008	2009	2010	2011
Revenues (Mil)	1,570	1,011	639	1,349	1,570
Net Income (Mil)	201	(11.6)	(49.1)	262	345
Price: high	35.0	27.7	26.0	33.2	41.7
low	25.4	10.3	11.4	20.6	26.2

Novellus Systems, Inc.
4000 North First Street
San Jose, CA 95134
(408) 943-9700
Website: *www.novellus.com*

SEMICONDUCTORS

ON Semiconductor

Ticker symbol: ONNN (NASDAQ) □ S&P rating: BB □ Value Line financial strength rating: B □
Current yield: Nil

Who Are They?

ON began as a spinoff of Motorola's semiconductor components group in 1999 and grew both organically and by a long series of acquisitions beginning in earnest in 2006. The most significant of the acquisitions were those of AMI Semi in 2008 and Sanyo Semi in 2011. Its product line is focused on discretes and power management applications, with a fair amount of signal management and processing and standard logic as well. The line is quite large and includes more than 1,000 discrete transistor types, 1,600 diodes, and 600 standard logic devices. It even makes memory and microcontrollers, and it sells capacity and design services.

Not surprisingly, its products end up pretty much everywhere, and end-market uses are split fairly evenly among the big five: Automotive, communications, computing, consumer, and industrial/military/medical each account for approximately 20 percent of shipments. The company has manufacturing facilities in ten countries around the world, fifteen design centers, and reports up through four major product groups, segmented largely by application. If someone were to ask you to draw a picture of a large, diversified semiconductor business, all you would need to do is lay a piece of tracing paper on ON and follow the lines.

Why Should I Care?

The entire semiconductor sector is in a bit of a funk right now due to the strong sentiment of uncertainty in the stock market. Is there room left to fall for ON? We can't say that the market won't drag this issue down further, but we'd be willing to bet that at $6.70 per share we're getting honest value. The lowest price this stock has seen following the recession was $6.20, and in 2011 has been below $10 only briefly prior to the current pullback in the market. The Sanyo acquisition appears to be going as well as could be expected, with a big bump to revenues and earnings, and operating margin has actually improved. This is a business ready to grow with the economy, so unless you're intent on socking your money away in gold, there's no reason (at these prices) not to make ON part of a solid tech portfolio.

How's Business?

To understand how well the Sanyo acquisition has been received you need only ask the folks who rate these things for a living. Standard & Poor's, following ON's purchase of Sanyo's semiconductor operations, raised ON's corporate credit and bond ratings to BB based on the business fit, ON's performance, and its business model.

The most recent earnings missed by 3 percent, while revenue beat the street by 3 percent. The company remains firm in its guidance through 2011, which at the current share price has it trading at a forward P/E of close to 5. There may not be a better bargain in the semi market right now.

Upside
- Well-diversified end markets
- Oversold
- In good position for more strategic acquisitions

Downside
- Sanyo had a big slug of inventory
- Some costs associated with shutdown of Phoenix fab
- Lingering production delays in Sanyo Japan

Just the Facts

SECTOR: Technology
BETA COEFFICIENT: 1.40
5-YEAR COMPOUND EARNINGS-PER-SHARE GROWTH: NA

	2007	2008	2009	2010	2011
Revenues (Mil)	1,566	2,055	1,769	2,314	3,600
Net Income (Mil)	242	173	74.0	402	510
Price: high	13.1	10.9	9.1	10.0	11.8
low	7.3	2.3	3.2	6.1	6.7

ON Semiconductor Corporation
5005 East McDowell Road
Phoenix, AZ 85008
(602) 244-6600
Website: www.onsemi.com

SOFTWARE/SERVICES

Oracle Corporation

Ticker symbol: ORCL (NASDAQ) ▫ S&P rating: A ▫ Value Line financial strength rating: A++ ▫ Current yield: 0.7%

Who Are They?

Oracle Corporation supplies the world's most widely used information-management software, the Oracle database. It is also the world's second-largest independent software company. In addition to its namesake database, Oracle also develops, manufactures, markets, distributes, and services middleware and applications software that help its customers manage their businesses.

Oracle is organized into three businesses: software, hardware systems, and services, which in FY2011 accounted for 68 percent, 19 percent, and 13 percent of the company's revenues, respectively. The company's software licenses segment includes the licensing of database and middleware software, which consists of Oracle Database and Oracle Fusion Middleware, as well as applications software.

Oracle's database and middleware software provides a platform for running and managing business applications for mid-size businesses and large global enterprises. Designed for enterprise grid computing, the Oracle Database is available in four editions, scaled to the size of the intended application. Oracle Exadata is a family of storage software and hardware products designed to improve data warehouse query performance. These products employ hardware developed internally, made possible by the recent acquisition of Sun Microsystems.

Oracle Consulting assists customers in deploying its applications and technology products. The company's consulting services include business/IT strategy alignment, business process simplification, solution integration, and product implementation, enhancements, and upgrades. The company provides training to customers, partners, and employees. Oracle offers thousands of courses covering all of its product offerings.

The company has more than 370,000 customers in 145 countries around the world, including all of the *Fortune* 100 companies. Worldwide sales in FY2011 were split 53/47, domestic/foreign.

Why Should I Care?

Oracle's new Exadata integrated systems are the focus of a lot of attention. The Sun acquisition made possible an integrated software/hardware product sold as a unit to run Oracle's database in an OLTP environment. It's designed to be easy to deploy and configure, and provide very high levels of performance due to its use of extremely low-latency storage. By all reports it has been selling well, but the numbers don't provide a lot of support for the claim—sales of hardware are down 9 percent over the year. However, the company has slashed hardware expenses to the tune of 23 percent, yielding an increase in earnings in hardware of about 7 percent. The company has originally forecast early sales of only $100 million per quarter for Exadata systems, so it's still too early to tell if the decline in revenues is due to lagging Exadata demand or simply the natural decline in sales of Sun's older x86 hardware.

How's Business?

One big question that arose concerning the Sun acquisition was what sort of synergies, if any, would result from the addition of a hardware segment to Oracle's business. So far the answer would have to be an emphatic "Some, but probably not as much as they would like you to think." Sun's traditional revenues are lumped in on the top line, the software and support revenues from each machine get bundled into the quarterlies as "hardware sales" to give the appearance of real synergy, and a few thousand systems per year from IBM, Dell, and HP get displaced by Sun hardware (which no doubt pleases Messrs. Ellison and Hurd). We're certain that Oracle will, over time, provide a more compelling reason to invest in its hardware, but for now the story appears to be driven more by marketing than engineering.

Upside
- Almost as much cash as Google (who they are suing)
- Earnings predictability
- Passed Recessionville without stopping for gas

Downside
- Three large hardware partners now selling against them
- Five billion shares out there
- Maybe a bit slow to move into some new ventures

Just the Facts

SECTOR: **Technology**

BETA COEFFICIENT: **0.95**

5-YEAR COMPOUND EARNINGS-PER-SHARE GROWTH: **22.5%**

	2007	**2008**	**2009**	**2010**	**2011**
Revenues (Mil)	18,208	22,609	23,495	27,034	35,900
Net Income (Mil)	5,295	6,799	7,393	8,494	11,400
Price: high	23.3	23.6	25.1	32.3	36.4
low	16.0	15.0	13.8	21.2	26.0

Oracle Corporation

500 Oracle Parkway

Redwood City, CA 94065

(650) 506-7000

Website: *www.oracle.com*

Orbotech

Ticker symbol: ORBK (NASDAQ) ❑ S&P rating: NA ❑ Value Line financial strength rating: B ❑
Current yield: Nil

Who Are They?

Orbotech develops and manufactures a number of high-value process tools
for the printed circuit board (PCB) and LCD flat-panel display industries.
Its product line includes computerized electro-optical systems for the automated inspection and repair of PCBs and displays, as well as laser-based
imaging systems for the production of PCBs, IC substrates, flex circuits,
and solder masks. It also designs and markets a number of software tools for
the preproduction optimization of PCB and panel designs, including simple
layout programs and very advanced tools for the parametric analysis of a
circuit's electrical properties.

The company, founded thirty years ago, has grown both organically
and through a series of strategic acquisitions, including the 2008 acquisition of Photon Dynamics, a Silicon Valley–based company engaged in test
and repair solutions for flat-panel displays. In 2009, the company established a joint venture with LT Solar for the manufacturing of solar energy
photovoltaics.

Why Should I Care?

The printed circuit board and flat-panel display manufacturing businesses
rely on high yields as much as they do low input costs and economic volumes. Just as in IC production, it's not practical to test products as they're
being built up layer by layer, and the manufacturer relies on their process
to generate functional products. By the time a PCB (or a flat-panel display)
gets to end-of-process testing there's already a great deal of material and process costs built into the product, and throwing out a large, complex assembly
because of a single defect is a major hit to operating costs. Orbotech's products are designed to reduce these losses to their practical minimum, if not
entirely eliminate them. Costly manual inspection and repair processes are
replaced with efficient automated processes; in many cases inspection and
repair is performed on products that simply can't be handled manually due
to the fine feature size of high-density layouts.

Another advantage of its technology is the flexibility it offers the manufacturer in terms of factory flow. Its laser direct-imaging products, while ideally suited for low-volume, high-mix production, can easily be ganged for high-volume production. This sort of repurposing assumes you have extra machines on hand, of course, so the benefits flow to the larger PCB manufacturers, which is exactly where the industry is moving. Smaller, specialty shops that can swing the up-front cost will benefit from the low operating costs and elimination of their dependence on many optical and chemical processes, and high-volume, lower-margin producers will appreciate the yield and throughput improvements. It's no wonder these tools are in high demand and that owners are willing to pay for Orbotech's service programs.

How's Business?

The company's first quarter results came with a nice earnings surprise and updated guidance for FY2011. Revenues were up 34 percent over 2010, with earnings up 200 percent to $.30 per share. The second quarter was equally positive, with a 14 percent increase in revenue and a 40 percent increase in earnings versus Q1. Guidance for the remainder of FY2011 is for 10 percent net margin, or $1.55 per share, up from analysts' consensus of $1.35 per share. The company expects to sell 170 of its direct-imaging systems this year, compared to 107 in 2010.

Upside
- Leading, disruptive technology
- Very attractive share price
- Aggressive tech company with proven demand

Downside
- Products priced at top of market
- Costly, sole-sourced inputs
- Shares may not be cheap for long

Just the Facts

SECTOR: **Technology**
BETA COEFFICIENT: **0.85**
5-YEAR COMPOUND EARNINGS-PER-SHARE GROWTH: **-24%**

	2007	2008	2009	2010	2011
Revenues (Mil)	361	430	378	529	570
Net Income (Mil)	15.8	12.5	9.9	34.0	53.0
Price: high	25.7	19.1	12.2	13.4	15.3
low	15.2	2.9	3.3	8.6	10.9

Orbotech Ltd.
Sanhedrin Blvd, North Industrial Zone
Yavne 81101, Israel
972 8-942-3533
Website: *www.orbotech.com*

Ormat Technologies

Ticker symbol: ORA (NYSE) ▫ S&P rating: NA ▫ Value Line financial strength rating: B ▫ Current yield: 0.8%

Who Are They?

Ormat is the largest geothermal energy pure play in North America. It operates in two segments: It builds, owns, and operates geothermal power plants, selling the electricity; it also sells power plant equipment using its proprietary geothermal technology to geothermal operators and to industrial users for remote power generation and recovered energy applications. Its geothermal plants (78 percent of revenue in 2010) top out at about 35 megawatts and are in approximately forty thermally active locations in the western United States, the Pacific Rim, and the Mediterranean. The power generation products are particularly attractive for harsh, remote locations as the technology requires very little in the way of management or maintenance. The vast majority of these units are currently sold outside of the United States. The recovered energy units are commonly used in gas pipeline compressor stations, but are suited to any process that generates significant waste heat.

The company owns a large number of patents on its very efficient energy conversion process. Its products do not require exotic manufacturing processes or materials, and the company builds almost all of its own products at its plants in Nevada.

Why Should I Care?

This is a stock you buy partly on the facts and partly on faith. There are few riskier stocks in this book, and while we feel this stock has significant potential, it will have to be watched closely. There's a significant level of speculative interest in this issue (the P/E has been as high as 100 in the last six months); strong rumors and a large camp of true believers have kept ORA's price above 20 even in the face of declining cash flow and ballooning debt. Ormat is a beneficiary of DOE cash grants and ARRA loan guarantees for geothermal projects, but its need for these funds begins to cast doubts on the stability of future earnings. The company currently has 553 megawatts of operating capacity, all of it presently at full utilization. It expects to bring another 228 megawatts of capacity online in the next three years.

Geothermal plants are quite a bit more expensive to bring online than, say, a gas turbine plant. A geothermal plant will cost approximately $2,500/kW installed versus $1,000/kW for a gas turbine facility. Operating costs are where the geothermal plant shines—generation costs are in the range of $0.01–$0.03 per kilowatt hour. Coal, the next cheapest alternative, yields costs of $0.02–$0.03 per kilowatt hour. Geothermal plants are also extremely reliable, with 24/7 availability and near 98 percent uptime, with very little maintenance and near zero environmental impact. Coal plants, on the other hand, average about 75 percent availability. These geothermal plants are very good solutions for particular needs in particular locations, but they cannot be plopped down just anywhere as they require a source of geothermal heat. Fortunately, the Department of Energy estimates there are a very large number of potential sites in the western United States.

How's Business?

The company has warned that it will likely lose money in the first half of FY2011. It expects the full year will be profitable, however. New capacity coming online and some enhancements to existing facilities are expected to make the difference. Ongoing production problems at the North Brawley plant in Southern California will impact earnings significantly in 2011, but the company is confident in greatly improved uptime in 2012. Backlog is growing and the future still looks tasty, but there are some growing pains here. If you buy in, buy in cheap.

Upside

- Unique technology
- Demonstrated success in narrow segments
- Governmental tailwind

Downside

- Emerging markets
- Large investment compared to alternative sources
- Debt will require attention

Just the Facts

SECTOR: **Energy**

BETA COEFFICIENT: **1.15**

5-YEAR COMPOUND EARNINGS-PER-SHARE GROWTH: **11%**

	2007	2008	2009	2010	2011
Revenues (Mil)	296	345	415	373	315
Net Income (Mil)	27.4	49.8	68.9	10.4	4.5
Price: high	57.9	57.7	44.1	38.8	31.2
low	33.5	21.8	22.8	23.0	15.4

Ormat Technologies, Inc.
6225 Neil Road, Suite 300
Reno, NV 89511
(775) 356-9029
Website: *www.ormat.com*

Photronics, Inc.

Ticker symbol: PLAB (NASDAQ) ❑ S&P rating: NA ❑ Value Line financial strength rating: C+ ❑ Current yield: Nil

Who Are They?

Photronics manufactures photomasks, which are basically stencils used in the production of integrated circuits. This is a very specialized and highly technical business, one requiring expensive tooling and the tightest of process controls. Customers supply Photronics with design data for their integrated circuits, and the company uses this data to produce the masks, which will later be used to produce the customer's part. Photronics does not perform the IC fabrication, but are often involved very closely during fabrication, as customers rarely produce a working design the first time through.

Why Should I Care?

The semiconductor fabrication process is a long and complicated one, requiring processes and tools that are used nowhere else in industry. The refinement of those tools and processes are what has made possible the continuous growth in the scale and sophistication of the final product, the integrated circuit. When we marvel at the history of the microprocessor and how far we've come in the past forty years, most commentators concentrate on the sophistication of the design and the increase in processing power. It's pointless, though, to design a large CPU if there's no way to execute the design in silicon. Intel recognized this very early on and so focused on developing its manufacturing capability in parallel with its CPU design expertise. And it's no stretch to say that its manufacturing skills kept them profitable when its designers faltered on the NetBurst architecture. The ability to realize large, complex parts is just as important as the ability to design them, and that's why the semiconductor toolmaker's margins are just as high, if not higher, than those of the product maker. That is, when there's work.

And now we come to the reason for the cyclical nature of the semiconductor business. Once you have a wrench that works, you don't really need another unless the one you have wears out or someone changes the size of the bolts. Companies such as Applied Materials and Lam Research sell the wrenches for crazy amounts of money, then work like crazy for a couple of years to shrink the bolts again. Each integrated circuit has associated with it a set of masks that are used to produce the part, and a complex part may have dozens of masks used sequentially as the part is built up layer by layer. Photronics's business is to supply the masks for new parts and to replace old masks when they wear out or, more commonly, when a part's design needs to be revised. Its business is thus not quite as cyclical as some, but it's still tied to the production level of the overall industry.

How's Business?

Photronics is in a recovery mode, both in the business cycle and its own financials. It has recently restructured its debt and is sound in terms of working capital and funding for R & D. Sales and earnings for the third quarter were above target, as were sales for the high-end products (65nm and smaller). Growth in flat-panel display masks nearly matched that of the high-end ICs, and year to date, Photronics has grown from 17 percent of the noncaptive world market share in 2010 to 22 percent market share in 2011.

Upside

- Very encouraging sales trends
- Good timing on semiconductor cycle
- Stock is undervalued at mid-$6

Downside

- Q4 unlikely to surprise on upside
- Double-dip on recession would sting here
- Good player in a risky industry

Just the Facts

SECTOR: **Technology**
BETA COEFFICIENT: **1.85**
5-YEAR COMPOUND EARNINGS-PER-SHARE GROWTH: **NA**

	2007	2008	2009	2010	2011
Revenues (Mil)	422	423	361	426	520
Net Income (Mil)	14.4	(11.2)	(27.2)	20.6	48.0
Price: high	17.0	12.9	5.5	7.3	10.0
low	8.9	0.3	0.7	3.5	5.5

Photronics, Inc.
15 Secor Road
Brookfield, Connecticut 06804
(203) 775-9000
Website: *www.photronics.com*

PMC-Sierra Inc.

Ticker symbol: PMCS (NASDAQ) ▫ S&P rating: NA ▫ Value Line financial strength rating: B ▫ Current yield: Nil

Who Are They?

PMC-Sierra designs semiconductors used in the local area network (LAN), wide area network (WAN), and other high-speed communications applications. It also produces microprocessor-based system-on-chip products for use in integrated networking gear and in intelligent printers; packet and cell processors for real-time state inspection and manipulation of network traffic; radio frequency transceivers for mobile devices; and line interface units for driving signals over distance on physical media.

PMC is in a number of interesting markets, but its largest is the enterprise storage market segment, where it provide chips that enable high-speed communications between the servers, switches, and storage devices that make up the backbone of all storage networks. Through its acquisition of Adaptec's RAID business, it also provides hardware for the infrastructure of the storage devices themselves. Other markets served include fiber access, supporting the passive optical networking business; wireless access for mobile networked devices; and metro transport and aggregation, the wireless backhaul infrastructure.

The company provides technical and sales support worldwide through a network of offices in North America, Europe, Israel, and Asia.

Why Should I Care?

PMCS is a stock some of you may remember from the heady days of the tech bubble. No, not that tech bubble, the other one. The first one. What did they call that . . . oh yes, the dot-com bubble. We've been resisting the temptation to dredge up the distant past, but the case of PMC serves to illustrate a point about dilution. In 1998 the company had 125 million shares outstanding and its stock was trading in the $6–$8 range. In 2000, because PMC's annual report included the word *network* in it somewhere, the shares were trading as high as $255 (putting its price/earnings ratio right about 255). As you might expect, some options got redeemed. In 2003 then, after the smoke cleared, PMCS was back to trading around $6–$8, but now had 175 million shares outstanding. It had essentially given away 40 percent of the company. Did it get anything in return? If so, it didn't show up in the numbers—in 2003 the company was losing money, and PMCS didn't get back to its 1998 per-share earnings until 2008.

We don't mean to pick on PMCS. In fact, we like it enough to include it in this book. But it's useful to look at its experience so that when you see management doing things like spending money foolishly, you know that's only the start of the trouble.

PMCS recently spent wisely when it picked up Wintegra, a designer of intelligent network controller chips. The $213 million purchase price was considerably less than the $300–$400 million Wintegra was rumored to be worth as it considered an IPO last year, but then the IPO market has changed significantly in a year. The addition to PMCS is a significant one as it adds a 4G backhaul exposure to the PMC's aging network processing line. The packet-based backhaul equipment segment is expected to grow 35 percent annually out to $5.5 billion in 2014, according to Infonetics.

How's Business?

The company's cash position will be pressured by the Wintegra acquisition at least until the beginning of calendar 2012, but we expect revenue growth to pick up sooner than that. However, bottom-line growth attributable to Wintegra may not show up until after the first quarter of 2012.

Upside

- Good markets to be in
- Very cheap at the moment (P/E is 10)
- Slow but steady revenue growth

Downside

- Cash flow could be better
- Earnings dilution
- MIPS line getting long in the tooth

Just the Facts

SECTOR: **Technology**

BETA COEFFICIENT: **1.15**

5-YEAR COMPOUND EARNINGS-PER-SHARE GROWTH: **30%**

	2007	**2008**	**2009**	**2010**	**2011**
Revenues (Mil)	449	525	496	635	695
Net Income (Mil)	15.9	66.9	90.4	151.2	140
Price: high	9.8	10.0	10.1	9.7	9.2
low	6.1	2.8	4.2	6.9	5.4

PMC-Sierra Inc.

1380 Bordeaux Drive

Sunnyvale, CA 94089

(408) 239-8000

Website: *www.pmc-sierra.com*

Power Integrations

Ticker symbol: POWI (NASDAQ) ❏ S&P rating: NA ❏ Value Line financial strength rating: NA ❏ Current yield: 0.5%

Who Are They?

Power Integrations, a fabless semiconductor company, designs and markets specialized integrated circuits for a wide variety of electronic devices in the commercial, consumer, and industrial markets. Its products accelerate the design of complex power supply circuitry and provide simpler designs. The resulting product will have fewer parts, higher performance, and better regulatory compliance than an identical circuit implemented with discrete components.

The company was founded in 1988 and re-incorporated in Delaware in 1997. PI ran into some problems with its financial statements in the early 2000s as a result of options backdating and had to restate earnings for the 2001–2006 period, but the problem appears to have been limited to two individuals, both of whom are long gone.

Why Should I Care?

PI's secret sauce is the way in which it combines several semiconductor technologies into one device. This technique allows the users of its products to avoid many of the pitfalls and compromises inherent in the power supply design process. How valuable is this, really? Consider PI's first product, released in 1994, which introduced this technology. Seventeen years later, this product (in newer iterations) still forms the core of PI's profitable product line.

A coming trend in the electronics industry is a mandated push for efficiency. Power supplies built on older technologies can be very inefficient, wasting as much as 40 percent of the energy supplied to them. Modern designs can also be costly to run—it's estimated that as much as 10 percent of residential energy usage is consumed by recently designed devices operating in standby mode. Recent industry initiatives such as EnergyStar have set guidelines for efficiency in electronic products, but compliance with the standards set by the programs has been voluntary, with no consequences for noncompliance. That situation is changing, however. The California Energy Commission mandated a set of efficiency standards for external power supplies beginning in 2007 and in July 2008, the Energy Independence and Security Act of 2007 implemented those standards nationwide. Similar standards have been adopted in the European Union, Australia, and New Zealand. The EISA further mandates significant improvement to the efficiency of lighting systems beginning in 2012. Fortunately, Power Integrations' products allow manufacturers to meet all current and proposed energy-efficiency regulations for electronic products, which puts PI in a very good position to capitalize on this enormous market opportunity. Going forward, we can expect to see EISA standards applied to many other classes of products, including televisions, audio equipment, and small appliances.

The semiconductor market tends to do very well during an economic recovery. Budgets are freed up to improve and modernize infrastructure and tools, and much of that spending is on new technology. New tech means new electronic devices, and all of those devices will require power supplies. We're in a recovery now, which is very good news for the semiconductor market in general, and the current focus on energy efficiency is particularly good news for PI.

How's Business?

The first half of 2011 came in right on target in terms of revenues and earnings, but the company warned that Q3 revenues would be 7–10 percent below expectations due to softness in the mobile market. Profitability is still good, however—the company's gross and net margins are approximately twice the industry average. Having proprietary products is as powerful in the semiconductor business as it is anywhere else.

Upside

- Well-regarded products and support
- The energy-efficiency trend is your friend
- Modular design gaining momentum in supply business

Downside

- Attractive acquisition target
- Market development could be lengthy
- Costly IP protection

Just the Facts

SECTOR: Technology
BETA COEFFICIENT: 1.38
5-YEAR COMPOUND EARNINGS-PER-SHARE GROWTH: 41%

	2007	2008	2009	2010	2011
Revenues (Mil)	191	202	215	300	305
Net Income (Mil)	26.6	1.8	23.3	49.5	48.0
Price: high	34.4	34.3	36.4	44.7	43.6
low	23.5	24.6	18.4	26.8	29.2

Power Integrations, Inc.
5245 Hellyer Avenue
San Jose, CA 95138
(408) 414-9200
Website: *www.powerint.com*

AGGRESSIVE GROWTH

Power-One, Inc.

Ticker symbol: PWER (NASDAQ) ❑ **S&P rating: NA** ❑ **Value Line financial strength rating: C++** ❑ **Current yield: Nil**

Who Are They?

Power-One is a leading supplier in the power supply and power conversion markets. Nearly every electrical device that you own uses a power supply of some variety. Power sources, such as batteries and the sockets in the wall, only provide power at a few select voltages. A device like a home theater receiver or a personal computer, however, may require power at many different voltages to operate the different kinds of electronic devices in the unit. When you plug something into the wall, the first place the power goes is into the power supply where the 120 volts AC from the electric company is converted into something the device can actually use. Power-One makes a range of supplies that are designed to fit established industrial form factors and electrical outputs, primarily for high-value equipment such as computer servers, telecommunications equipment, medical devices, and industrial equipment.

With the growing popularity of alternative energy programs such as photovoltaics (solar panels) and wind power, Power-One has capitalized on its expertise in converting AC (alternating current) to DC (direct current) and has created a range of products that go the other way: They convert the DC output from wind turbines and solar panels back to AC power suitable for use or for simply feeding back into the power grid. These products are called inverters.

Power-One thus operates two business units: its traditional power supply business, and its new Renewable Energy BU (inverters and power management tools).

Why Should I Care?

Governments in many E.U. countries and the United States have provided strong tax incentives in order to subsidize the growth and development of green alternative energy programs such as wind and solar. Every wind or solar installation requires an inverter to connect to the grid, and a number of smaller niche players produced inverters for the market that operated with varying levels of reliability. For an established tier-one supplier like

Power-One, the growth of this new market was essentially found money. It produced its first photovoltaic inverters in late 2006 and is now the second-highest volume supplier of PV inverters in the world. In less than two years, it has grown from 3 percent market share to 13 percent, while revenues from its inverter business grew from $12 million in Q2 2009 to $260 million in Q4 2010. In 2010 it shipped over 2.6 gigawatts of inverter capacity, which is about the output of two mainline nuclear facilities.

How's Business?

The company's $148 million in earnings in FY2010 represented the first profits in the prior nine years. The current management team, all new since 2008, have overseen a remarkable turnaround in the company's direction and fortunes. The company was barely breathing at the start of 2009, with no cash flow and an inventory value representing three months of sales. It now has one-third the debt, very healthy cash flow, greatly reduced inventory (even though revenue has doubled), and $200 million cash in the bank. Revenues for 2011 have so far met expectations and are expected to continue to do so through the year. Earnings in the second quarter were $.21 per share, a 25 percent increase over the prior year. The solar market is quite volatile at the moment, with both economic and social policies at the government level affecting the global demand for product. Power-One is responding with a broader range of products tailored to meet local needs. As volatile as this market is, Power-One is in the business to stay.

Upside
- Right place, right time with regard to renewable energy
- Management making the correct calls
- Innovative products lead the way

Downside
- Share price may have lost momentum
- Tax incentives may not last much longer
- When do Chinese loss leaders appear?

Just the Facts

SECTOR: **Technology**

BETA COEFFICIENT: **1.50**

5-YEAR COMPOUND EARNINGS-PER-SHARE GROWTH: **NA**

	2007	2008	2009	2010	2011
Revenues (Mil)	512	538	432	1,047	1,150
Net Income (Mil)	(36.4)	(17.5)	(63.3)	148	110
Price: high	7.8	4.1	4.8	13.0	11.8
low	3.3	0.9	0.3	3.0	6.7

Power-One, Inc.

740 Calle Plano

Camarillo, CA 93012

(805) 987-8741

Website: *www.power-one.com*

COMMUNICATIONS

Powerwave Technologies, Inc.

Ticker symbol: PWAV (NASDAQ) ▫ S&P rating: NA ▫ Value Line financial strength rating: C ▫ Current yield: Nil

Who Are They?

Powerwave Technologies is a global supplier of products and technologies for wireless communication network infrastructures, including PCS, 3G, 4G, and cellular. The company designs, manufactures, and markets products such as antennas, boosters, cabinets, electrical filters, amplifiers, repeaters, and networks of these products for complete end-to-end hardware solutions. These products are most often sold to integrators (such as Alcatel, Motorola, etc.), which in turn sell to end providers of cellular and other wireless services (such as AT&T and Verizon). Powerwave also sells individual components directly to end providers, typically for support as spares or repair.

Founded in 1985, the company's first products included radio frequency power amplifiers for use in analog wireless networks and the air-to-ground market, then ultimately in digital cellular networks. The company's IPO in 1996 marked the beginning of a period of substantial organic growth and selective acquisitions, greatly expanding its product line and applications.

Why Should I Care?

The company made a number of acquisitions over the past decade that gained it entry to and strengthened its presence in a number of key markets (Europe, particularly). However, these acquisitions also burdened it with some extraordinary integration costs, negatively impacting its bottom line over multiple fiscal years. Complicating this situation was a multiyear downturn in orders from three of its primary customers: AT&T, Nokia, and Nortel. The result was a period of losses that drove the stock price into the sub-$1 range for several quarters. The company was able to maintain market share through this period while reducing costs through consolidation of manufacturing resources.

In mid-2009, as the general business environment began to recover from the financial crisis, Powerwave's customers started investing in new infrastructure and the company finally began to see the full benefits of their acquisition strategy. It is now on track to ship $720 million in 2012 with very strong margins.

In February 2011, the company introduced a new MIMO (multiple-input, multiple-output) tower antenna for the rapidly expanding mobile broadband market, which nearly doubles the current standard coverage pattern and reduces power consumption by 40 percent. This will greatly reduce the operational costs for wireless broadband providers, allowing them to provide higher levels of coverage for a lower investment. At the same time, the company introduced proprietary technologies that will allow wireless operators to quickly deploy 4G services over existing 2G/3G wireless networks. The combination of the two should permit operators to selectively upgrade services in high-demand areas while enhancing service and coverage in adjacent areas without the burden of upgrading hardware in every tower.

How's Business?

In August the company reconfirmed analysts' estimates for FY2011 for revenues in the range of $650–$680 million, representing a 13.8 percent increase over FY2010. Earnings are expected to increase 136 percent to $40 million, a very significant recovery from the two consecutive years of losses in 2006–2007. Cash flow, which had been under pressure of late, has recovered to a healthy $.55 per share and is expected to increase another 20 percent in 2012, more than enough to support its low debt service and maintain a reserve for strategic growth opportunities.

Upside

- Broad customer base
- Global presence
- Strong buying opportunity with shares below $2

Downside

- Tail of the wireless market dog
- Rapidly evolving technology
- No "killer" tech as yet

Just the Facts

SECTOR: **Technology**

BETA COEFFICIENT: **2.9**

5-YEAR COMPOUND EARNINGS-PER-SHARE GROWTH: **NA**

	2007	2008	2009	2010	2011
Revenues (Mil)	781	890	568	592	665
Net Income (Mil)	(66.0)	19.6	3.2	17.2	35.0
Price: high	7.0	5.1	1.7	2.7	4.7
low	4.5	0.4	0.3	1.2	1.6

Powerwave Technologies, Inc.
1801 East St. Andrew Place
Santa Ana, CA 92705
(714) 466-1000
Website: *www.powerwave.com*

NETWORKING

QLogic Corp.

Ticker symbol: QLGC (NASDAQ) ❑ S&P rating: NA ❑ Value Line financial strength rating: A+ ❑ Current yield: Nil

Who Are They?

QLogic designs and markets high-performance adapters, switches, and routers for storage and networking applications. It also designs and uses its own ASICs for this purpose. Its board-level adapters implement SCSI, iSCSI, Fiber Channel, Infiniband, and converged FCoE protocols on standard server architectures. Its switches include Fiber Channel and Infiniband implementations and support QLogic's internally developed fabric management software.

The company includes among its customers all the usual suspects: Dell, HP, IBM, Cisco, NetApp, and Oracle.

Why Should I Care?

QLogic has now had sixty-four consecutive quarters of profitable operations (yes, it remained profitable through the 2001 tech collapse). This successful run is largely a result of being a preferred supplier of essential, high-end hardware to so many of the industry's largest OEMs (and most of its smaller ones, as well). What has also helped is the enormous success of the Fiber Channel protocol for storage interfaces. FC (and its variants) has been the most commonly deployed technology for storage networks for nearly fourteen years. Over that period, its supported speed has increased by a factor of 20, and implementations exist for every interface and in every OS on the market. This stability and ubiquity has been a cash cow for QLogic, which was early to market with one of the better and more efficient ASICs for the acceleration of the protocol on a host bus adapter. Its early success and subsequent improvements and support cemented its position in the industry. In 2010, QLogic had a 55 percent market share in Fiber Channel adapters and was present in more than 70 percent of the blade servers sold.

The company's acquisition of NetXen in 2009 is paying benefits. The networking expertise acquired in the deal has led directly to QLogic's latest line of HBAs, the converged network adapter. This card supports Ethernet protocols and FCoE simultaneously, with both being fully offloaded from the host CPU. These adapters are doing very well in the market, as they permit SAN implementations over an Ethernet-based infrastructure with full FCoE support.

As a provider of higher-end I/O hardware, QLogic has been shielded from the pricing pressures prevalent in the consumer space and has benefited from a largely stable customer base. As a supplier to the largest OEMs, though, it is at some risk from displacement. QLogic's top three customers (HP, IBM, and Oracle/Sun) account for 55 percent of fiscal year 2010 sales, and should any one of them jump ship, QLogic's business would be impacted more than a little bit.

The bottom of QLogic's Fiber-Channel-over-Ethernet market is under some cost pressure from Intel, which has modified its own line of Ethernet adapters to perform some FCoE functions on-board. The remainder of the FCoE protocol is, however, implemented in a software stack that executes on the host CPU, so while the channel throughput can be comparable to QLogic's converged products, the CPU loading would be unacceptable for all but low-end SMB (small/medium business) applications.

Like many of the companies in this book that participate in the storage market, QLogic also gets a nice push from the wave that is the ever-expanding need for data space.

How's Business?

Steady, if unspectacular. We like the business here, but we also like where the balance sheet is at the moment. The company is sitting on nearly $400 million in cash with zero debt. It has already rejected one buyout bid (and has adopted a few poison pill provisions), so if the right offer comes along, it's sure to be a big one. In the meantime, it can look at fill-in acquisitions.

Upside
- Market leadership
- No game-changing tech on the horizon
- Got that cash money

Downside
- No major growth on the horizon
- Earnings flattening a bit
- Continued pressure on low end

Just the Facts

SECTOR: Technology
BETA COEFFICIENT: 0.95
5-YEAR COMPOUND EARNINGS-PER-SHARE GROWTH: NA

	2007	2008	2009	2010	2011
Revenues (Mil)	598	634	549	597	645
Net Income (Mil)	96.2	109	54.9	139	130
Price: high	22.5	20.2	19.6	22.4	18.8
low	11.5	8.7	8.8	14.3	12.3

QLogic Corporation
26650 Aliso Viejo Parkway
Aliso Viejo, CA 92656
(949) 389-6000
Website: *www.qlogic.com*

Radware, Ltd.

Ticker symbol: RDWR (NASDAQ) ❏ S&P rating: NA ❏ Value Line financial strength rating: NA ❏
Current yield: Nil

Who Are They?

Radware, founded in 1996, develops, manufactures, and markets computer-networking products for the application delivery and network security markets. Its products consist mainly of internally developed applications that run exclusively on Radware's intelligent network switch. The switch and the applications are modular and upgradeable in response to the need for more ports, higher bandwidth, higher speed, or other considerations. It competes with all of the big players in this market (Cisco, 3Com/HP, Juniper, F5) but has established a beachhead by focusing on a specific set of needs common to small and mid-sized businesses. Its targeted applications include data center management, firewall and application gateway management, management of multiple wide-area networks (WANs), packet inspection, and traffic prioritization.

The company also provides:

- Intrusion prevention and other security products to protect against worms, bots, viruses, malicious intrusions, and denial of service attacks
- A device that provides online network-based pervasive monitoring solution
- An appliance-based management and monitoring system

Its primary customers include banks, insurance companies, manufacturing, retail, government agencies, media companies, and service providers worldwide.

Why Should I Care?

Radware addresses the two main concerns of businesses with regard to their networking infrastructure: delivery of service and data security. *Delivery of service* is a broad term, but it basically means striving for a situation in which all applications receive the level of service from the network that's appropriate for their needs. Some applications require high throughput, some require low latency, some require tight synchronization with other services, and some require all three and several other things as well. The goal of load-balancing software and hardware is to provide optimum levels of service to all demands at all times, within the limits of external constraints. Radware's value proposition is the intelligence with which its products perform this optimization, their awareness of enterprise-wide resources, and their real-time response to threats to data security. Radware data security provides protection against threats on WAN storage, a feature that will become even more valuable as backup services move to the cloud.

All of these services can be run on the actual server itself, and in many cases, they still are. But going forward, for a number of sound technical and economic reasons, it often makes more sense to aggregate these activities in an intelligent switch, which is what Radware has done. This is the key to the future of the company: As customers adopt Radware's proprietary hardware and software platform, the company creates lock-out potential. It's critical to establish a solid customer base as quickly as possible, and 2010's results are very encouraging in this regard.

How's Business?

After five years of losses, Radware turned the corner in 2010 with nearly $10 million in earnings. Its marketing strategy had been to build the brand recognition while developing support for the product concept. It was early to the party, and as other better-known players announced similar products, the market has warmed to the idea and Radware's sales have begun to meet expectations. Revenue was up 40 percent in 2010 and estimates are for another 20 percent growth in 2011, with per-share earnings of $1.31 (versus $.44 in 2010).

Upside
- Market support for the technology
- Small share base (20 million)
- Solid financing and no debt

Downside
- Big, healthy competitors
- Dynamic technological battlefield
- Proprietary tech can also work against you

Just the Facts

SECTOR: **Technology**

BETA COEFFICIENT: **1.2**

5-YEAR COMPOUND EARNINGS-PER-SHARE GROWTH: **NA**

	2007	2008	2009	2010	2011
Revenues (Mil)	88.6	94.6	109	144	169
Net Income (Mil)	(12.0)	(31.0)	(5.93)	9.63	12.0
Price: high	16.8	14.4	15.1	39.8	42.7
low	12.3	5.2	5.4	15.1	26.7

Radware Ltd.
22 Raoul Wallenberg Street
Tel Aviv, 69710, Israel
(972) 3-766-8666
Website: *www.radware.com*

SOFTWARE

Red Hat, Inc.

Ticker symbol: RHT (NYSE) ❑ **S&P rating: BB+** ❑ **Value Line financial strength rating: B+** ❑ **Current yield: Nil**

Who Are They?

Red Hat is the leading distributor of open-source Linux software. Linux is a Unix-like operating system that runs on a variety of hardware platforms, including PCs, tablets, game consoles, servers, and mainframes. In fact, Linux runs on some of the most recent smartphones and runs the ten fastest supercomputers in the world. One of the very powerful features of Linux is its modularity and ease of customization—a builder can add or remove functionality as needed to meet the requirements of use. The only common thread among these various installations is that they run the Linux kernel.

Red Hat builds configurations of Linux (called distributions), which are customized for the intended application: There are different builds for desktop users, workstations, and so on. Server bundles are optimized for the intended hardware and intended function—there are distributions specifically tuned for running SAP, for example.

Red Hat's business model is built around its subscription-based support services, although it also collects revenues on the initial sale of the distribution.

Why Should I Care?

Five years ago an IT manager making a strategic commitment to a Linux-based platform for mission-critical applications would have met with resistance, or at least a great deal of skepticism from his peers. That's not the case today. Hotels, banks, airlines, national postal systems, railroads, telephone systems, hospitals . . . the list of real-time, transaction-intensive installations that rely on Linux (and Red Hat) is growing quickly, particularly in international markets. Red Hat, as the largest of the value-added distributors with the most highly developed support channels, will benefit as a result. These task-oriented machines are the strength of Red Hat's product line.

The Red Hat Enterprise Linux distribution is very well regarded against the competition and appears to be emerging as the OS of choice for private cloud computing architectures, according to analysts. Cloud computing is a recent trend in information services in which pools of computing resources are dynamically allocated among users and applications. An application might draw computing resources from several different virtualized machines simultaneously, for example. Cloud computing's goal is to make computing resources more available, more flexible, and less expensive to acquire and use. Virtualization is an important first step in creating a cloud architecture, and Red Hat's powerful virtualization tools make it an excellent platform on which to build cloud computing architectures. Its virtualization tools also make it a favorite for data center application servers.

We like Red Hat's healthy cash balance and absence of debt. The company recently acquired cloud software developer Makara to supplement its own JBoss middleware platform. Additional acquisitions during the year would not surprise us.

How's Business?

We've had concerns about Red Hat's profitability even as its revenues have increased and its products have been more broadly accepted. Results for the first quarter of 2012 show a favorable trend in earnings growth, and the company has given guidance for improved profitability through the year. Revenues and earnings for the quarter were up 26.6 and 28.6 percent over the prior year respectively, with earnings beating estimates. Net margin was up 60 basis points in the quarter. Interestingly, the increase in revenues was driven largely by higher demand for cloud computing technologies.

Upside

- Secure, high-performance OS
- Cost-effective versus Microsoft
- Persuasive virtualization story

Downside

- Mid-40s share price deserves scrutiny
- Competitors (HP, Oracle) are larger, better-established
- Top-line growing—operating margin still needs help

Just the Facts

SECTOR: **Technology**

BETA COEFFICIENT: **1.1**

5-YEAR COMPOUND EARNINGS-PER-SHARE GROWTH: **29.5%**

	2007	2008	2009	2010	2011
Revenues (Mil)	523	653	748	909	1,080
Net Income (Mil)	76.7	78.7	87.3	107	125
Price: high	25.3	24.8	31.8	49.0	47.7
low	18.0	7.5	13.0	26.5	35.0

Red Hat, Inc.
1801 Varsity Drive
Raleigh, NC 27606
(919) 754-3700
Website: *www.redhat.com*

Riverbed Technology, Inc.

Ticker symbol: RVBD (NASDAQ) ◻ S&P rating: NA ◻ Value Line financial strength rating: C ◻ Current yield: Nil

Who Are They?

Riverbed Technology, founded in 2002, designs and markets hardware and software appliances that address some of the operational problems arising when companies deploy wide area networks (WANs). Most of its products are designed simply to speed up operations across the WAN by a variety or a combination of methods, including data compression, smart caching, and bottleneck identification.

Riverbed's products address networks for branch offices, mobile workers, private data centers, private clouds, and cloud computing. The company's hardware products include the Steelhead line and the Cascade line. Steelhead products are designed to accelerate application and data delivery through local caching, data compression, and other methods, while the Cascade line is a collection of network diagnostic tools for troubleshooting and monitoring network performance. An integrated solution, the Riverbed Optimization System (RiOS), consists of hardware and software products that address distributed computing environments. In July 2011, the company acquired Zeus Technology, a software-based load-balancing and traffic-management solution for virtual and cloud environments.

Why Should I Care?

The core Internet protocols were designed at a time when the scope of most companies' IT infrastructure was a data center and a bunch of attached terminals. The most distant user was perhaps 1,000 feet from the server, and networks were often point-to-point, running proprietary protocols under proprietary operating systems. Today it's not at all unusual for a company to have a far more robust and powerful IT service, even though the data center may be a bunch of wires and three metal boxes in a broom closet at remote—even international—branches and two or three more boxes at headquarters. The core resources in this new model are the connections between the branches and headquarters and the Internet. Riverbed's products are not servers or traditional routing tools that make up the core of the data path. Rather they are adjuncts that optimize the use of those connections.

The company designs the products to be largely self-configuring and simple to use during operation. The products provide the greatest benefit to companies that do not have a dedicated IT staff to troubleshoot network problems. The products also allow companies to avoid the cost of investing in those resources before deploying WAN technologies. In the case of the Cascade line, the troubleshooting expertise is built into the product, freeing up personnel resources and providing a comprehensive, updateable knowledge base for the entire network at one location. The Steelhead products reduce the load on existing links and can eliminate the need for additional or higher bandwidth connections as the network grows. These are useful tools that work across networks of dissimilar hardware and software platforms and which can be installed at remote locations by untrained personnel.

How's Business?
The results for second quarter 2011 were very good, with revenue up 35 percent and earnings up 81 percent year over year. In our book on aggressive investing, we talked about Riverbed's performance versus the analysts' forecasts, mentioning the burden of high expectations that came with consistently hitting the numbers. Well, it came back to bite the company earlier this year—it missed earnings by a penny per share, and the stock dropped 30 percent. While we feel this was very much an overreaction by the market, it shows what can happen even when you've done your homework and invested wisely. What to do in that situation? Never waste a crisis—buy in at the lower price and cost average your holdings.

Upside
- Product positioned well for market trends
- Solid financing
- Management depth

Downside
- Tough competition
- P/E ratio 70-plus
- IT spending still in recovery

Just the Facts

SECTOR: **Technology**

BETA COEFFICIENT: **1.60**

5-YEAR COMPOUND EARNINGS-PER-SHARE GROWTH: **NA**

	2007	**2008**	**2009**	**2010**	**2011**
Revenues (Mil)	90.2	236	333	394	552
Net Income (Mil)	(15.8)	20.0	2.3	11.4	57.0
Price: high	24.0	11.7	12.0	38.4	44.5
low	13.2	4.2	4.9	11.2	23.0

Riverbed Technology, Inc.

199 Fremont Street

San Francisco, CA 94105

(415) 247-8800

Website: *www.riverbed.com*

SanDisk Corporation

Ticker symbol: SNDK (NASDAQ) ❑ S&P rating: BB- ❑ Value Line financial strength rating: B ❑ Current yield: Nil

Who Are They?

SanDisk is one of the world's largest suppliers of the various types of flash memory products. Flash memory is a type of solid-state memory that, unlike standard random-access memory, retains the data written to it after its power has been removed. Growth in market acceptance has largely paralleled the advances in the technology, with density (size) increasing 16,000-fold and speed increasing by a factor of ten since the introduction of the devices in the early 1990s.

SanDisk's products are distributed through retail and OEM channels. Its products are sold as standalone devices, such as removable memory cards, and as embedded devices such as packaged memory die and their associated controllers. Most of its products include memory and a controller; SanDisk produces the bulk of its memory components in venture relationships with Toshiba foundries, and designs its controllers in-house for production by third parties.

The flash memory market has generally been price elastic; the lower the price per unit of capacity, the higher the demand and the greater the number of new applications for the product. As such, SanDisk's strategy is to remain the highest-volume supplier, allowing it to open new markets and drive revenues with volume.

Why Should I Care?

Flash memory's distinguishing property—the nonvolatility of its data—has enabled more new products and applications than almost any other single product in the semiconductor industry. Digital cameras, smartphones, portable music players, and so many other electronic devices we now take for granted would be impossible to produce had it not been for the advent and rapid development of flash memory. A relatively new application, the solid-state drive (SSD), has the potential to become a very large revenue generator for flash manufacturers and SSD OEMs. The SSD is essentially a flash-based replacement for many applications where a disk drive is the current storage medium of choice. SSDs are currently at about a ten-to-one cost disadvantage to disk drives, but their performance, particularly in use profiles with a high transaction rate (such as servers), far exceeds that of disk drives. As the cost of SSDs continues to drop due to density improvements, demand will reach some critical inflection points where their production economies of scale override the disk-drive cost advantage and SSDs will become the dominant storage medium for sub-terabyte applications. In May 2011, SanDisk completed its $725 million (cash and stock) acquisition of Pliant Technology, a developer of enterprise SSDs. Pliant now becomes SanDisk's Enterprise Storage Solutions business.

Flash memory is into its twelfth generation. There's room for perhaps four or five more generations before the memory architecture runs into physical limits beyond which it no longer scales. SanDisk is already working on alternative technologies to replace/augment flash in the market when flash can no longer scale effectively.

How's Business?

SanDisk has turned in record revenue for each of the first two quarters of FY2011 and expects more of the same for the remainder of the year. With more than 2,800 U.S. and international patents, SanDisk's licensing is a significant part of their business; from 2008 through 2010, SanDisk generated $1.28 billion in revenue through license agreements, or roughly 11 percent of its total revenue.

Upside

- Popularity of tablet products
- Stock is very cheap at mid-40s
- Semiconductor boom cycle—hop on

Downside

- State-of-the-art fabs are not cheap
- Wide adoption of cloud streaming could reduce flash demand
- Solid competition in Samsung and Hynix

Just the Facts

SECTOR: Semiconductor
BETA COEFFICIENT: 1.35
5-YEAR COMPOUND EARNINGS-PER-SHARE GROWTH: 18.1%

	2007	2008	2009	2010	2011
Revenues (Mil)	3,896	3,351	3,567	4,827	5,650
Net Income (Mil)	218	(572)	415	1,100	1,085
Price: high	59.8	33.7	52.3	53.6	53.2
low	32.7	5.1	7.5	24.9	36.1

SanDisk Corporation
601 McCarthy Boulevard
Milpitas, CA 95035
(408) 801-1000
Website: *www.sandisk.com*

Sanmina-SCI

Ticker symbol: SANM (NASDAQ) ❏ S&P rating: B+ ❏ Value Line financial strength rating: C+ ❏ Current yield: Nil

Who Are They?

Sanmina is one of the larger players in the electronic manufacturing services sector. SCI (originally called Space Craft Inc.) was the first large-scale EMS provider in North America, serving the nascent aerospace industry out of its base in Huntsville, Alabama. The EMS industry grew with the founding of Solectron in the late seventies and really accelerated in the eighties and nineties as large manufacturing companies began aggressively outsourcing their printed circuit assembly and other high labor content operations. In early 2001, Sanmina (already an established but niche player) bought SCI and catapulted itself into the top echelon of end-to-end suppliers. Since then it's been a bit of a wild ride, as the industry as a whole has been whipsawed by boom/bust cycles in the computing and consumer electronics sectors. The company stock went from $143 down to $9 in 2002, back up to $77 in 2003, back down to $9 in 2007 and then $1 in 2009, back up to $20 in 2010 and then back down to a recent price in the mid-$8 range.

Why Should I Care?

The EMS industry has evolved greatly over the past thirty years. All of these businesses began as outsourced labor, then added purchasing and inventory management, then added test capability, and then grew from a business that acted simply as the printed circuit and cable supplier to a large standalone integrated business that manufactures a product through to final assembly. Now many of the larger players design, manufacture, and support complete products and product lines on behalf of a client. As such, there are benefits to size other than simply the ability to take on higher volumes and provide purchasing power. Size allows you to support increasing levels of R & D and to sell those R & D services for far higher value-add than a smaller assembly house can hope to garner. As the underlying hardware for many products have become commoditized (we love our big words here at *100 Best*), general-purpose machines, the underlying product value is provided less by the appliance and more by its intellectual property content. Companies are now often founded using business models with completely outsourced manufacturing—some of the most important value providers in a company may never see a finished product except in an advertisement or at a trade show. In this sort of model, Sanmina is more than just an outsourced service provider; it is an extension of the client company. Its broad geographic coverage in both design and manufacturing capability provides real advantages in terms of response time and content localization.

How's Business?

Sanmina has sorted out some of the problems driving its multiyear funk of the mid-decade. Out of eight years starting in 2002, the company had one year of profitability. Operating margins began to improve in 2009, however, and in 2010 its operating margin rose to greater than 5 percent for the first time since 2001. The predictions for 2011 and 2012 look steady, with improving operating margin and greatly improved cash flow. This is a risky stock, no question, but the company appears to have turned the corner on its cost model and, as such, buying here is less of a bet on the company and more of a bet on the recovery of the electronics sector as a whole. Closely watched, Sanmina could be a very worthwhile addition to an otherwise conservative portfolio.

Upside

- Increased margins holding steady for eight quarters
- Good projections for 2012
- Two dividend increases in one year

Downside

- Management advising on "sales headwinds" through end of 2011
- Large price swings
- Very competitive market with thin margins

Just the Facts

SECTOR: **Industrials**

BETA COEFFICIENT: **1.70**

5-YEAR COMPOUND EARNINGS-PER-SHARE GROWTH: **NA**

	2007	2008	2009	2010	2011
Revenues (Mil)	10,384	7,202	5,178	6,319	6,600
Net Income (Mil)	(33.0)	55.3	(43.0)	107	130
Price: high	23.6	16.0	11.4	20.3	16.9
low	9.7	1.6	1.1	8.9	7.9

Sanmina-SCI Corporation
2700 First Street
San Jose, CA 95134
(408) 435-8444
Website: *www.sanmina-sci.com*

SEMICONDUCTORS

Semtech Corp.

Ticker symbol: SMTC (NASDAQ) ❑ **S&P rating: NA** ❑ **Value Line financial strength rating: B** ❑ **Current yield: Nil**

Who Are They?

Semtech, a fabless semiconductor company, is one of the niche players in the analog and mixed-signal integrated circuit market. The company was founded in 1960 to serve the military and aerospace markets, where it established a reputation for performance and reliability. It did not transition to the commercial markets until the early 1990s, which is around the same time the military softened its stance on using commercial-spec parts in noncritical applications. The company followed this with a series of acquisitions in the commercial space, picking up niche players in the communications and low-power markets, and adding engineering talent along the way (more than 60 percent of the company's employees are engineers).

Since "going commercial," the company has expanded its customer base from one to nearly 5,000. It makes more than a thousand products for customers worldwide. It has sales, application, and design resources throughout the United States, the United Kingdom, Western Europe, the Asia-Pacific region, and China.

Why Should I Care?

Here's another company that's in the right place at the right time with all the right ingredients. While the traditional computer/PC markets continue to founder, markets such as those served by Semtech are the new hotness. Communications, interface, and power management are key growth sectors in the IC market, and Semtech's product line is full of new designs in all of those areas. Five years ago you might not have predicted a lot of growth potential for these products, but that was before the iPhone. The dramatic shift in consumer electronics toward mobile devices has driven strong demand in all of these areas, and Semtech was ready.

One of its traditional strengths has been in protection devices. The parts of an electronic product that face the outside world (buttons, display panels, connectors) face a risk that the internal parts do not: static discharge. Consequently, things like touchscreens, USB ports, and all the other interfaces to an electronic device have to be protected from the threat of high-voltage transient events that might otherwise destroy the expensive parts inside. This protection is a function that every device requires, and Semtech is one of the leaders in the market. As the number of human interfaces on an electronic device increases, so does the need for this protection, and the growth in the personal electronics and mobile markets has lot to do with Semtech's success.

We've mentioned how some analog IC businesses can leverage fab expertise into a strategic advantage via owning and running their own fabrication facility. While Semtech would seem to fit that profile, it still doesn't have a fab. The fact that it hasn't gone out and bought a facility is something for which we give the company a great deal of credit. Smaller design houses, even those with the expertise that Semtech has, have gone belly-up trying to keep a fab happy and fed. The simple fact is that until 2010 it has lacked the volume and revenue to justify the expense, but if its business continues to prosper it may benefit from picking up a small process for its higher volume and more profitable segments.

How's Business?

Semtech's quarterlies for the past two years have been up and to the right. It has a great balance sheet, with no debt and cash equal to six months of revenue. Don't be surprised to see further acquisition activity here.

Upside

- Diversified product line
- Growth in its highest-margin products
- Solid financials

Downside

- Everybody else likes Semtech, too
- Highest revenue segment (protection) is lowest margin
- Long-term growth prospects less clear

Just the Facts

SECTOR: **Technology**
BETA COEFFICIENT: **1.00**
5-YEAR COMPOUND EARNINGS-PER-SHARE GROWTH: **7.5%**

	2007	2008	2009	2010	2011
Revenues (Mil)	285	295	287	455	525
Net Income (Mil)	48.8	40.2	40.2	90.3	110
Price: high	21.1	18.6	19.2	25.0	29.0
low	12.7	8.8	10.2	14.6	19.5

Semtech Corporation
200 Flynn Road
Camarillo, CA 93012
(805) 498-2111
Website: *www.semtech.com*

Solutia Inc.

Ticker symbol: SOA (NYSE) ▫ S&P rating: NA ▫ Value Line financial strength rating: B ▫ Current yield: Nil

Who Are They?

Solutia is a manufacturer of performance materials (mainly films) and specialty chemicals used in the manufacture of a number of consumer and industrial goods. Solutia also makes a number of end-user products for consumer and commercial applications. The company has customers in more than fifty countries worldwide, and serves them through twenty-two manufacturing facilities, seven technical centers, and thirty sales offices located in the United States, Europe, Latin America, and the Asia-Pacific region.

It's been a bumpy ride for the Solutia brand. The company began in 1997 as a spinoff from Monsanto's chemical business. Six years later, under heavy financial obligations assigned to it as part of the divestiture and under the additional threat of litigation for environmental wrongdoings while under Monsanto's management, the company filed for Chapter 11 protection. Five years after that, the company emerged from Chapter 11 and began operations under its original name and most of its original senior management. The timing couldn't have been much worse, as the doors opened the very same week that the economy officially entered the recession of 2008–2009.

Why Should I Care?

The automotive market uses two particular products from Solutia in critical applications, and its technology is such that the products have thoroughly dominant market shares. Their Saflex PVB sheet has been used as an interlayer reinforcement for laminated glass for more than seventy years and is widely used in automotive windshields for nearly every make and model of car. The plastic film, bonded between layers of glass, greatly increases the shatter resistance of the glass and makes it lighter as well. A special version of the film also acts as a sound-deadening layer, a feature that has caught on very well recently with makers of luxury automobiles. Another variation on Saflex PVB is now used as an encapsulant for thin-film photovoltaic panels. The PVB film protects the photovoltaic materials from weather and corrosive elements while maintaining transparency. The other major automotive product, Crystex, is used in nearly every automobile tire manufactured, as it promotes a more secure bond between the rubber and the steel belts during the vulcanization process. Another of its chemical products, Skydrol, is the most commonly used hydraulic fluid for commercial aircraft.

The company's film products are also widely used across a number of markets and applications. Its Flexvue films are used in the electronic displays of many book readers and touchscreens, where they can provide characteristics such as conductivity or insulation, reflectivity or anti-reflectivity, removability, or hard coating. These film coatings, with some variation, are also used in architectural applications, where they are used to block UV energy from passing through exterior windows, providing significant energy savings in air-conditioned buildings.

How's Business?
Product demand has been good and is increasing. A turnaround in the automotive market will drive volumes even higher, but the company is already in good shape from a top-line perspective. Margins on these products are very good and the overall net (currently 13 percent) is healthy and getting healthier. Solutia's products are in critical applications and in high-value products, which is a great place to be. We think there's great growth potential here if its solar applications catch on.

Upside
- Good mix of cash cows and leading-edge products
- Excellent profitability
- Good localization

Downside
- Some volatility here
- Raw material costs rising
- Pricing competition in films

Just the Facts

SECTOR: **Technology**

BETA COEFFICIENT: **1.95**

5-YEAR COMPOUND EARNINGS-PER-SHARE GROWTH: **NA**

	2007	2008	2009	2010	2011
Revenues (Mil)	—	1,775	1,667	1,950	2,145
Net Income (Mil)	—	(14.0)	56.0	188	275
Price: high	21.8	20.5	13.8	24.0	26.4
low	17.0	3.6	1.0	11.8	15.7

Solutia Inc.

575 Maryville Centre Drive

St. Louis, Missouri 63166–6760

(314) 674-1000

Website: *www.solutia.com*

SEMICONDUCTORS

STMicroelectronics

Ticker symbol: STM (NYSE) ❑ S&P rating: BBB+ ❑ Value Line financial strength rating: B+ ❑ Current yield: 4.2%

Who Are They?

STM was originally named SGS-Thomson after the merger of SGS Micro-elettronica and Thomson Semiconducteurs in 1987, and taken public in 1994. It was renamed STMicroelectronics in 1998 and is headquartered in Switzerland, though the original founding companies were Italian and French. Take notes, because there's a quiz at the end of the book (just kidding, don't look). Just letting you know that this is a company with some history behind it (and how—its founder, Elihu Thomson, was born in England in 1853).

STM is now the largest semiconductor manufacturer based in Europe and one of the largest in the world. The company's products are divided among five product groups: automotive, consumer, computer and communications infrastructure, wireless, and the industrial and multisegment sector. The bulk of its product line consists of discrete power devices, analog devices, microcontrollers, and MEMS devices.

Why Should I Care?

ST is one of the core suppliers to companies such as Apple, Bosch, Cisco, HP, LG Electronics, Motorola, Nokia, Philips, Samsung, and most all of the top industrial and consumer electronics manufacturers in the world. It supplies everything from garden-variety operational amplifiers up to the ARM processor cores used in nearly all of the smartphones and tablets now entering the market. Like most semiconductor businesses, it is subject to the cyclical nature of the market, but it has diversified its applications and customer base probably more than any other producer. Diversification is just good business if you have the resources to support it, but it's particularly so in the case of STM because it has captive fabs that need to be kept busy. Designers and researchers can generate economic value even when sales are off. Fabs and their associated labor cannot. This diversification also creates opportunities for product integration that other players may not have. Using combinations of its internal CMOS, bipolar CMOS, diffused MOS, BCD, and embedded memory technologies, the company has created SoC (System on a Chip) and SiP (System-in-Package) products using exclusively its own designs combined in one part to perform very high-level functions. These integrated products are in high demand from product designers looking for complete solutions for finished products, which integrate RF, CPU, power management, and other technologies in one package.

STM is now one of the largest volume suppliers of micro-electromechanical systems (MEMS) in the world. These devices are not that well known by name, but their functions are seen in many smartphones and other hand-held products. These are the devices that tell the CPU the orientation of the product and alter the display accordingly. MEMS functions also include compasses, gyroscopes, and accelerometers and are widely used in medical and automotive applications. STM is significantly increasing its MEMS production capacity to more than 3 million units per day in order to keep up with demand.

How's Business?

The big rebound in 2010 following a dismal 2009 had the look of a dead cat bounce, as earnings had already been unsteady leading into the recession. The first quarter of 2011 was encouraging, but the company missed badly in the second quarter, posting EPS of $.14 versus the $.21 that was expected. Still, for the year, the company is on target to post a 22 percent increase in year-over-year earnings with just an 8 percent bump in sales.

Upside

- Maintained 2010's earnings momentum through 2011
- Healthy product pipeline
- Trading at an attractive 6 forward P/E

Downside

- Nokia represented 14 percent of FY2010 sales
- ST-Ericsson joint venture remains unprofitable
- Operating margin low-ish for an R & D-reliant company

Just the Facts

SECTOR: Semiconductor
BETA COEFFICIENT: 1.83
5-YEAR COMPOUND EARNINGS-PER-SHARE GROWTH: NA

	2007	2008	2009	2010	2011
Revenues (Mil)	10,001	9,895	8,510	10,346	11,150
Net Income (Mil)	674	410	(628)	666	885
Price: high	20.8	14.4	10.3	10.7	13.5
low	14.2	5.9	3.7	6.5	6.3

STMicroelectronics N.V.
39 Chemin du Champs-des-Files Plan-les-Quates
Geneva 15, Switzerland
(602) 485-2061
Website: *www.st.com*

Stryker Corp.

Ticker symbol: SYK (NYSE) ❑ S&P rating: A+ ❑ Value Line financial strength rating: A++ ❑ Current yield: 1.5%

Who Are They?

Stryker Corporation, founded in 1941, is one of the larger players in the $12 billion global orthopedic implants industry. The company operates in two segments: orthopedic implants and medical/surgical equipment.

The implants segment produces artificial hips, prosthetic knees, and trauma products, as well as prosthetic shoulder and spinal implants. The medical/surgical equipment segment produces powered surgical tools, powered instruments and endoscopic systems, and specialty stretchers. Most of the products from medical/surgical are targeted for implant procedures and follow-on care but find use in many other applications.

Late in 2009, the company acquired the privately held Ascent Healthcare Solutions, the market leader in reprocessing and remanufacturing of medical devices. In January 2011, Stryker completed its acquisition of Boston Scientific's neurovascular unit for $1.5 billion in cash. Stryker's revenue is split roughly 60/40 between implants and equipment and 65/35 between domestic and international.

Why Should I Care?

Formerly known only for its orthopedics-based businesses, Stryker's newly diversified product line provides some hedges against any significant sales shortfall in economic downturns. And, as it turns out, the orthopedic industry is showing signs of recovery from its slowdown at the bottom of the recession, and the company is guiding for FY2011 year-over-year sales growth of 11–13 percent.

Stryker continues to achieve healthy revenues, fueled by growth across the company's business segments, particularly in its medical/surgical segment. Sales there have been boosted by the Ascent acquisition and sustained growth across its surgical equipment and surgical navigation systems, as well as the endoscopic and communications systems.

Stryker's product pipeline has been on the mend as well. Regular product introductions have kept its offerings up-to-date, including several new hip systems, Restoration ADM, and Rejuvenate. Recently Stryker secured

FDA approval for its MDM X3 (Modular Dual Mobility) mobile bearing hip system, representing an important addition to its portfolio of next-generation hip replacement systems. Stryker has committed to lead the mobile bearing hip market with products that address the shortcomings of metal-on-metal hip implants. Its aggressive transition to next-generation hip systems should provide a revenue tailwind.

Stryker's acquisition of Boston Scientific's neurovascular unit offers the company an opportunity to diversify into a fast-growing therapy market. The business complements the company's existing neurosurgery products and positions it as the leading player in the neurovascular market. The neurovascular business performed strongly in the most recent quarter and should help Stryker in expanding its top line moving forward.

The company has a solid balance sheet, healthy free cash flow, and very good earnings leverage. Stryker's gross margins rose another percentage point during the year, helping to fund a large R & D initiative that took more than two points out of operating margin. The company also raised its dividend by 20 percent and announced an additional $500 million share repurchase program, which should further shore up the share price.

How's Business?
Steady as she goes. The company has been delivering in line with most estimates, with strong revenue growth over the past two years. As organic top-line growth starts to taper due to an unpredictable health care environment, expect the company to make several more (smaller) acquisitions to boost revenues and provide further diversification.

Upside
- Well positioned for further acquisitions
- Increased diversification
- Strong product demand

Downside
- Medicare environment hazy
- Material cost increases
- Pricing pressure as market leader

Just the Facts

SECTOR: **Health Care**
BETA COEFFICIENT: **0.80**
5-YEAR COMPOUND EARNINGS-PER-SHARE GROWTH: **NA**

	2007	**2008**	**2009**	**2010**	**2011**
Revenues (Mil)	6,001	6,718	6,723	7,320	8,390
Net Income (Mil)	1,001	1,148	1,107	1,329	1,450
Price: high	76.9	74.9	52.7	59.7	65.2
low	54.9	35.4	30.8	42.7	43.8

Stryker Corporation
2825 Airview Boulevard
Kalamazoo, MI 49002
(269) 385-2600
Website: *www.stryker.com*

Suntech Power ADS

Ticker symbol: STP (NYSE) ❑ S&P rating: NA ❑ Value Line financial strength rating: B+ ❑ Current yield: Nil

Who Are They?

Suntech is, in terms of capacity, the world's largest producer of solar panels. On an annual basis, it can produce 2,200 megawatts of capacity, or the equivalent output of two and a half mainline nuclear power plants. It has an installed base of 15 million panels in eighty countries, including the largest single photovoltaic plant in the western hemisphere, a 14-megawatt facility at Nellis Air Force Base in Nevada.

The company, founded in 2001, completed its IPO in 2005 and has grown rapidly since then, increasing its capacity by a factor of eight. Suntech's manufacturing process consists of producing cells and assembling them into finished panels, ready for installation. Suntech does not produce any of the silicon wafers on which its products are based. It buys raw mono-crystalline and polycrystalline silicon from wafer producers in China (where there is no shortage of ready suppliers), processes it using a number of proprietary and patented methods, and then creates the cells.

Suntech's products are designed mainly for commercial and utility-scale programs. It also makes a panel appropriate for residential programs, but the company focuses its process on the market for the higher-output panels desired by large-scale users. Suntech does not sell inverters or installation services, relying instead on an extensive network of independent dealers and partners to complete the project configuration and installation processes.

Why Should I Care?

In the past five years, solar stocks have sprung up like desert flowers after a spring rain. China, in particular, has built up enormous capacity in its solar industry from start to finish. There are dozens of silicon foundries, wafer manufacturers, finished cell manufacturers, and panel assemblers, and all of them built up on a very large scale with the new industrial money that China can't seem to stop making. Making the situation very attractive for a company like Suntech is the overcapacity in the foundry and wafer manufacturing sectors. The tonnage of polysilicon that has come online in the past five years has more than tripled the world supply. Total polysilicon capacity will increase by more than 35 percent in 2011 alone, with most of that increase coming in China. This glut of raw material has kept input prices down for Suntech, at least as far as polysilicon goes. The price of silver, however (used in the cell production process), has climbed along with the prices of other special metals as people seek a cash refuge during the economic recovery. This is not a sustainable trend, though, and its effect on the company's earnings is just a few cents per share in any case.

What drives Suntech's future success will be less a matter of production costs and more a matter of demand, and that picture is starting to improve of late. Germany, one of the largest supporters of the entire industry through its tax incentives to solar power users has, after a turn away from the subsidy model, returned to the fold after rejecting a future of nuclear power.

How's Business?

Could be brighter. The recent news on the industry in general has been downbeat, with Evergreen filing for bankruptcy and LDK Solar revising its second quarter guidance downward 40 percent. As we go to press the Guggenheim Solar ETF is trading very close to its fifty-two-week low. Make no mistake, the solar industry is as risky as it's always been, but Suntech has solid financing and is trading at a very attractive price.

Upside
- Massive capacity
- Encouraging results from installed base
- Living on the value end of the solar chain

Downside
- Uncertain worldwide demand
- Strong competition
- U.S. tax incentives fading

Just the Facts

SECTOR: Technology

BETA COEFFICIENT: 1.95

5-YEAR COMPOUND EARNINGS-PER-SHARE GROWTH: NA

	2007	2008	2009	2010	2011
Revenues (Mil)	1,348	1,923	1,693	2,902	3,350
Net Income (Mil)	171	88.2	91.5	136	190
Price: high	88.6	90.0	21.4	18.8	10.7
low	31.4	5.4	5.1	7.1	5.1

Suntech Power ADS

17-6 Changjiang South Road, New District

Wuxi 214028, China

8651-0534-5000

Website: *www.suntech-power.com*

TE Connectivity, Ltd.

Ticker symbol: TEL (NYSE) ❑ S&P rating: NA ❑ Value Line financial strength rating: BBB ❑ Current yield: 2.0%

Who Are They?

TE Connectivity, formerly known as Tyco Electronics when it was spun off from Tyco International in 2007, is a provider of engineered electronic components, cable systems, connectors, telecommunication systems, and specialty products. The company changed its name in March 2011 to more closely match its position as a component and communications manufacturer. The company was put together out of a series of acquisitions made in the early part of the past decade. The connector manufacturer AMP Inc., Raychem Corporation, the components division of Siemens, and the OEM division of Thomas & Betts were joined in 2000 to form the core of the business when it was part of Tyco International. The company has more than 97,000 employees in nearly fifty countries.

TE operates four reporting segments: electronic components, network solutions, specialty products, and undersea telecommunications. The specialty new segment is made up of smaller operations—aerospace, defense, and marine; touch systems; medical; and circuit protection businesses. All of these segments provide connectoring, wire and cable, tubing, and circuit-protection devices. The company also designs and produces custom electronic solutions for customers in all of its markets. Two-thirds of the company's revenue is derived from the sale of electronic components, with just over one-third of sales going to the automotive industry.

Why Should I Care?

One of the company's core competencies—the design and manufacturing of telecommunications systems—is in high demand at the moment. Its most recent quarter's results bear this out, as it was able to post better-than-expected results in spite of the slowing of the Japanese market. Telecommunications companies in Australia, China, and Europe are making big investments in broadband networks outside the United States, driving demand for its products.

The company's performance in the Chinese automotive market has been better than expected. While the market grew by nearly 50 percent,

TE's revenues in the market grew 66 percent to $500 million. The improved revenues helped justify and fund a 45 percent growth in engineering investments in China, Brazil, and India. Total revenue for the three countries in FY2010 was $2.4 billion, with significant growth expected in FY2011. The Chinese automobile manufacturing sector is expected to produce very significant growth over the next ten years, and developing a solid vendor relationship early in the process will benefit TE greatly down the road.

TE has one of the most unique businesses found anywhere on the planet. Its SubCom subsidiary supplies undersea communications systems and services. It has laid more than 300,000 miles of fiber-optic cable on the seafloor, making broadband available for the first time to Africa, Australia, Indonesia, and throughout the Asia-Pacific region. This is a vertically integrated business with a tremendous moat (more like an ocean, really). The demand for this service keeps it operating pretty much full time with a backlog extending several years.

How's Business?

The company will probably report revenues and earnings perhaps 3 percent higher than early-year predictions. Revenues will increase 19 percent over the prior year, while earnings will improve over FY2010 by 21 percent. These numbers would have been better still but for the downturn in the Japanese economy.

TE spent much of the past three years reducing its manufacturing footprint by 25 percent, and the results are showing up in improved operating and net margins. We expect 2012's results to benefit even further from TE's cost-control efforts.

Upside
- Very specific and necessary expertise
- Good total return
- Solid financials

Downside
- Increasing material costs
- Moderate exposure to Japanese downturn
- Pricing competition in several markets

Just the Facts

SECTOR: **Technology**

BETA COEFFICIENT: **1.95**

5-YEAR COMPOUND EARNINGS-PER-SHARE GROWTH: **NA**

	2007	2008	2009	2010	2011
Revenues (Mil)	13,460	14,834	10,256	12.070	14,100
Net Income (Mil)	1,061	1,296	379	1,158	1,350
Price: high	41.3	40.3	25.0	35.7	38.5
low	31.3	12.9	7.4	23.8	28.0

TE Connectivity Ltd.

Rheinstrasse 20, CH-8200

Schaffhausen, Switzerland

41-52-633-66-61

Website: *www.tycoelectronics.com*

Tech Data Corporation

Ticker symbol: TECD (NASDAQ) ❑ S&P rating: BBB- ❑ Value Line financial strength rating: B++
❑ Current yield: Nil

Who Are They?

Tech Data Corporation is one of the top-tier providers of information technology products and logistics management and other value-added services.
Incorporated in 1974 and based in Clearwater, Florida, the company is the
second-largest distributor of IT products worldwide with offerings that
cover 75 percent of the total market. It has more than 125,000 customers
in over 100 countries.

The company offers microcomputer hardware and software products
to value-added resellers (half of FY2011 revenue), direct marketers and
retailers, and corporate resellers. These products are sourced directly from
manufacturers and publishers for sale and are provided in a variety of IT
segments, including peripherals, systems, networking, and software. Tech
Data distributes consumer electronics products from leading hardware and
software vendors such as Apple, Panasonic, HP, Adobe, Autodesk, and Cisco
Systems, among others.

Tech Data also provides pre- and post-sale training services and technical support, external financing options, configuration services, outbound
telemarketing, and marketing services. In addition, the company provides
e-commerce solutions, including online order entry, product integration
services, and electronic data interchange services.

The company generates just over half of its revenues from Europe, with
the remainder from the Americas.

Why Should I Care?

Tech Data is in a good position for strong top-line and bottom-line growth
over the next two years. Its bet on higher IT spending and its diversification into new technologies should continue to pay off in 2012, as Gartner
expects worldwide IT spending to increase 7.1 percent through fiscal 2011.
Tech Data's well-timed entry into data center, mobile technology, consumer
electronics, software, and integrated supply chain has helped to produce
top-line growth of 15 percent so far in 2011. The expectation for FY2012
is for a further 8.0 percent increase. In addition, stronger demand for

technology products, particularly from the small and medium-sized business (SMB) customer segment in several countries, will boost profitability going forward. The company's management is providing guidance on operating margins, which are currently in the range of 1.2 percent. TECD maintains that by the end of 2013 it will be turning at a 1.5 percent rate, which would impact earnings dramatically. A shift in the product mix, pent-up demand in the United States, and geographic growth in Europe would be the main drivers for such a move, and we think management has a good story around that.

You can't talk about the distribution business without mentioning acquisitions, and Tech Data has not been idle on that front. In 2011 it was very busy, acquiring five companies in Europe and expanding its footprint significantly in the Nordic countries. It also formed a number of joint ventures, many of which are focused on mobile communications. Earlier this year, the company announced a distribution agreement with Webroot, a well-known Internet security provider, which will allow Tech Data's resellers to offer their products as part of its security solutions offering.

How's Business?

Tech Data's balance sheet is in great shape and provides the flexibility to buy market share through discounts, pursue acquisitions, pay down debt, and repurchase shares. The company ended the first half of 2012 with $418 million in cash after spending nearly $150 million in the second quarter to repurchase shares. Since 2005, Tech Data has repurchased 20 million shares for approximately $800 million, representing over a third of its outstanding shares.

Upside
- Management pulling all the right strings
- Excellent cash generation
- Conservative expansion

Downside
- HP represents 27 percent of sales
- Strong pricing pressure in Europe
- Moving into higher-complexity lines

Just the Facts

SECTOR: **Distribution**
BETA COEFFICIENT: **0.95**
5-YEAR COMPOUND EARNINGS-PER-SHARE GROWTH: **9.5%**

	2007	**2008**	**2009**	**2010**	**2011**
Revenues (Mil)	23,423	24,080	22,100	24,376	26,300
Net Income (Mil)	137	124	175	214	225
Price: high	41.4	37.9	47.8	48.8	53.8
low	33.0	14.1	16.2	34.8	39.1

Tech Data Corporation
5350 Tech Data Drive
Clearwater, FL 33760
(727) 539-7429
Website: *www.techdata.com*

TECHNE Corporation

Ticker symbol: TECH (NASDAQ) □ S&P rating: NA □ Value Line financial strength rating: A+ □
Current yield: 1.4%

Who Are They?

TECHNE Corporation, incorporated in Minnesota in 1981, is a holding
company for two wholly owned operating subsidiaries: Research and Diagnostic Systems, Inc. (R & D Systems), located in Minneapolis; and R & D
Systems Europe Ltd. (RDSE) located in Abingdon, England. R & D Systems
is a specialty manufacturer of biological products, specifically purified proteins
and antibodies sold primarily to the research market, and assay kits, which are
sold to the research and clinical diagnostic markets. The company manufactures and sells more than 11,000 different protein bases and related biotech
products, accounting for 93 percent of its sales. Other major product lines
include hematology controls, which are used in hospitals and clinical laboratories to check the accuracy of blood analysis instruments.

More than 95 percent of TECHNE's revenues are derived from products manufactured by R & D Systems. RDSE sells and distributes R & D
Systems' biotechnology products in Europe. RDSE also has a German sales
subsidiary, R & D Systems GmbH.

Why Should I Care?

The problem for an individual investor putting money into a biotechnology
company is usually one of volatility. Many of these businesses are built on
the thinnest of revenue streams, and the stock price often reflects not the
health of the ongoing business but the prevailing opinion on the future of
the company's research and development. If the active research turns out to
be marketable, the share price appreciates significantly; if not, then the share
price . . . well, let's not talk about that. But that's the sort of share price volatility we worry about when we buy stock—the volatility that comes from
pure, unprotected risk. That sort of volatility is one of the criteria we use
here at *100 Best* to separate our picks from the others.

TECHNE's value proposition is quite the opposite. Its stock price is
largely a reflection of the value investors put in TECHNE's steady and predictable earnings, which at the moment are selling at quite a premium. Three
dollars' worth of TECHNE's earnings will cost you in the range of $75 by
the time you read this. Okay, it turns out that there's still some speculative

value in the share price, but that's where the fun is. If you're comfortable with a P/E of 25, then this is a stock that should provide the potential for buzz on the upside without the potential for a massive sting on the backside.

The "bet" on TECHNE right now comes from three bits of news: good growth in the Chinese market, a terrific balance sheet (fueling internal research and speculation about acquisitions), and the recent purchase of Tocris Holdings for $124 million. A cash deal, the Tocris acquisition dovetails with TECHNE's existing R & D with new disease assays and should add $18–$20 million per year to the top line going forward.

How's Business?

Steady growth in both revenues and earnings are in the forecast through FY2012. Business in China could be key to any potential upside surprises— while sales for the larger company grew 7.8 percent in FY2010, sales from the Chinese operation grew 26 percent.

Upside

- Low-risk play in a high-growth market
- A good time for acquisitions
- Outstanding business moat

Downside

- Weaker sales through 2011 likely
- Long product-development cycles
- Slow organic growth

Just the Facts

SECTOR: **Health Care**

BETA COEFFICIENT: **0.75**

5-YEAR COMPOUND EARNINGS-PER-SHARE GROWTH: **NA**

	2007	2008	2009	2010	2011
Revenues (Mil)	224	257	264	269	290
Net Income (Mil)	85.1	104	105	110	116
Price: high	72.0	82.9	69.9	69.8	85.1
low	54.5	57.1	45.4	55.6	66.0

TECHNE Corporation

614 McKinley Place, N.E.

Minneapolis, MN 55413

(612) 379-8854

Website: *www.techne-corp.com*

Teradata Corp.

Ticker symbol: TDC (NYSE) ❑ S&P rating: NA ❑ Value Line financial strength rating: A+ ❑ Current yield: Nil

Who Are They?

Teradata is one the largest players in the enterprise data warehousing (EDW) market. What is EDW? We don't normally quote directly from company reports, but we can't do much better than this for clarity: "Data warehousing is the process of capturing, storing and analyzing data to gain insight. This process is built on an enterprise data warehouse, which is a single, centralized application-neutral repository of an organization's current and historical data."

And there you have it. All of your data, current and future, in one place. Safe, secure, and accessible. Of course, Teradata doesn't stop there. It also sells all of the tools that help you understand what you have and how you can put it to its best use.

Why Should I Care?

There are two basic ideas behind all of this data warehousing. One is operational: Your people will make better day-to-day decisions if they are better informed. If you give reasonably intelligent people perfect data (or as perfect as you can get it), then they will make reasonable, intelligent decisions based on the best information at hand. The challenge (and the business opportunity) is to provide that information where and when it is needed, without unnecessary data clouding the issue. The second reason for warehousing is strategic: What can we learn from this data that we didn't know before? Are there some larger truths hiding in this pile of seemingly disconnected facts that will show us how to run our current business better or allow us to grow our business into new and profitable areas? Teradata's business is the collection and provisioning of this raw data for later analysis to suit the needs of the data's owners.

Data, for what it's worth, is being collected at a staggering rate. What kind of data? In many cases, it is collected long before there's any purpose identified for it or value assigned to it, which makes it all the more important to collect and save the data as soon as it's available. You never know what you'll need or when you'll need it.

This data packrat mentality is sweet, sweet music to the ears of companies such as Teradata, which provide the hardware and service for these storage installations. Using what is essentially standard server hardware and a Linux operating system, Teradata has managed to snag margins that are decidedly un-standard. It has also been able to generate cash sufficient for acquisitions, killing off the smaller competitors before they can get a foothold in a business that is very scalable. The company's recent acquisitions of Aprimo and Aster Data also provides Teradata with a better set of capabilities in the cloud (applications service) space.

How's Business?

Incorporated at the very start of the most recent recession, the company has produced in the past ten quarters some impressive growth in revenues, earnings, and cash flow. Teradata trades at a fairly high multiple (25-ish), but high multiples are par for the course for the vertical players in this space. Its major competitors in the "big data" market include IBM, HP, and Oracle.

Upside

■ Revenue growth of 20 percent through 2012 likely
■ Well-entrenched in a growth market
■ Management projecting conservatively

Downside

■ Big, motivated competitors
■ Some exposure to Japanese downturn
■ Growth worth the price?

Just the Facts

SECTOR: **Technology**
BETA COEFFICIENT: **0.90**
5-YEAR COMPOUND EARNINGS-PER-SHARE GROWTH: **NA**

	2007	2008	2009	2010	2011
Revenues (Mil)	1,702	1,760	1,709	1,936	2,300
Net Income (Mil)	200	250	254	301	310
Price: high	30.1	27.9	32.2	43.8	62.3
low	22.3	11.1	12.8	26.8	41.6

Teradata Corporation
10000 Innovation Drive
Dayton, OH 45342
(866) 548-8348
Website: *www.teradata.com*

INSTRUMENTS

Trimble Navigation

Ticker symbol: TRMB (NASDAQ) ❑ S&P rating: NA ❑ Value Line financial strength rating: B+ ❑
Current yield: Nil

Who Are They?

Trimble Navigation designs and manufactures positioning, surveying, and machine control products. Though handheld and automotive consumer GPS (global positioning system) is a well-developed market, Trimble instead concentrates on the commercial end user. It makes and sells handheld units for surveying and mobile applications, but it also provides integrated systems that employ GPS, laser, optical, and inertial techniques with wireless communications and application software. These systems are sold into commercial and industrial markets that require precise location and positioning tools. As such, Trimble operates as four business segments: field solutions, mobile solutions, engineering and construction, and advanced devices.

The field solutions products are used in agriculture to guide, and in some cases, auto-pilot farming equipment such as tractors and combines. The systems also include software for the mapping of utility assets (power, sewage) and terrain mapping for groundwater analysis. Mobile solutions produces hardware and software fleet management tools for the concrete trucking and waste management trucking end markets. The systems also provide direct store delivery applications and are used by law enforcement, fire, rescue, and other public safety agencies. The engineering and construction products are used for surveying, machine control, and layout by the building, highway, marine, mining, and general construction markets. The advanced devices business produces Trimble's GPS chipsets and other hardware and licenses the technology to major OEMs, primarily for the automotive and wireless communications infrastructure end markets.

Why Should I Care?

Trimble is one of the leading players in the GPS market, particularly in the agricultural market, where it enjoys a 25 percent market share. In addition, the markets served by Trimble are relatively underpenetrated, creating real opportunities for expansion and premium pricing through innovation.

Trimble, along with Caterpillar (its partner/customer in several markets), develops fully integrated product platforms that yield strong revenues and margins. The product line is made up of generally higher-end commercial products that have high barriers to entry. And since the company's technology drives productivity gains for its customers, demand tends to be very stable even when (and perhaps especially when) the larger economy turns flat. Trimble's innovative products lead to pricing power, which shows up in its gross margins (45–50 percent over the past two years).

The company has made international expansion a priority, particularly into the Asian markets of China and India. Most of Trimble's growth in the region has come from those two countries. While the growth has been inconsistent, the potential is enormously attractive and the actuals have served to balance the downturn in the domestic markets somewhat. The company is putting further resources into the dealer networks in both countries.

Trimble remains a nonplayer in the consumer market, leaving this lower-margin business to the more cost-competitive, high-volume players. Trimble's focus on innovation and commercial applications has provided better margins and a more dependable revenue stream.

How's Business?

Trimble has been aggressive in its acquisitions, and by the time we go to press it should have completed its largest acquisition yet: $485 million for Tekla, a building-modeling company based in Finland. There are many potential synergies here, and the move has been viewed positively, though it will dilute 2011 earnings a bit.

Upside
- Key partnerships in key markets
- Good reputation among customers
- Application base continues to grow

Downside
- Not the cheapest earnings in the book
- Construction markets still weak
- Volume growth biased toward lower-margin products

Just the Facts

SECTOR: **Technology**
BETA COEFFICIENT: **1.35**
5-YEAR COMPOUND EARNINGS-PER-SHARE GROWTH: **9.0%**

	2007	2008	2009	2010	2011
Revenues (Mil)	1,222	1,329	1,126	1,294	1,550
Net Income (Mil)	117	142	63.4	127	170
Price: high	43.2	41.4	26.2	42.2	51.9
low	25.0	14.4	12.0	22.8	32.6

Trimble Navigation Ltd.
935 Stewart Drive
Sunnyvale, CA 94085
(408) 481-8000
Website: *www.trimble.com*

Triumph Group, Inc.

Ticker symbol: TGI (NYSE) ❑ S&P rating: NA ❑ Value Line financial strength rating: B++ ❑ Current yield: 0.3%

Who Are They?

Triumph Group is an international supplier of aircraft components, structures, accessories, subassemblies, and systems. Its forty-four component companies design, manufacture, repair, overhaul/maintain, and distribute products to customers in the aerospace industry, including OEMs and suppliers to the aircraft industry. End users include operators of commercial, regional, business, and military aircraft, as well as commercial and regional airlines and carriers.

The company's component organizations are organized into three major segments: aerostructure, aerospace, and aftermarket services. The aerostructure group produces wings, fuselage sections, tail assemblies, nacelles, control surfaces . . . basically everything you see when you look at the outside of an airplane, other than landing gear. It also produces cabins for helicopters. The aerospace unit produces electronic and hydraulic control systems, gearboxes, actuators, and other nonstructural components. The services arm is a classic MRO (maintenance, repair, and overhaul) operation with inventory management services for the commercial and military aviation sectors.

Why Should I Care?

In June 2010, Triumph completed the acquisition of Vought Aircraft, more than doubling net sales and nearly doubling earnings, and operating margin barely budged. The integration has continued to progress smoothly, and the company expects to eliminate redundancies over the next few years, providing cost savings estimated at $50 million per year by mid-2013. This would add 1.4 percent to the already healthy operating margin. The company has also won a number of important contracts recently, including wings for Bombardier and significant business for the air force's new refueling tankers. Boeing, which represents 45 percent of Triumph's sales, has released its long-term market forecast, which calls for 3.6 percent annual growth in the number of operating planes over the next twenty years. Triumph's business grows not only with sales of new aircraft, but also with the expansion of the installed base of existing airframes. Its maintenance business, which represents about 10 percent of net sales, grew earnings by 156 percent last year on a 21 percent increase in net sales. According to the company, the majority of the earnings gain was based primarily on increased sales volume, indicating some underutilization of assets. Comps should look much better going forward with increases in the serviceable installed base.

Lastly, this stock has some solid fundamentals. Its price-to-book value is about half of its competition's, its price-to-cash flow is about 60 percent of its competition's, and its forward P/E of 10 is about 40 percent lower than the rest of the aerospace market. For a company with strong financials in a rebounding market, it is trading fairly cheap. We're value investors, but these are some standout numbers.

How's Business?

Carlyle Group, which acquired close to 7.3 million shares in the sale of Vought to Triumph, recently completed a public sale of 2.5 million shares at $92.75 (Triumph had only 24.5 million shares outstanding at the time). Triumph has since split 2-for-1, effectively pricing those shares at $46.37, and the stock has since traded as high as $53.50. Carlyle can sell off the remaining shares over the next two years, but Triumph shareholders would appear to have little to fear from those sales.

Upside
- Synergy from Vought purchase
- Significant long-term contracts
- Outstanding financials

Downside
- Military exposure a double-edged sword
- Recent Boeing stumbles
- A cheap buy-in may not be in the offing

Just the Facts

SECTOR: Manufacturing
BETA COEFFICIENT: 1.10
5-YEAR COMPOUND EARNINGS-PER-SHARE GROWTH: 33.0%

	2007	2008	2009	2010	2011
Revenues (Mil)	1,151	1,240	1,295	2,905	3,460
Net Income (Mil)	75.7	97.8	85.3	165	215
Price: high	43.2	41.8	25.5	46.3	50.5
low	25.8	23.5	15.6	23.8	21.7

Triumph Group, Inc.
899 Cassatt Road, Suite 210
Berwyn, PA 19312
(610) 251-1000
Website: *www.triumphgroup.com*

TSMC Ltd.

Ticker symbol: TSM (NYSE-ADR) ❑ S&P rating: NA ❑ Value Line financial strength rating: B+ ❑
Current yield: 4.0%

Who Are They?

Taiwan Semiconductor Manufacturing Company is the world's largest independent semiconductor foundry. Started in 1987, it was also the first dedicated foundry, meaning that its production was sold only to its clients and not on the open market. This is still the case today, as the dedicated foundry model has become standard and has spawned several competitors, including UMC and Global Foundries.

TSMC provides state-of-the-art facilities for many of the world's leading semiconductor design firms, such as Nvidia, Broadcom, Marvell, and Conexant. Volumes are significant, and customer designs are on the cutting edge—Nvidia's graphics processing chips are the largest and most complex semiconductors made, with more than 3 billion transistors on a single die. TSMC also provides capacity to a number of companies that have their own fabrication facilities, including Intel. Its production facilities include one 150mm fab, four 200mm fabs, and two 300mm fabs, as well as the former Fujitsu 200mm fab in Washington State (run as WaferTech, a subsidiary), and a joint venture with the former Philips semiconductor facilities in Singapore, now known as NXP semiconductors. A third 300mm fab should come on-line early in 2012.

Why Should I Care?

The reason Intel is one of the few remaining companies that continue to build their own die is because of its history of manufacturing expertise with its existing facilities and the volumes that support them. For nearly everyone else on the planet, the dedicated fab model that TSMC created is the only practical solution. Foundries are so expensive to build, operate, and update that a business model like this is simply a no-brainer. Even Intel's main competitor, AMD, recently sold off its fabs to Global Foundries, principally to reduce the impact on cash flow. Like Global Foundries, TSMC has also grown through the attrition of captive fabs and has managed its acquisition business very well, upgrading the older fabs to viable, in-demand processes. It is also one of the top R & D firms in the world, behind perhaps only Intel in semiconductor manufacturing research. It will be on the leading edge of the development of 450mm wafer processes—not due for another five years, but already well into development. TSMC is a tremendous growth story with an impeccable reputation, and if you're a fabless semiconductor outfit, TSMC is simply The Man. There are less expensive shops, but no one has the breadth of process expertise and the flexibility to meet as many needs as does TSMC. As former customers of the company, we have to say we're also fans. So shoot us.

How's Business?

One year after the Great Rebound of 2010, TSMC's business is still vigorous, and 2011 revenues should finish up 15 percent above 2010's record high. High capacity utilization should keep net margins in the mid-30 percentage, just a few points under the company's all-time high. Demand has fallen off among a few of TSMC's key customers of late, however (notably Nvidia), and the new fab may not find full utilization for a few quarters. This understanding appears to be cooked into the current mid-$12 price, though, so any significant uptick in volumes should bode well for investors.

Upside
- Accelerating revenue
- Leading-edge technology
- Flexible capacity models

Downside
- Taiwanese dollar getting stronger
- Demand for 450mm process uncertain
- Earnings tapering after a big 2010

Just the Facts

SECTOR: **Semiconductor**

BETA COEFFICIENT: **1.05**

5-YEAR COMPOUND EARNINGS-PER-SHARE GROWTH: **13.0%**

	2007	2008	2009	2010	2011
Revenues (Mil)	9,949	10,609	9,256	13,322	15,600
Net Income (Mil)	3,390	3,194	2,792	5,132	5,460
Price: high	11.6	11.6	11.4	12.7	13.9
low	9.4	6.5	7.5	9.5	10.9

TSMC, Ltd.

No. 8, Li-Hsin Road 6

Hinschu Science Park, Hinschu, Taiwan

(866) 3-578-0221

Website: *www.tsmc.com*

COMPUTERS

TTM Technologies

Ticker symbol: TTMI (NASDAQ) ❑ S&P rating: BB- ❑ Value Line financial strength rating: NA ❑ Current yield: Nil

Who Are They?

TTM Technologies is the largest printed circuit board manufacturer in North America and the fifth largest in the world. A printed circuit board (PCB) is the platform onto which integrated circuits and other electronic components are mounted in order to build a functioning product like a PC motherboard or any of thousands of other electronic products. Building a PCB is a rather specialized process requiring customized fabrication equipment and, in the more exotic applications, unique design expertise. The vast majority of PCBs are manufactured by companies such as TTM rather than by the companies that assemble the finished circuit board.

The company is based in the United States, with fifteen specialized facilities split roughly equally between the United States and China. The Chinese facilities, acquired in the 2009 purchase of Meadville, focus primarily on high-volume products for the consumer electronics market. The U.S. facilities build mainly lower-volume designs for the networking and military markets.

Why Should I Care?

If you've read anything about the electronics industry in the last twenty years, you may be thinking: "North America? I thought all this stuff was built in China." You would be mostly right, as only 8 percent (by revenue) of the world production is U.S.-based. Still, this is a $3.9 billion market; TTM's China facilities have close access to the $28.6 billion market there.

What makes the U.S. market attractive is the product mix: The U.S.-based production addresses customers that need more complex designs with specific performance characteristics. As products reduce in size and increase in operating speed, the connections between the electronic components become more and more critical to the operation of the product. If you've ever looked inside an iPhone, you've probably seen examples of these rather exotic PCB technologies. The trends toward further miniaturization, higher-speed operation, and higher circuit complexity will only accelerate the demand for improved interconnect performance.

TTM also supplies the companies that build electronic gear for the U.S. military. These contracts are only let to a small number of qualified suppliers, most often based only in the United States. The technologies employed in some of TTM's products are very sophisticated and difficult to manufacture, but are irreplaceable in many of the military's designs. Military PCBs also are typically ruggedized for operation in extreme environmental conditions and often have unique form factors. These state-of-the-art PCBs are just the sort of product that TTM specializes in, and these products are, on a per-unit basis, far more profitable for TTM than the higher-volume, consumer-grade designs built in its facilities in China.

The company also provides extensive quick-turn capability, delivering prototypes quickly and offering fast ramps into production volumes. This service is valued highly in competitive bid cycles and time-limited market opportunities.

How's Business?

TTM's acquisition of Meadville was a bit of a surprise, given TTM's closing of three facilities due to the economic downturn, but the move looks like it will pay off brilliantly. The price was very reasonable, the debt was attractively priced, and the effect on the income statement has been impressive. The FY2011 second quarter revenues grew 148 percent year over year, while non-GAAP earnings are more than $66 million for the first half. The GAAP earnings are quite a bit lower due to an impairment charge taken in the second quarter, resulting in a net loss of $20.9 million. Still, operating profit and cash flow for the year will show impressive gains. High volumes in touchpad tablets and smartphones account for a large part of the increases.

Upside
- Very broad technical capability
- Volumes adequate to compete on cost
- Big fish in the profitable military market

Downside
- Cyclical businesses
- Somewhat speculative price
- Manageable, but significant debt

Just the Facts

SECTOR: Manufacturing
BETA COEFFICIENT: 1.7
5-YEAR COMPOUND EARNINGS-PER-SHARE GROWTH: NA

	2007	2008	2009	2010	2011
Revenues (Mil)	669	681	582	1,180	1,450
Net Income (Mil)	35.4	34.7	(36.9)	4.9	71.5
Price: high	14.0	14.7	12.4	15.3	19.1
low	9.5	4.2	4.3	8.4	9.6

TTM Technologies, Inc.
2630 South Harbor Boulevard
Santa Ana, CA 92704
(714) 241-0303
Website: *www.ttmtech.com*

SEMICONDUCTOR EQUIPMENT

Ultratech Inc.

Ticker symbol: UTEK (NASDAQ) ❑ **S&P rating: NA** ❑ **Value Line financial strength rating: NA** ❑ **Current yield: Nil**

Who Are They?

Ultratech is a semiconductor process equipment manufacturer based in San Jose, California. The company, founded in 1979, was a subsidiary of General Signal until 1993, the same year the company had its IPO as Ultratech Stepper.

The company's main product lines are steppers, packaging equipment, and laser processing tools. Steppers are machines that expose silicon wafers with the patterns that create integrated circuits on the surface of the silicon. The packaging equipment is not for boxes and such but rather for the placement of minute connectors directly onto the surface of the silicon die. These connectors are later attached to external metal pads, allowing the die to be integrated onto a circuit board. The company's laser processing tools are used to enhance the performance of a finished circuit, a process that benefits a number of mainstream applications.

The company designs and manufactures its products in California, with a fair amount of subassembly work handled by subcontractors. The company's marketing activities are also headquartered in California, with eight sales and marketing offices in technology centers worldwide.

Why Should I Care?

We tend to think of high-tech companies as being either on the leading edge or failing, with nothing much in the middle. This used to be closer to the truth, but as very highly capable processors and other circuit blocks have come way down in price and are showing up in modestly priced consumer goods, the tools used to produce them have formed a stratified market, from machines that cost as much as some companies themselves, to machines that simply get the job done. Ultratech's main line of products, its photolithography tools, are not state of the art in terms of feature size. They are not used to build the incredibly dense and advanced dies of the latest CPUs from Intel or the high-density memory used in modern servers and PCs. The optical design they employ would not permit it. What they give up in terms of ultimate resolution, though, they gain in ease of use, flexibility, and overall cost of ownership. You wouldn't lease a stable of Ferraris to deliver newspapers, and you wouldn't use the latest twenty-eight-nanometer IC process to make inkjet print heads. Horses for courses is the game here, and Ultratech's workhorses are the machines used to make print heads, thin-film heads for disk drives, laser diodes, and LEDs, as well as digital integrated circuits. It's a good business to be in, as Ultratech's fairly steady revenues and remarkably stable stock price have shown.

In 2004, however, the company advanced the state of the art with an interesting new process they call Laser Spike Annealing. LSA is a variation on an established process that uses highly localized heat during the IC fabrication process in order to improve the performance characteristics of certain structures in the circuit. It has been shown to provide benefits in customer designs all the way down to 45nm (so far) and has been well received in the market overall.

How's Business?

Business is good, and thanks for asking. One of the bright spots in semiconductor packing recently has been the growing use of "flip-chip" packaging, due to the advantages it brings in terms of reduced size, improved thermal characteristics, and the potential for higher speed operation. Ultratech makes some of the better flip-chip equipment, and sales of that equipment have been driving a very strong first half of 2011. The company is very optimistic about its prospects through 2012.

Upside

- Bump packaging becoming more widely adopted
- LED volumes increasing
- Ultratech one of the lowest-cost suppliers

Downside

- Competition for laser process arriving soon
- Used equipment competes in Ultratech's market
- Earnings highly volume sensitive

Just the Facts

SECTOR: **Technology**

BETA COEFFICIENT: **0.5**

5-YEAR COMPOUND EARNINGS-PER-SHARE GROWTH: —

	2007	**2008**	**2009**	**2010**	**2011**
Revenues (Mil)	113	132	95.8	141	210
Net Income (Mil)	(1.04)	11.8	2.13	16.8	38.0
Price: high	14.4	17	15.7	20.8	33.5
low	11.4	9.0	10	12.8	18.5

Ultratech Inc.

3050 Zanker Road

San Jose, CA 95134

(408) 321-8835

Website: *www.ultratech.com*

COMMUNICATIONS

Vicor Corporation

Ticker symbol: VICR (NASDAQ) ❏ S&P rating: NA ❏ Value Line financial strength rating: B ❏ Current yield: 2.7%

Who Are They?

Vicor Corporation designs, develops, manufactures, and markets modular power components and complete power systems for use in the higher-performance, higher-power segments of the power systems market. You would not normally find a Vicor supply in a consumer-grade piece of equipment, as consumer gear is too highly cost driven, and the need for performance is just not there. You *would* find Vicor gear in applications such as commercial telecommunications and networking infrastructure, enterprise and high performance computing, industrial automation, vehicles and transportation, and defense electronics. It builds to a set of performance and form-factor requirements, and while cost is important, it is in many cases not the primary concern.

The company is organized into three business units that reflect the three key product lines: the Brick Business Unit, the V*I Business Unit, and the Picor Corporation business unit. The company doesn't make bricks, obviously, *brick* being the semi-affectionate term used in the industry to refer to any heavy, dense, roughly rectangular device. The V*I business unit provides small, lightweight integrated design for variable output and POL (point of load) uses. The Picor business unit consists of Picor Corporation, a majority-owned subsidiary of Vicor and a fabless designer, developer, and marketer of high performance integrated circuits and related products for use in a variety of power system applications. Picor products are sold both to Vicor business units and to customers who use them in their own designs.

Why Should I Care?

The company is making a number of internal changes to address the declining gross margin percentage. Part of the problem is due to a high level of product line churn, but structural changes are being made to improve Vicor's biggest area of need. The CEO is confident that the rework will bear fruit in calendar 2012. This would be a very positive move, as the company is able to generate strong earnings with higher volumes, but it's clear the fixed costs are challenging.

The requirements of Vicor's traditional customer base have led to high-efficiency, high power-density designs for compact, high-performance applications. These designs are apparently becoming attractive to an entirely new class of customers, as Vicor has been messaging since the June shareholder's meeting. The company has plans for several new product platforms and will aggressively pursue new markets. It is also working on a new multitiered distribution model, which to us sounds as if it may be going direct on some new high-volume accounts. Maybe that's wishful thinking, but whatever the reasons, shaking up the channel is usually only done when you're certain you can be doing better.

How's Business?
Revenues were off somewhat in the second quarter of 2011. According to what sounded like a rather frustrated Patrizio Vinciarelli, chief executive officer, "Vicor's bookings and revenues during the second quarter were negatively impacted by curtailed demand for bricks and custom products because of continued deferral of funding for defense electronics projects." Dealing with the government has its pluses and minuses, but it sounds like the third-quarter's comps are going to get a bump on the high side.

Upside
- Good revenue growth foreseen
- Bookings up 50 percent in Q1 (y/y)
- No debt

Downside
- SG&A will almost certainly bump up in early 2012
- Some manufacturing outsourcing may be needed
- Will require a close watch

Just the Facts

SECTOR: **Technology**
BETA COEFFICIENT: **1.35**
5-YEAR COMPOUND EARNINGS-PER-SHARE GROWTH: **57%**

	2007	**2008**	**2009**	**2010**	**2011**
Revenues (Mil)	192	196	205	198	251
Net Income (Mil)	(29.1)	5.34	(3.6)	2.8	33.3
Price: high	15.1	14.7	9.9	18.7	17.3
low	8.9	4.1	4.1	8.4	9.7

Vicor Corporation
400 Federal Street
Andover, MA 01810–5499
(978) 470-2900
Website: *www.vicr.com*

Vishay Intertechnology

Ticker symbol: VSH (NYSE) ❑ S&P rating: BB+ ❑ Value Line financial strength rating: B+ ❑
Current yield: Nil

Who Are They?

Vishay Intertechnology designs, manufactures, and markets discrete semi-conductors and passive electronic components. These components are used in a very wide range of consumer, commercial, and industrial products, as well as defense, medical, and aerospace. It would be difficult to find an electronic product of any complexity for which Vishay could not supply at least some components.

The company's products include semiconductors (55 percent of 2010 revenue) and passive components. The semiconductor products include MOSFETs, diodes, and optoelectronic components. It manufactures a very limited line of ICs and specializes in the simpler elements of circuitry, the two-terminal or three-terminal passives, sensors, and switches. Its passive components include resistors, capacitors, inductors, and transformers. Taken as a whole, Vishay's product line represents every type of solid-state component that existed prior to the development of the integrated circuit. This is not to say that the company is performing the electronic equivalent of stamping out license plates. The parts it produces require a great deal of R & D at a very basic physical level. In many ways, the work Vishay does has to be at the very leading edge of materials science, but since the functions its products perform are so basic (in most cases), the technology behind them is often overlooked.

Why Should I Care?

What's attractive about Vishay is not so much its technology, but its ubiquity. Yes, it has a number of technical innovations that set it apart in a number of its markets: It has very dense charge storage with its Micro-Tan capacitor line, and it has some very advanced switches that utilize its Trench-FET technology. It is also a market share leader in resistors, rectifiers, infrared components, and a few other markets. But the real appeal for us is that Vishay's products are used everywhere, in every class of hardware from the least expensive consumer tchotchkes to the most expensive scientific instruments and exotic defense gear. They cover all the markets and all the applications, and so when the market moves up Vishay is very likely to move with it.

We also like Vishay's free cash flow of nearly $400 million over the past six quarters. While we don't expect it to continue indefinitely at this pace, it shows us what it is capable of on an up cycle, which tells us a lot about the company's earnings leverage. The $1 billion it currently has in the bank will almost certainly be put to use in acquisitions in order to take advantage of that leverage.

There is some seasonality to this stock, possibly due to its exposure in consumer goods. We would recommend waiting until late summer to catch a good entry price when VSH stock is at a seasonal lull.

How's Business?

The company's 2012 second-quarter results, while encouraging, were not enough to please the street and the stock fell to the $13 range. In the recent market pullback, the stock has again felt the brunt of lowered expectations for an economic recovery in 2012 and the shares are now in the $10–$11 range. This is a very attractive entry point, reflecting a forward multiple of less than 5 for a company with anticipated organic growth of 4 percent and acquisitions on the horizon.

Upside

- Broad, deep market presence
- Good acquisitions experience
- Longer-term promise

Downside

- Not a lot of pricing power
- Increasing tantalum prices
- Above-average volatility

Just the Facts

SECTOR: **Technology**
BETA COEFFICIENT: **1.20**
5-YEAR COMPOUND EARNINGS-PER-SHARE GROWTH: **NA**

	2007	**2008**	**2009**	**2010**	**2011**
Revenues (Mil)	2,833	2,822	2,042	2,725	2,850
Net Income (Mil)	140	(15.6)	3.3	301	350
Price: high	18.2	11.6	8.8	15.6	19.1
low	10.9	3.2	2.2	6.9	9.9

Vishay Intertechnology, Inc
63 Lancaster Ave
Malvern, PA 19355
(610) 644-1300
Website: *www.vishay.com*

VMware, Inc.

Ticker symbol: VMW (NYSE) ❑ S&P rating: NA ❑ Value Line financial strength rating: B++ ❑
Current yield: Nil

Who Are They?

VMware is the world's largest supplier of virtualization software, platforms, and tools. Virtualization is a growing trend in IT that encompasses many concepts, offering the primary benefit of a higher utilization of expensive hardware, improved security, ease of administration, and improved data integrity.

VMware's products are widely used across many industries. They are present in all of the *Fortune* 100 companies, and in 96 percent of the *Fortune* 1,000. Their economic benefits are quickly realized in use.

The majority of VMware's sales are through indirect channels, including software distributors, hardware bundlers, and other value-added-resellers. It also develops custom solutions in collaboration with manufacturers such as Intel and Cisco to optimize performance on their hardware.

Why Should I Care?

In virtualized architectures, a computer can run several operating systems simultaneously. In most virtualization schemes, there is a host operating system (the one the machine boots with), and there are one or more guest operating systems (the virtualized machines). The virtualized operating systems permit applications written for that particular OS to run as though they were running on dedicated hardware. The VMware products (called hypervisors) are the software that create these virtual machines on the host OS. In some cases, the host OS is itself a VMware product. This hypervisor is the basis for the virtualization scheme, as it permits access to the hardware from not only the host operating system but also from guest operating systems and applications being used by those guests. In most user environments, Windows would only permit one user at a time to be logged on to a machine, but in a virtualized environment many applications can have access to the CPU and memory of that machine, putting to economic use what would otherwise be sitting idle. IDC estimates that the typical Intel server is utilizing only 10–15 percent of its capacity. With virtualization, a single server could then reasonably be expected to do the work of six to ten servers, generating enormous cost savings in multimachine environments.

The coming wave of cloud computing environments, by the way, relies on virtualized architectures as a foundation. You can use your current dedicated hardware as the basis for a cloud configuration, but you must first virtualize the hardware and operating systems.

VMware's revenues come from licenses (the initial sale of the software and other proceeds) and services, which includes support, training, etc. As late as 2007, revenue from services was less than half of that from licenses. In 2008, however, service revenue began to increase far more quickly than license fees. In 2010, revenue from services exceeded licenses for the first time. Since 2006, service revenue has increased seven-fold. This bodes very well for steady revenue in the future, given VMware's large installed base and rapidly consolidating position as the dominant player.

How's Business?

As widespread as VMware is at the moment, the potential for growth is still there. Every new machine installation, whether it's in a Windows, OSX, or Linux environment, is a potential VMware seat. On top of that, there are a great many data centers that are still running dedicated hardware, and these all represent potential sales waiting to happen. The company's finances are exceptionally strong, with $3.3 billion in cash, zero short-term debt, and rock-solid net margins in the mid-teens.

Upside
- Nearly 80 percent market share
- Ten-year lead on Microsoft
- Oracle, HP . . . all pushing cloud architectures

Downside
- Shares won't be cheap
- Hard to capture more market share
- Revenue is 65 percent international—currency exposure

Just the Facts

SECTOR: **Technology**
BETA COEFFICIENT: **1.15**
5-YEAR COMPOUND EARNINGS-PER-SHARE GROWTH: **28.0%**

	2007	2008	2009	2010	2011
Revenues (Mil)	1,326	1,881	2,024	2,857	3,635
Net Income (Mil)	218	290	197	357	550
Price: high	125.3	86.9	45.6	91.9	107.8
low	48.0	17.3	19.2	41.1	74.8

VMware, Inc.
3401 Hillview Avenue
Palo Alto, CA 94304
(650) 427-5000
Website: *www.vmware.com*

COMPUTING

Western Digital Corp.

Ticker symbol: WDC (NYSE) □ S&P rating: NA □ Value Line financial strength rating: B+ □ Current yield: Nil

Who Are They?

Western Digital is one of the largest hard disk drive (HDD) manufacturers in the world. By the time you read this, it may well be the largest. The European Commission is reviewing its proposed acquisition of Hitachi Global Storage Technologies and should issue a ruling by Q4 of 2011. Of course, by that time WDC's major rival, Seagate, may have completed *its* acquisition of Samsung's data storage operations, putting WDC and Seagate back into a race for the number-one spot, with WDC having about an 8 percent lead at 48 percent market share.

WDC began as a supplier of controllers, the interface between the HDD and the rest of the computer. The controller business turned out to be a bit more profitable than the early HDD business though, and as HDD manufacturers one by one bit the dust, WDC found itself in good position to expand its business through acquisition. With the market exits of Quantum, Maxtor, and later IBM, WDC and Seagate were left as the only two U.S.-based HDD suppliers. Soon the global market will be simply WDC, Seagate, and Toshiba, and if we were Toshiba, we'd be nervous.

In addition to disk drives, WDC also designs and manufactures HDD-based products such as external storage products, home entertainment devices, and a powerline networking product line.

Why Should I Care?

If there was one thing we'd add to death and taxes on the list of inevitables, it would have to be increased demand for fast digital storage. Every Goliath of the online world—Google, Amazon, eBay, plus all the thousands of wannabe Goliaths, plus all the video servers such as Netflix, Comcast, Dish networks, plus all of the current and planned cloud services . . . all of them, everywhere in every market in every country on the planet—rely on the continued availability of fast, cheap, hard drive space. Count on WDC being a major supplier for all of these applications.

One might think a company that can double revenue and quadruple earnings over a four-year period might get some attention in the form of higher share price, but WDC's stock has struggled for as little as a 25 percent increase. The problem is that this is the tech market, and that market has long treated the HDD as a commodity item with very little speculative value. So WDC does what a smart company does in a commodity market: It develops vertical integration and attempts to acquire market share through any means possible. In early 2010, WDC announced a deal to buy Hitachi Global Storage, whose volumes were roughly equivalent to both WDC and Seagate. Assuming the deal goes through, WDC will be the clear market leader in terms of revenue and volume and will have acquired a very important toehold in the enterprise storage market, which has been its only weak spot in terms of market share. WDC will now be the dominant player in the overall HDD market, with only Seagate's presence in enterprise keeping it from leading all the product categories as well.

Western also has its own solid-state drive technology as well, with its SiliconDrive controllers and SiliconEdge drives.

How's Business?

Pricing competition and a flat PC market have depressed revenues somewhat in 2011. Sales will be down nearly 5 percent, although unit volumes were up about 8 percent. The company saw a strong recovery in net margins in the June 2011 quarter and feels confident that profitability will recover, perhaps not to 2010 levels, but at least 3 percentage points.

Upside

- Picking up Hitachi and IBM tech in one purchase
- Solid financial ground—room for more acquisitions
- HDD market pricing environment should improve

Downside

- Earnings reliability, not so much
- Significant SSD earnings still a few years out
- Tablet sales displacing traditional PCs

Just the Facts

SECTOR: **Technology**

BETA COEFFICIENT: **1.33**

5-YEAR COMPOUND EARNINGS-PER-SHARE GROWTH: **34.5%**

	2007	2008	2009	2010	2011
Revenues (Mil)	5,468	8,074	7,453	9,850	9,330
Net Income (Mil)	438	976	574	1,382	720
Price: high	31.7	40.0	45.0	47.3	41.2
low	16.2	9.5	11.5	23.1	29.1

Western Digital Corporation

20511 Lake Forest Drive

Lake Forest, CA 92630

(949) 672-7000

Website: *www.wdc.com*

Zygo Corp.

Ticker symbol: ZIGO (NASDAQ) ❑ S&P rating: NA ❑ Value Line financial strength rating: B ❑ Current yield: Nil

Who Are They?

Zygo Corporation, with a current market cap of $175 million, is the smallest company we review in the book. It has been in business for more than forty years but has remained small-ish even as its reputation in the market has grown.

The company operates two business segments: the metrology solutions division and the optical systems division. The metrology division manufactures high-accuracy, high-precision measurement products and tools, mainly for technology companies. Its products are used to measure displacement, surface shapes, and textures as well as film thickness. The optical division provides product development and manufacturing services for medical, defense, semiconductor, optics research, biomedical, and other industrial markets. Many of the tools and advances produced by the optical division are put to use in the metrology division, as the measurement tools in metrology all rely on optical techniques for their high performance.

Zygo is part of the important but fairly niche market of metrology. Metrology is literally the science of measurement, and metrology specialists such as Zygo have been in business since the start of the industrial revolution. Any company whose product or process depends on very accurate measurements of mechanical properties will use very accurate and reliable measurement tools, and Zygo supplies extraordinarily accurate and versatile tools. Measurements made with Zygo equipment were part of the repair process for the optics on the Hubble Space Telescope.

Why Should I Care?

Zygo's business prospects have turned around as optical technologies have become more prevalent in high-volume markets and as current optical markets have grown in size. It's a bigger pie now, and Zygo's slice looks to be scaling up. Applications for the company's optical systems include medical laser delivery (such as LASIK equipment), Department of Defense (all of the ultra-high quality optics used nowadays), 3D medical imaging, and semiconductor lithography. The semiconductor industry relies on ultra-flat silicon wafers for high yields. When the wafers were four inches in diameter and the surfaces were not so critical, optical tools were fairly fast and inexpensive. As the wafer size has increased and the geometries of the active die have decreased, measuring flatness is more critical and takes more time, meaning you need better and better measuring tools as you upgrade your process. The completed dies, in addition to being characterized electrically, also have to be inspected mechanically to ensure they can be correctly packaged, and semiconductor packaging is in the midst of a regime change. Packaging methods are moving toward much higher-density interconnect schemes, whereby there are no longer external leads but simply solder bumps on the bottom of the package. The profile and positioning of these bumps are critical to the assembly process, and some of these parts have more than a thousand bumps. Rapid and accurate inspection of these dimensions is critical to some of the highest-volume, highest-value, and highest-margin parts currently in production. Zygo makes inspection and measurement equipment for all three of these processes, and we expect that demand for this equipment will increase significantly as devices shrink in size but increase in complexity.

The medical use of implants and other engineered materials is on the rise both in the United States and worldwide, as the availability of these devices and the training to use them becomes more widespread. The testing and inspection of these implants and devices are done at the 100 percent level (each and every device made gets a full characterization), and their mechanical dimensioning is critical to their successful operation. Zygo makes equipment specifically for this application, and we would expect to see these volumes grow as these procedures become even more commonplace and the demand for the devices increases.

How's Business?
The company's recently announced FY2011 actuals exceeded expectations by a fair margin. Revenues and earnings were expected to post at $145 million and $14 million, and instead came in at $150 million and $19.1 million. Bookings for the year came to $167 million, a 55 percent increase over 2010's bookings of $108 million.

Upside
- Niche market, but growing
- Zero debt
- Good customer base

Downside
- Cyclical markets
- Some exposure to federal budget
- Operating margin a little thin

Just the Facts

SECTOR: **Industrials**
BETA COEFFICIENT: **1.25**
5-YEAR COMPOUND EARNINGS-PER-SHARE GROWTH: **NA**

	2007	2008	2009	2010	2011
Revenues (Mil)	181	159	116	101	150
Net Income (Mil)	15.1	1.2	66.1	3.6	19.1
Price: high	17.1	13.8	7.9	13.1	16.2
low	10.6	4.7	3.1	6.5	9.5

Zygo Corporation
Laurel Brook Road
Middlefield, CT 06455
(860) 347-8506
Website: *www.zygo.com*